9187
α.
8⁴

D1550270

HARVARD STUDIES
IN COMPARATIVE LITERATURE

HARVARD STUDIES
IN COMPARATIVE LITERATURE
FOUNDED BY WILLIAM HENRY SCHOFIELD

20

PERSPECTIVES OF CRITICISM

Sarcophagus of the Muses, The Louvre. Photographs, Giraudon

PERSPECTIVES
OF CRITICISM

Walter Jackson Bate

William C. Greene

John V. Kelleher

Perry Miller

Renato Poggioli

Alfred Schwarz

Jean Seznec

Geoffrey Tillotson

Harry Levin, *Editor*

HARVARD UNIVERSITY PRESS · CAMBRIDGE · 1950

TO THE MEMORY OF
THEODORE SPENCER

PREFACE

This is the twentieth volume of a series which began almost forty years ago with the publication of George Santayana's *Three Philosophical Poets*. If I venture now to recall that book, with its fine combination of philosophic range and aesthetic insight, it is not because we would brave comparison with it or disparage the usefulness of the intervening volumes. A glance down the list of titles will indicate some of the trends that were being pursued in those years, not merely by students of Comparative Literature at Harvard, but by literary scholarship in this country at large. Broadly speaking, the focus has shifted from medieval to modern culture, while the approach has shifted from philology to the history of ideas. Locally these shifts are associated with the respective influences of G. L. Kittredge and W. H. Schofield, on the one hand, and Irving Babbitt and Fernand Baldensperger on the other. Recent years and younger generations, coming to graduate study already schooled in the need for intercultural understanding, have raised further questions: the synthesis of our monographic research, the revaluation of our humanistic curriculum, the reciprocation between the study and the practice of literature.

Positive answers to any or all of these questions give a new centrality to the hitherto somewhat peripheral subject of Comparative Literature. This indeed is one of the many suggestive points that are scored by René Wellek and Austin Warren in their recently published *Theory of Literature*. They go on to suggest that the history of criticism, perhaps the most central of literary disciplines, can scarcely be studied except by comparative methods. Now criticism, a generation ago, bore almost as strained a relation to scholarship as it did, on the other side, to artistic

creation. Scholars who turned critic, like J. E. Spingarn and Stuart
Sherman, broke with their academic affiliations. When, about fifteen years ago, the tide began to turn, R. S. Crane counseled
teachers of English to abandon literary history for literary criticism. But, though the emphasis has since been shifting in that direction, it has not proved necessary to regard the two spheres as
mutually exclusive. Their common ground is precisely the history
of criticism, for neither history nor criticism can operate in the
vacuum created by the absence of the other. Criticism, without
historical perspective, is forced to fall back on obsolete dogmas or
subjective impressions; history, without critical perspective, bogs
down into the sheer accumulation of irrelevant detail.

Meanwhile, along with such thoughtful reconsiderations of
scholarly method as Messrs. Wellek and Warren have presented,
there has been a kind of critical renewal. Spingarn had called for
"the new criticism" in 1910, without receiving very much response.
John Crowe Ransom called again in 1941—and this time spirits
came from the vasty deep. It is salutary that criticism, which is
bound to admit a good deal of extraneous matter, should thus
renew itself for each generation by returning to the direct contemplation of the artistic object. The danger is that the critic who
limits his purview too narrowly is apt to misinterpret the text upon
which he dwells. Critics of the new critics, however, have adduced
enough specific reminders that interpretation of the present requires acquaintance with the past. The striking fact about the
contemporary movement is that it has turned so many writers
into teachers. This may provide a negative comment on the haz-
ards that make it all but impossible for a man of letters, particularly for a serious critic, to be a free lance today: Edmund Wilson
is possibly the exception that proves the rule. More positively, by
its preoccupation with craftsmanship, this new criticism provides
a special impetus for, and exerts a leavening influence over, our
students of literature.

Even now the Modern Language Association is beginning to
quibble as ponderously over the symbolism of twentieth-century
fiction as it used to do over the syntax of Middle English poetry.
We may well be faced, when the situation crystallizes, with a new
academism. The issue will then be whether it is more enlightening,

less occult than the old. At all events, the term "academic" ought
not to frighten anyone who does not harbor the latent preconceptions of romantic Bohemianism. Criticism, since the days of the
classical rhetoricians, has largely functioned under academic auspices; critics like A. W. von Schlegel and Sainte-Beuve and Arnold
put some of their best efforts into lectures; and an increasing
number of our poets, on the more mundane plane of their existence, dwindle into professors. Given the pressures of journalism
and commercialism, or the partisan animus of coteries, the college
or university does seem to be a more favorable place for the culti-
vation of that "disinterestedness" which—today more desperately
than in Arnold's day—critics need. It is also a place which, by its
very nature, brings out the interrelationships between reading
and writing, studying and teaching, as well as the status of these
related pursuits within the domain of knowledge as a whole.

Like any other body of human opinion, with its contradictions
and controversies, its trials and errors, the corpus of literary
criticism seems to include an overwhelming amount of misapplied
ingenuity and wasted endeavor. More often than not, argues
Henri Peyre, it has missed its mark. To support this argument
Mr. Peyre, himself an accomplished scholar-critic, instances many
great works which were not as highly valued by their contemporaries as he would value them now. In short, he identifies criticism
with reviewing, and treats values as ultimate discoveries rather
than as developing conceptions. Yet, if we stress the evaluative
function of criticism, it seems tautological to conclude that critics
disagree, and unfair to belabor them for their disagreement. It
seems fairer and more revealing to consider their numerous and
various responses as relevant aspects of a long-range process by
which a given work attains a collective significance and occupies
a dynamic position. Though the vast majority of man's hypotheses
are sooner or later refuted by experiment, they are incidentally
justified by experience, since every test brings him closer to an
awareness of the limits of possibility and thereby plays its part
in his own intellectual development.

It may well be that critical discussion has placed too much
stress upon evaluation and not enough upon the more objective
function of analysis. Dr. Johnson, according to our tastes, under-

rated the Metaphysical Poets; yet he analyzed them with clearer penetration than most of their later apologists have shown. It is salutary to remember that the Greek root for "criticize" meant "to cut, to distinguish" before it meant "to judge." Judgment is based upon criteria which in turn depend upon some act of faith; hence the Aristotelian, the Thomist, the Marxist can appeal to standards of "correctness"; but the standards vary drastically and are too often imposed on situations to which they do not pertinently apply. For those who do not wish to simplify the problem by ignoring its complexities, the actual variations are significant. It is fruitful to observe what attitudes persist, what views are modified by changing circumstance, and what ephemeral formulations break down. Though there may not be progress in the arts, our knowledge of the arts is cumulative and in this respect comes closer to the sciences. Though the critic, like the scientist, may not be as big a man as some of his predecessors, he enjoys the benefit of their contributions; he utilizes techniques and draws on perceptions which transcend any single period or individual.

It should not be surprising, then, that our age is nothing if not critical. Among its augmenting critical publications, reviews and journals, surveys and anthologies, manifestoes and polemics, the present volume can exert but a modest and marginal claim on the reader's attention. It is rather a miscellany than a symposium: that is to say, its contributors were not asked to frame their articles within a prearranged scheme. Each of them, as it happened, was interested in some particular question which broadly fell within the history of criticism. All of them, working in different fields independently, share certain premises and meet at certain points. But the collection is quite unsystematic, and the authors in no sense form a school of thought. If continuities or principles emerge, where the attempt has simply been variety, the result attests the unity of our subject. Thus our first essay is the explication of a single poem, whereas our second surveys a whole critical tradition. Mr. Seznec, vitalizing archaeology, shows a living poet figuratively and literally inspired by the very sepulcher of the Muses. Mr. Greene, showing that even Greek poetry is not entirely subsumed by ancient criticism, offers a helpful caveat to those—

and there are still many—who would rigidly judge the moderns by classical canons.

Certainly Newman, as Mr. Tillotson expounds him, was a rather wayward Aristotelian; his moral fervor and evangelical afflatus range him—in terms of Coleridge's polarity—among the Platonists. Coleridge himself tried to mediate between extremes; and Mr. Bate, for whom classicism and romanticism are not polar but continuous, reconstructs the Coleridgean fragments and adumbrates that wholeness toward which they strive. Mr. Miller, concerned with the rhetorical implications of empirical philosophy, lays bare the idea at its critical moment of mediation between the word and the thing; while the essay on convention defines this concept, historically and semantically, as a mean between art and nature. On rare occasions, as Mr. Kelleher demonstrates, a gifted critic may misconstrue his theme so evocatively that he helps to launch a whole new movement. On others, as Mr. Schwarz points out, a creative writer who fails to live up to his own intentions may cast illumination on the work of a vastly more creative writer. But criticism, though it controls a much wider area of agreement than its critics suppose, cannot always reconcile opposites; there are times when it must sharpen alternatives; and Soviet Russia bears witness, in the remarkable case that Mr. Poggioli interprets, to the most acute phase of the recurrent conflict between culture and anarchy.

The fact that all the contributors are teaching in the Divisions of Ancient and Modern Languages at Harvard University, or were when the material for this volume was being gathered, is merely coincidental. If circumstances warrant, and it proves possible to devote future volumes in this series to collaborative and illustrative discussions of other broad topics within the realm of Comparative Literature, we should welcome contributions from elsewhere. Meanwhile, it remains to be acknowledged that Mr. Seznec's paper was first read at Dumbarton Oaks on January 20, 1947; that Mr. Greene's, in part, was read at a meeting of the American Philological Association in December 1947, at New Haven, Connecticut; that Mr. Tillotson's is a revision and elaboration of an article which first appeared in *Newman Centenary Essays* (London, 1948), and is printed here by permission of the original publishers, Messrs. Oates and Washburne; that Mr. Poggioli's, in part, was accepted by the editors of *Partisan Review* in 1948 and was subsequently withdrawn by request of the author. I cannot conclude these prefatory remarks without thanking my fellow contributors for their forbearance as well as their coöperation; Miss Eleanor Towle, secretary to the Department of Comparative Literature, for her valued assistance; and Mr. Thomas J. Wilson, Director of the Harvard University Press, for his interest in reanimating the Harvard Studies in Comparative Literature.

HARRY LEVIN

15 Holyoke House
Cambridge, Massachusetts
September 1949

CONTENTS

PERSPECTIVES
OF CRITICISM

PAUL CLAUDEL
AND THE SARCOPHAGUS
OF THE MUSES

Jean Seznec

I

To the first of his five great odes, "Les Muses," [1] published
in 1905, Paul Claudel has set a footnote which says: "Sarcophagus found on the road to Ostia, now in the Louvre." [2] (See
frontispiece.) The sarcophagus, which served as a basis for the
poem, belongs to the second century. It happens to be one of the
most beautiful, and also one of the most interesting, that antiquity
has left us. What I propose to do is to consider the relationship
between this piece of sculpture and the text of Claudel.

It is not the first time, of course, that an ancient work of art
has inspired a modern poet. We find a famous precedent in the
case of Keats and his "Ode on a Grecian Urn"; and the parallel
that could be drawn here would be a close one; for in spite of its
title, the inspiration for Keats's poem came not from any definite
vase, but from various sculptural sources, among them the Elgin
marbles, and specifically that part of the frieze of the Parthenon
which shows the cattle being brought to sacrifice. [3]

Now I should like to analyze Claudel's poem in order to study,
first, his description of the sarcophagus: it will be very easy to
check this description with our own eyes; second, I want to study
his interpretation of the sarcophagus—and here we shall have to
contrast his poetic, intuitive, personal construction with the scientific and scholarly version of the archaeologists. This is not to say,
of course, that Claudel is a simple layman in the matter: he possesses a strong classical background; [4] he is familiar with the
Greek genius, "saturé d'hellénisme," as Péguy once described him;
indeed, he had already translated, at the time when he was writing his ode to the Muses, Aeschylus' *Agamemnon*. But he was ob-

viously unaware of the discoveries made by classical scholars
about the deep significance of such funerary documents as this
one; actually, the most remarkable of these discoveries have taken
place only in recent years.

II

"The nine Muses!" So starts the poem. And Claudel proceeds
to call each of them, characterizing at the same time her attitude,
her function, and her role in the choir.

First comes Terpsichore, who stands in the middle. "Les neuf
Muses, et au milieu, Terpsichore!" I recognize you, he says, and
I know what you mean:

. . . cette grosse flûte toute entrouée de bouches à tes doigts in-
dique assez
   Que tu n'as plus besoin de la joindre au souffle qui t'emplit
   Et qui vient de te mettre, ô vierge, debout!
   Point de contorsions: rien du cou ne dérange les beaux plis de ta
robe jusqu'aux pieds qu'elle ne laisse point voir!
   Mais je sais assez ce que veulent dire cette tête qui se tourne vers
le côté, cette mine enivrée et close, et ce visage qui écoute, tout ful-
gurant de la jubilation orchestrale!
   Un seul bras est ce que tu n'as point pu contenir! Il se relève, il
se crispe,
   Tout impatient de la fureur de frapper la première mesure!

.   .   .   .   .

   Terpsichore, trouveuse de la danse!

She is the soul of the whole group, the animating force that brings
and weaves the others together:

   Où serait le choeur sans la danse? quelle autre captiverait
   Les huit soeurs farouches ensemble, pour vendanger l'hymne
jaillissante, inventant la figure inextricable?

Then the poet goes on to call the other Muses. On the left
side, he recognizes Clio and Thalia, and the one he calls Mnemosyne:

   Du même côté j'ai reconnu Clio, j'ai reconnu Mnémosyne, je t'ai
reconnue, Thalie!

Mnemosyne is the elder sister, the one who never speaks: she only listens and remembers; Thalia is the one who goes in quest of material, through the grotesque and terrible comedy of life:

. . . pourvoyeuse, infatigable Thalie!

.   .   .   .   .

O batteuse de buissons, on t'a bien représentée avec ce bâton à la main!
Et de l'autre, prête à y puiser le rire inextinguible, comme on étudie une bête bizarre,
Tu tiens le Masque énorme, le mufle de la Vie, la dépouille grotesque et terrible!

As for Clio, she is the recorder; she waits, and registers history.

Mais Clio, le style entre les trois doigts, attend, postée au coin du coffre brillant,
Clio, le greffier de l'âme, pareille à celle qui tient les comptes.

These, then, are the silent Muses, the secret providers of the soul. On the other side are the inspired, the industrious ones:

J'ai dit les Muses respiratrices, et maintenant je dirai les Muses inspirées . . .
. . . les grandes Muses intelligentes.

First comes Euterpe, with her lyre:

Voici celle qui tient la lyre de ses mains, voici celle qui tient la lyre entre ses mains aux beaux doigts,
Pareille à un engin de tisserand . . .
Euterpe à la large ceinture, la sainte flamine de l'esprit, levant la grande lyre insonore!
La chose qui sert à faire le discours, la claricorde qui chante et qui compose.
D'une main la lyre, pareille à la trame tendue sur le métier, et de son autre main
Elle applique le plectrum comme une navette.

May the poet perceive and embrace the whole universe through the strings of her lyre—the earth with its lights, and the sky with its stars:

Que je voie tout entre tes fils bien tendus! et la terre avec ses feux, et le ciel avec ses étoiles.

But the lyre is not sufficient to cross and to measure the immensity of space or the intervals of thought. The compass is needed; and that is why Urania stands next to Euterpe:

Il faut l'Angle, il faut le compas qu'ouvre avec puissance Uranie, le compas aux deux branches rectilignes.

.   .   .   .   .

Aucune pensée . . .
Dont le compas ne suffise à prendre tous les intervalles, calculant chaque proportion comme une main écartée.

At the other extremity of the sarcophagus is Melpomene, Muse of Tragedy; she looks like a military chief and like a builder of cities:

Et à l'autre extrémité du long coffre, vide de la capacité d'un corps d'homme
On a placé Melpomène, pareille à un chef militaire et à une constructrice de cités.
Car, le visage tragique relevé sur la tête comme un casque,
Accoudée sur son genou, le pied sur une pierre équarrie, elle considère ses soeurs.

So, then, Clio stands at one extremity, Melpomene at the other.

Clio à l'un des bouts est postée et Melpomène se tient à l'autre.
Quand les Parques ont déterminé
L'action, le signe qui va s'inscrire sur le cadran du Temps comme l'heure par l'opération de son chiffre,
Elles embauchent à tous les coins du monde les ventres
Qui leur fourniront les acteurs dont elles ont besoin . . .

.   .   .   .   .

Et maintenant, chorège, il faut recruter tes acteurs, afin que chacun joue son rôle, entrant et se retirant quand il faut.

History unfolds according to a superior Fate; but to perform the fatal deeds that make history, actors are to be selected among men; and the poet evokes the frightful apparitions of Greek tragedy, Clytemnestra the murderess, and Oedipus with his eyes torn out:

Clytemnestre [apparaît], la hache à la main, les pieds dans le sang de son époux, la semelle sur la bouche de l'homme
Et Oedipe avec ses yeux arrachés, le devineur d'énigmes!
Se dresse dans la porte Thébaine.

Finally, he reverts to the veiled Polyhymnia, who stands among her sisters, leaning on the pulpit—now she can begin to sing:

Et maintenant, Polymnie, ô toi qui te tiens au milieu de tes soeurs,
enveloppée dans ton long voile comme une cantatrice,
Accoudée sur l'autel, accoudée sur le pupitre,
C'est assez attendu, maintenant tu peux attaquer le chant nouveau!
maintenant je puis entendre ta voix.

Such is Claudel's description of the Muses. Physically, so to speak, it is accurate and vivid and full of vigor. You may have noticed, however, that he mistakes Calliope for Mnemosyne, who actually is not a Muse herself, but Memory, the mother of them all. You may have noticed also that one of the Muses is not described, namely Erato. But she is not forgotten, as we shall see when we come to the conclusion of the poem.

As for the respective attributes of these divinities, Claudel, on the whole, follows the orthodox line. It should be remembered that, for a long period of time, the types of the Muses in art were not even differentiated. Only in the Alexandrian period were they assigned specific functions, each of them becoming the sponsor of a peculiar discipline. We must wait until the Roman period before their iconography and their roles are definitively codified. What is more interesting is that the poet, as we have seen, tried to link them together in well-balanced and harmonious groups:

Les hautes vierges égales, la rangée des soeurs éloquentes,
Je veux dire sur quel pas je les ai vues s'arrêter et comment elles
s'enguirlandaient l'une à l'autre.

Here, obviously, he reflects the intention of the artist, who skillfully introduced such unity in the grouping of the figures and arranged them in a garland, according to Claudel's own expression. This is not the archaic, rigid pattern, where the Muses stand isolated, but the Hellenistic tradition which seems to connect them gracefully through the community of thoughts.

We now come to the general interpretation that runs through the poem. Claudel uses the relief as a medium to express his own concepts about poetic inspiration; it is at the same time a program and an apology. He defines inspiration as a drunkenness.

The poet must be out of his senses, possessed by a sort of frenzy. He must lose his reason, "sa raison grossière et basse," before he can sing. The Muses themselves are inebriated; and Claudel calls Terpsichore "Maenad." This is actually one of the ideas that are symbolized on the sarcophagus. For that is the meaning of the Bacchic figures sculptured on the lid of the tomb: Satyrs and Maenads, lying on cushions, are drinking cups of wine; and some of them look already inebriated. What is the relationship between this orgy and the chaste virgins underneath? How can the Muses be compared to Maenads?

The answer is to be found in Plato's *Phaedrus:*

There is a possession, a madness inspired by the Muses, which seizes upon a tender and virgin soul, stirring it up to rapturous frenzy. But whosoever without the madness of the Muses comes to knock at the doors of poesy from the conceit that haply by force of art he will become an efficient poet, departs with blasted hopes, and his poetry, the poetry of sense, fades in obscurity before the poetry of madness.[5]

So again in *Ion,* Socrates declares—somewhat sarcastically, it is true—and here I quote Shelley's translation:

The authors of these great poems which we admire do not attain to excellence through the rules of any art, but they utter their beautiful melodies of verse in a state of inspiration and, as it were, possessed by a spirit not their own. Thus the composers of lyric poetry create those admired songs of theirs in a state of divine insanity, *like the Corybantes,* who lose control over their reason in the enthusiasm of the sacred dance; and, during this supernatural possession, are excited to the rhythm and harmony which they communicate to men; *like the Bacchantes,* who, when possessed by the gods, draw honey and milk from the rivers, in which, when they come to their senses, they find nothing but simple water . . .

For a poet is indeed a thing ethereally light, winged and sacred; nor can he compose anything worth calling poetry until he becomes inspired, and, as it were, mad, or whilst any reason remains in him. For whilst a man retains any portion of the thing called reason, he is utterly incompetent to produce poetry or to vaticinate.[6]

This conception is Claudel's own, as expressed not only in this first ode, but still more explicitly in the fourth, entitled "La Muse qui est la Grâce." There he confesses that he had hoped, with age, to be liberated from the fury of the Bacchic spirit: "J'attendais que l'âge me délivrât de la fureur de cet esprit bachique."[7] But in vain. He is still intoxicated, still possessed by a god: "Ah, je suis ivre! Ah! je suis livré au dieu!"[8] He confides to the Muse that "he is a little drunk, the way she likes"; and she starts a rather jovial comparison between the poet and the drunkard:

> Celui qui a bu seulement plein son écuelle de vin nouveau, il ne connaît plus le créancier et le propriétaire;
> Il n'est plus l'époux d'une terre maigre et le colon d'une femme querelleuse avec quatre filles à la maison;
> Mais le voici qui bondit tout nu comme un dieu sur le théâtre, la tête coiffée de pampres, tout violet et poisseux de pis sucré de la grappe . . .
> Telle est la vertu de cette boisson terrestre: l'ivrogne peu à peu, plein de gaieté, voit double,
> Les choses à la fois comme elles sont et comme elles ne sont pas et les gens commencent à ne pas comprendre ce qu'il dit.[9]

Does it mean that the poem is just the overflowing of that drunkenness, and that the poet must go adrift, reeling and staggering? No—for in the very midst of his rapture, intelligence retains her control and her moderating influence:

> Mais vous ne m'abandonnerez point, ô Muses modératrices.

This Claudel explains very clearly in his "Lettre à l'Abbé Brémond sur l'inspiration poétique":

> Of course, poetry is primarily emotion; it is a movement of the soul; it is essentially imagination, fired by desire; and it requires a certain state of rapture. But the poet is precisely the man who knows how to put himself, at will, in such a state; and intelligence does not surrender all her rights; she plays some part in the creation of the poem. She does not make it; but she looks at it while it is being made—and she introduces some light and order and proportion into it. That is why the final outcome of emotion is not obscurity, but a superior kind of lucidity.[10]

Urania, with her compass, is here to remind the poet that he cannot sing well if he does not sing according to measure:

> O poète, tu ne chanterais pas bien
> Ton chant si tu ne chantais en mesure.

But, on the other hand, this does not mean that the poet has to follow the traditional patterns or tie himself down to formal rules of composition. He will not imitate the great epic models. He will write no *Odyssey:*

> O mon âme impatiente! nous n'établirons aucun chantier! nous ne pousserons, nous ne roulerons aucune trirème
> Jusqu'à une grande Méditerranée de vers horizontaux,
> Pleine d'îles, praticable aux marchands, entourée par les ports de tous les peuples!
> Nous avons une affaire plus laborieuse à concerter
> Que ton retour, patient Ulysse!
> Toute route perdue! sans relâche pourchassé et secouru
> Par les dieux chauds sur la piste, sans que tu voies rien d'eux que parfois
> La nuit un rayon d'or sur la voile, et dans la splendeur du matin, un moment,
> Une face radieuse aux yeux bleus.

He will not even follow the wake of Aeneas:

> Et toi aussi, bien que ce soit amer
> Il me faut enfin délaisser les bords de ton poème, ô Enée.

Nor the steps of Dante, going up and down, from Heaven to Hell:

> O rimeur Florentin! nous ne te suivrons point, pas après pas, dans ton investigation,
> Descendant, montant jusqu'au ciel, descendant jusque dans l'Enfer.

No, nothing of that sort; none of those tracks already known, already beaten:

> Rien de tout cela! toute route à suivre nous ennuie! . . . toute échelle à escalader!

The poet should not even devise any plan, any itinerary beforehand. His verse should be free, like a flight of swallows:

> O mon âme, il ne faut concerter aucun plan! ô mon âme sauvage, il faut nous tenir libres et prêts,
> Comme les immenses bandes fragiles d'hirondelles quand sans voix retentit l'appel automnal!

It should be sudden and violent as the flash of lightning: nobody knows where it is going to strike:

> Pour toi, Mnémosyne, ces premiers vers, et la déflagration de l'ode soudaine!

Ainsi subitement du milieu de la nuit que mon poème de tous côtés frappe comme l'éclat de la foudre trifourchue!
Et nul ne peut prévoir où soudain elle fera fumer le soleil.

Finally, he compares himself to the eagle, too impatient even to build his nest:

O mon âme impatiente, pareille à l'aigle sans art! comment ferions-nous pour ajuster aucun vers? à l'aigle qui ne sait pas faire son nid même?

Let the verse be like a sea hawk, which darts upon a fish, in a splashing of foam:

Que mon vers ne soit rien d'esclave! mais tel que l'aigle marin qui s'est jeté sur un grand poisson,
Et l'on ne voit rien qu'un éclatant tourbillon d'ailes et l'éclaboussement de l'écume!

This rebellious, intolerant attitude, this apparent rejection of any discipline, has led some critics to describe Claudel as a wild and brutal genius—and even as a barbaric one. They claim that he does not belong to the classic Mediterranean tradition of orderly eloquence. But a more perspicacious critic, J. de Tonquédec, has observed that, on the contrary, the characteristics of Claudel's style are identical with those of a Greek poet, namely, Pindar.[11]

Pindar himself is remembered by Claudel in connection with the Muses. He is the one who celebrates the victors of the Olympic games:

L'ode pure comme un beau corps tout nu, tout brillant de soleil et d'huile
Va chercher tous les dieux par la main pour les mêler à son choeur,
Pour accueillir le triomphe à plein rire, pour accueillir dans un tonnerre d'ailes la victoire
De ceux qui par la force du moins de leurs pieds ont fui le poids du corps inerte.

What has been said about the ancient poet applies exactly to the modern one. Croiset writes about Pindar:

His real characteristic is a thoroughly original manner of seeing things in a general view or collectively with a searching, yet synthetic

and summary glance. He does not analyze. In this respect he is not
Attic, not even Ionic. In the depiction of an object, or an idea, he
gives at once the dominant impression, and that with a concentrated,
quick vigor. A trait, a word is sufficient; but the word is incisive, the
trait shines like an electric spark . . .

His sentences are never periodic after the manner of oratory, but
are a flood of souvenirs and images, recalling each other in the poet's
mind as his song proceeds. He advances by brusque association of
ideas, not by logical succession.

The absence of analysis brings into relief his summary style . . .
but the general movement of his thought is noble and magnificent.
Horace compares him to an overflowing river. The image is a beautiful
and just one. A torrent with its mass of water, troubled and deep, well
represents the immense effectiveness of his synthetic style, sometimes
tumultuous in detail, yet animated, as a whole, by an impetus simple
and imposing.[12]

There is not a word in that page which does not fit Claudel;
and Claudel himself has warned the critics, disconcerted by what
they consider incoherent or erratic in his poetry, to take the compass of Urania; then they will find, not the way, but the center,
the secret unity which runs through the poem:

O grammairien dans mes vers! ne cherche point le chemin, cherche
le centre! mesure, comprends l'espace compris entre ces feux solitaires!

This is the theory of inspiration as expressed in the "Ode to
the Muses." Of course, this analysis does not claim to be exhaustive. Claudel's thought on the subject is far more complex and
elaborate; I have limited myself to pointing out the contacts between the Greek conception and his own. It is remarkable indeed
that his definition should be so close to the pagan one, and that
the pagan color should be so strong in his poem. At the time
when he started writing his ode, Claudel had been converted to
the Catholic faith for nearly fifteen years; still the Christian poet
does not emerge clearly, despite some mysterious allusions to the
Creator. In his fourth ode, "La Muse qui est la Grâce," which is
dated 1907, the Muse gradually transforms herself into divine
Grace to whom, however, the poet still refuses to yield. Finally,
in the fifth ode, "La Maison Fermée," he turns from the nine
Muses to the four Cardinal Virtues, who from now on will be his
inspiring guides:

Jadis j'ai célébré les Muses intérieures, les neuf soeurs indivisibles,
Mais voici que dans cette maturité de mon âge, j'ai appris à recon-
naître les Quatre Assises, les Quatre grandes Extérieures . . .

.   .   .   .   .   .

Je chanterai les grandes Muses carrées, les Quatre Vertus cardinales
orientées avec une céleste rectitude.

However, in Claudel's interpretation of the sarcophagus, there
is one point on which he departs strikingly from classical standards. You may remember that in his description of the nine sisters
he had left out the ninth one, Erato. Now, at the very end of the
poem, he suddenly turns to her in a dramatic and magnificent
outburst.[13] "O Muses," he says, "wise sisters, too wise—even thou,
inebriated Terpsichore! How did you ever think that you were
going to keep this one, this mad one, as a prisoner in your choir,
as a bird in a cage?"

O sages Muses! sages, sages soeurs! et toi-même, ivre Terpsichore!
Comment avez-vous pensé captiver cette folle, la tenir par l'une et
l'autre main,
La garrotter avec l'hymne comme un oiseau qui ne chante que dans
la cage?

This is the one who is really drunk, drunk not with water and air
only, but with red wine and the powerful perfume of roses—this
is the real Maenad and the real Bacchante! For the syllables of
her name spell Love.

Voici celle qui n'est point ivre d'eau pure et d'air subtil!
Une ivresse comme celle du vin rouge et d'un tas de roses! du
raisin sous le pied nu qui gicle, de grandes fleurs toutes gluantes de
miel!
La Ménade affolée par le tambour! au cri perçant du fifre, la
Bacchante roidie dans le dieu tonnant!
Toute brûlante! toute mourante! toute languissante!

This foolish virgin will not stay among the wise virgins, the
active, the industrious ones. She will break away; she will rush
to her lover, the poet. She begs him now, impatiently, ardently,
to take her away:

"Ami!
C'est trop, c'est trop attendre! prends-moi! que faisons-nous ici?

> Combien de temps vas-tu t'occuper encore, bien régulièrement,
> entre mes sages soeurs,
> Comme un maître au milieu de son équipe d'ouvrières? Mes sages
> et actives soeurs! Et moi je suis chaude et folle, impatiente et nue!
> Que fais-tu ici encore? Baise-moi et viens!
> Brise, arrache tous les liens! prends-moi, ta déesse, avec toi!"

Under the spell of all-powerful desire, the poet forgets his task,
his duty. He interrupts the orderly rhythm of the choir and flees
away, with Erato:

> Que m'importe la mesure interrompue de votre choeur?
> Je vous reprends ma folle, mon oiseau!

All this part of the poem is strangely, movingly personal. Indeed, it sounds almost like a confession; there are transparent
allusions in the last verses to a woman, to a crossing which they
made together—and the figure of that woman identifies itself with
the profile of Erato.

> O mon amie! ô Muse dans le vent de la mer . . . !
> Erato! tu me regardes . . . !

Other echoes of this earthly passion are to be found in that most
human of Claudel's tragedies, *Le Partage de Midi*.

So the poem ends on this note, intensely passionate and personal. The irresistible call of life, the burning voice of Love, has
upset the serenity of art; Claudel leaves behind him a disrupted
choir, a mutilated sarcophagus.

III

Let us try to reconstruct it, this time through the patient, penetrating studies of archaeologists. Claudel does not stress the fact
that the Muses are carved on a tomb. He does mention it once
or twice, for instance:

> A l'autre extrémité du coffre, *vide de la capacité d'un corps
> d'homme* . . .

or again:

> O Muses patiemment sculptées *sur le dur sépulcre*.

But he does not elaborate further. Now this fact is a mystery which calls for an elucidation. We have a number of these sarcophagi ornamented with the Muses. Why are the Muses represented on them? What is their relation to the dead man?

Of course there is an obvious, if rather flat, explanation. It may mean simply that the dead man was a learned person, a poet or a scholar who had cultivated the Muses in his lifetime. Indeed, some among the most eminent archaeologists cautiously refuse to go beyond that interpretation: "He was a cultivated man." [14]

The next step is to point out the traditional relation of the Muses to the idea of immortality. Those who will have illustrated themselves in poetry or in the arts will live long after their death in the memory of men. Immortality in that sense means only the prolongation of worldly fame beyond the grave; it is that sort of fictitious and shallow survival of which Paul Valéry spoke so bitterly and so derisively:

> Maigre immortalité noire et dorée,
> Consolatrice affreusement laurée
> Qui de la mort fais un sein maternel,
> Le beau mensonge, et la pieuse ruse!
> Qui ne connaît, et qui ne les refuse,
> Ce crâne vide, et ce rire éternel? [15]

But in recent years some scholars have offered a deeper and, as it seems, a well-substantiated interpretation of immortality, gained thanks to the Muses. I have in mind the studies of Pierre Boyancé, *Le Culte des Muses chez les philosophes Grecs;* of Henri Marrou, Μουσικὸς 'Ανήρ, *Etudes sur les scènes de la vie intellectuelle figurant sur les monuments funéraires romains;* and, above all, the monumental work published by Franz Cumont in 1942: *Recherches sur le symbolisme funéraire des Romains.*

Let us again consider the relationship between the group of the Muses and the group of the Bacchantes on the lid. We have seen that, according to Plato, their association symbolizes the affinity between drunkenness and poetic inspiration. But this assimilation must be enlarged and completed. We must remember that the wine in pagan theology had become par excellence the drink of immortality. "Among the votaries of Dionysus the feasts

of the mysteries in which the consecrated wine was drunk gave
a foretaste of the joys reserved for the initiate in the Elysian
Fields. Drunkenness, which frees from care, which awakens un-
suspected forces in man, was looked upon as the indwelling of
the god in the hearts of the Bacchantes." [16]

In the same way, "all those who have given themselves up to
the works of the intellect had a part in the godhead"; minds that
had experienced in this earthly life the *sober intoxication* of that
spiritual ecstasy given by the contemplation of truth had actually
foretasted eternal beatitude; and they had prepared themselves
for it, because "they were purified by the high pursuit of intellectual joy, and freed thereby from the passions of the body, and
the oppression of matter." [17] For this reason the Muses are frequently represented on tombs. They were the ones to deliver mortals from earthly miseries and lead them back toward the sacred
light of the heavens. By learning their gifts, you took with you, so
to speak, a passport to these heavenly places; and you were sure
to listen one day to the music of the spheres of which, through the
Muses, you had heard some echo here below. Thus, to dedicate
one's life to culture was a way of acquiring much more than
glory; it was a way of winning *astral* immortality. And when a
poet like Horace, for instance, said, *non omnis moriar*, he promised himself more than the applause of posterity; he meant literally that his mind would live forever among the planets and
the fixed stars.

The doctrine is Pythagorean in origin, but it pervaded all
Greek thought, and its most eloquent exponents are the Neoplatonists. This is, for example, how Philo describes the rapture
of intelligence:

The human mind . . . carrying its gaze beyond the confines of
all substance discernible by sense, comes to a point at which it reaches
out after the intelligible world, and on descrying in that world sights
of surpassing loveliness . . . it is seized by a sober intoxication *like
those filled with Corybantic frenzy.*

From then on, the mind will long to see the object of its
yearning; and Philo addresses to his soul this vibrant exhortation:

Therefore, my soul, leave not only thy land, that is the body, thy kinfolk, that is the senses, thy father's house, that is speech, but be a fugitive from thyself also and issue forth from thyself. Like persons possessed *or Corybantes*, be filled with inspired frenzy. For it is the mind which is under the divine afflatus, and no longer in its own keeping, but is stirred to its depths and maddened by heavenward yearning, drawn by the truly existent and pulled upwards thereto, with truth to lead the way and remove all obstacles before its feet;—such is the mind which has the inheritance of divine things.[18]

As for Proclus, who has been called the last priest of the Muses, he begs the nine sisters to take his soul to the circles of Heaven:

> Listen, divinities, you who hold
> The reins of sacred wisdom,
> Who set men's souls on fire
> With flames indomitable
> Drawing them, through the cloudy depths,
> Far up to the Immortals.

These lofty speculations constitute the spiritual substratum of our sarcophagus; and if we doubt it, let us look at the faces of the monument. One of them represents Homer with Calliope, the other one, Socrates with Erato [19] (see frontispiece). It seems very natural that Homer should be represented with the Muse of the epic poem, who is invoked in the first line of the *Iliad* and in the first line of the *Odyssey*. But actually Homer appears on the tomb to complete the allegory which is expressed in its decoration; he appears as an example of a great man, deified for his wisdom. His apotheosis exemplified the heavenly reward due to the studious mind. As for Socrates, we know through his own words why he is associated with Homer on the sarcophagus. At his trial, before being condemned to death, he explained to his judges that he was quite willing to die, for he hoped to meet in the afterlife the great intelligences of the past:

If death is, as it were, a change of habitation from here to some other place, and if what we are told is true—what greater blessing could there be? What would any of you give to meet with Orpheus and Musaeus and Hesiod and Homer? I am willing to die many times over if these things are true; for I personally should find the life there wonderful, when I meet these people.[20]

Socrates is therefore another example of this beatification which awaits the follower of the Muses, the poet, the scientist, the artist, or the philosopher.

Such beliefs were apparently those of the literati under the Empire; for them, intellectual culture had acquired a sort of mystic value; indeed, it had almost become a religion. What they expected from it was more than a refined pleasure or a means of gaining distinction in the world: it was the purification of their soul, and sometimes its salvation.

We seem to have come a long way from Paul Claudel; and indeed there is a curious contrast between his passionate dialogue with Erato and Socrates' serene conversation with the same Muse. I merely wanted to show that this sarcophagus is a sort of meeting ground between great minds of antiquity and a great mind of our own time. It embodies some of the noble thoughts of Pythagoras, of Plato, of Philo; it crystallizes the religious hopes of an intellectual aristocracy at the end of the pagan era. At the same time, it kindles the imagination of a modern poet, whose intuition recreates part of its symbolism, while his lusty genius restores to these cold marble figures a new flesh and a new soul.

Notes

1. *Cinq grandes odes* (Paris, 1913). Selections from these poems are quoted here by permission of Librairie Gallimard, Paris.

2. *Catalogue sommaire des marbres antiques* (Paris: Musée National du Louvre, 1922), no. 475, p. 116 and plate lii.

3. Amy Lowell, *John Keats* (Boston, 1925), II, 241; S. A. Larrabee, *English Bards and Grecian Marbles: The Relationship Between Sculpture and Poetry, Especially in the Romantic Period* (New York: Columbia University Press, 1943), p. 212. Cf. also Maurice de Guérin's *Le Centaure* and *La Bacchante*, partly inspired by ancient marbles; see Elie Decahors, *Les poèmes en prose de Maurice de Guérin et leurs sources antiques* (Toulouse, 1932).

4. Henri Peyre, "Le Classicisme de Claudel," *Nouvelle revue française*, September 1, 1932.

5. *Phaedrus*, 245a.

6. *Ion*, 533.

7. *Cinq grandes odes*, p. 122.

8. *Ibid.*, p. 119.

9. *Ibid.*, pp. 128, 129.

10. *Positions et propositions* (Paris, 1928), pp. 91–100, particularly pp. 94, 96, 97.

11. J. de Tonquédec, "L'oeuvre de P. Claudel," in *Etudes*, April 20, 1917, pp. 182–189.

12. A. and M. Croiset, *An Abridged History of Greek Literature*, tr. Heffelbower (New York, 1904), p. 143.

13. According to André Gide (*Journals*, tr. Justin O'Brien [New York: Alfred A. Knopf, 1947], I, 162), Claudel did not know "how to finish" his Ode, begun in 1900; it was only in 1904 that he added the invocation to Erato and the end.

14. A. D. Nock, "Sarcophagi and Symbolism," *American Journal of Archaeology*, vol. L (1946), no. 1.

15. Paul Valéry, "Le Cimetière marin," in *Charmes* (Paris, 1933), p. 162. Quoted by permission of Librairie Gallimard, Paris.

16. Franz Cumont, *Afterlife in Roman Paganism* (New Haven, 1922), p. 120.

17. *Ibid.*, p. 115. On the "sober intoxication," see H. Lewy, Μέθη Νηφάλιος, Untersuchungen zur Geschichte der Antiken Mystik (Berlin, 1929).

18. *Quis rer. divin. heres*, XIV, 69–71.

19. Cumont's tentative interpretation; see *Recherches sur le symbolisme*, pp. 310 ff.

20. *Apologia*, 41.

THE GREEK CRITICISM OF POETRY
A RECONSIDERATION

William C. Greene

I

It would be pleasant to suppose that artists always knew from the beginning what they were about: that poets and sculptors had clear notions of the meaning and methods and function of their arts before they set to work. Seldom, however, is this true; blundering experiment and many a failure, with here and there a happy intuitive venture, usually precede theory. Yet artistic achievement is the ultimate sanction of theory. Only after continued and solid achievement has established trends and traditions does limping criticism struggle forward to generalize and appraise what has been done, or make bold to ordain what may be done in the future. Thus the more considerable Greek critics come long after the greatest Greek poetry has become the familiar possession of the Greek people. If not merely the general public but even persons in the learned world today have a less intimate knowledge of Greek literature than in various periods in the past, the world at least still pays it respect and is willing to believe that the Greek criticism of poetry must be of value both for Greek poetry and for poetry more generally. Such modern readers are not wholly mistaken in their belief. But they need guidance if they are to understand the limits within which the criticism is valid even for Greek poetry, and discretion if they are to apply it to poetry in general.

For Greek criticism tends to generalize from a selection, sometimes arbitrary, of available literature (virtually all of it being Greek); tragedy is criticized very fully, but not with finality, comedy in fragmentary form, epic inadequately, lyric only tardily. Moreover, the Greek critics had an inadequate notion of historical method, and their method of classification by genres, based on their assumption that literature has already achieved in each kind its natural limits, imposes on criticism itself a limitation that would be disastrous if Greek literature were not indeed so varied and far developed. Specialists today, and the educated public, understand Greek literature in its historical and social development better than did Plato and Aristotle, for all their greatness of mind and their close acquaintance with works lost to us. Through historical and anthropological and comparative methods, for example, we have a better understanding of the social background and the oral composition of early epic; of the ritual elements in drama; of the response of the tragic poets to their environments; of the several periods in the work of Sophocles. Moreover, the Greek criticism was at first, as with Pindar, Aristophanes, and Plato, incidental to other purposes; only with Aristotle did it become self-contained. And after Aristotle it tended, with one notable exception, to confine itself to questions of style. It will therefore be necessary to ask why the Greek critics wrote about poetry, how far their several writings are polemic or apologetic, how far their conclusions now seem adequate for this literature, and how far their ideas can be carried over, with due supplements, to the newer developments of modern literature. To grasp these essentials is well worth the effort, for some few of them are of lasting value and were never more needed than now. They comprise what may be called in the true sense, not in the narrow and dated sense, the doctrine of "classicism": the belief that certain experiences and forms of expression are more vital and universal than others, and that those who drink deeply of these living springs are continually refreshed, whatever their personal experiences may be.[1]

II

Two attitudes toward poetry, two ideas of its purpose and effect, meet us in the earliest period: poetry charms and delights; and poetry reveals the truth. In Homer, it is chiefly the former that is stressed. Eumaeus, wishing to convey to Penelope the "charm" of the newly arrived stranger (Odysseus) and his tale, declares: "Even as when a man gazes on a minstrel whom the

gods have taught to sing words of yearning joy to mortals, and
they have a ceaseless desire to hear him so long as he will sing,
even so he charmed me, sitting by me in the halls." [2] If we ask
what pleasure there can be in hearing of the "pitiful return of
the Achaeans"—and indeed Penelope protests against the theme
—Telemachus will answer us: "Why grudge the sweet minstrel
to gladden us as his spirit moves him? . . . It is no blame if he
sings the ill-faring of the Danaans; for men always prize the song
most that rings newest in their ears." [3] In these minstrels, singing
for the rapt ears of princes in the heroic age or of later aristocratic
listeners in an Ionian society, and in their successors, the rhapsodes of the classical period, who recited Homeric passages to
large audiences and communicated to them their own intense
feeling (as Plato's *Ion* suggests), the purpose is to delight and
"lead" the soul; indeed, the word *psychagogia* will presently be
used of their attitude.

The Homeric minstrel and "Homer" himself and poets in the
epic tradition claim that they are "taught" or "moved" or, as a
later age will say, "inspired," by the Muses or by a god. But for
Hesiod, the epic chronicler of the farmer's ceaseless round of
toil, and for the Boeotian school of poetry that gathered about
him, it is not enough to delight; the end of poetry is to impart
truth. Nor is it enough to be taught by the Muses, for even the
Muses can deceive. The poet of the *Theogony* proclaims that "the
Muses who once taught Hesiod glorious song" has appeared to   *have*
him, too, and before giving him a laurel bough and inspiring him
to sing the past and the future, they have declared: "Many a
feigned thing [ψεύδεα] like to the truth we know how to tell; yet
we know how, when we will, to utter what is true." [4] Here begins
the long war between the poetic and the scientific spirit. Solon
will echo the thought: "The poets feign many a thing." [5] Par-
menides will distinguish in his Proem the Way of Opinion and
the Way of Truth, and Plato will contrast appearance (δόξα)
and truth (ἀλήθεια). Xenophanes will condemn Homer and Hesiod
for immoral myths and for anthropomorphism. Not without reason
will Plato, who himself subjects Homer and drama to criticism
on moral grounds and is not content with allegorical interpretation of objectionable myths, remark that "there is an ancient

quarrel between philosophy and poetry." [6] But the discovery of the nature of poetic truth is slow in coming to light.

Pindar more than once takes note soberly of the illusions of poetry. "Wonders indeed are many, and as for the tale that is told among mortals, transgressing the language of truth, it may haply be that stories cunningly embroidered with lies lead them astray. But the charm [*charis*] of song, that maketh for mortals all things that soothe them, by adding her glory, full often causeth that which is past belief to be believed; but the days that are still to come are the wisest witnesses." [7] "I deem that Odysseus hath won fame far beyond his sufferings, thanks to the sweet lays of Homer; for on Homer's fiction and on his winged skill there resteth a solemn spell [σεμνὸν ἔπεστί τι]; and the poet's lore beguileth us, leading us astray with legends; but the mass of men have a heart that is blind." [8] For all that, Pindar has an exalted conception, not so much of his personal gifts as of his sacred office—one might almost say, of his priestly if not prophetic role. Thus, continuing the conception of the poet as taught or inspired by the gods or the Muses, he gives to the conception a special form and initiates a controversy that is not even yet silenced. For with Pindar inspiration is not so much the external prompting of the poet by supernatural powers, or the madness or ecstasy of the Dionysiac mystics and their followers—doctrines which we shall meet elsewhere—as it is the normal activity of a specially gifted nature (φυά), of a genius, as we should say. Thus it is nothing that can be acquired by taking pains, or by art (τέχνη). Here begins, then, the problem of the relative claims of "Nature" and "Art": are poets "born" or "made"? Pindar takes his stand generally on the side of Nature. "That which cometh of Nature is ever best; but many men have striven to win fame by means of excellence that cometh from mere training [διδακταῖς ἀρεταῖς]; but any thing in which God hath no part is none the worse for being quenched in silence." [9]

Before Pindar died, Greek tragedy had reached nearly its most perfect and characteristic form; but it had hardly occurred to anyone that prose was capable of achieving artistic form. The impulse toward artistic prose came chiefly from the sophists and rhetorical teachers who offered, in the last third of the fifth century, to teach young Athenians how to succeed in public life in a now democratic state, where the art of persuading assemblies and juries was the most important of tools. With Gorgias, prose was poetic in coloring and technique, while poetry was encouraged to be rhetorical; both are productive of pleasure and dispel sorrow, and both seek to "charm" and "persuade" the soul by a sort of "magic." Holding, if we may trust Plutarch,[10] that tragedy deceives, but thus gratifies, its audience, and that poetry affects its hearers with "shuddering awe and tearful pity and a yearning for sorrow and a fellow-feeling for the fortunes of others," Gorgias seems to anticipate certain famous Aristotelian views of tragedy; and his emphasis on "persuasion" in prose, as well as in poetry, will reappear, in modified form, in Aristotle and in other writers on rhetoric.

Beyond the criticism of drama involved in the competitions of the dramatic festivals, which resulted in a relative ranking of the plays presented—a crude use of the comparative method, like the drawing up of lists—we find in the plays themselves criticism of earlier plays and of rival poets; and now for the first time the criticism is not merely general, but is directed to specific artistic matters. Thus tragedy criticizes tragedy. Still more pointed is the criticism of tragedy by comedy. It is in the *Frogs* that Aristophanes gives most fully his considered judgment of tragic poetry. If he does not formulate abstract critical principles, he provides a comparison of two actual but dead poets, candidates for resurrection from Hades to Athens. Of the three great tragic poets, Aeschylus and Euripides, extremes in art and attitude as well as in time, afford the greatest contrast, and Sophocles is represented as preferring not to enter the contest. For a contest, or *agon*, it is, something familiar in Greek life and especially familiar as one of the regular parts of the Old Comedy. In this, the first example of extended literary criticism in European literature, we observe that the contest is concerned with two matters: artistic and moral standards, that is, "skill in the art, and wise counsel for the state, making men better citizens." [11]

From the licensed jester Aristophanes, it would be as idle to expect sober aesthetic criticism as it would be to look for sound historical perspective in Aristophanes the reactionary; we must take him for what he is, a comic poet having his fun with matters of great interest to his public. We may agree with him that the majestic dramas of Aeschylus represent a great tradition and a school of character: of their probing of moral problems Aristophanes has nothing to say. We may recognize with him that there is something disturbing, as well as appealing, in the new drama of Euripides, with its broad humanity, its realism, its reckoning with contemporary experience and thought. Further than that we need not go; his criticism, though it has the merit of dealing with actual poetry, not with mere theory, is narrowly dated and springs from a nostalgic longing for a past to which there could be no return. For an attempt at universal principles, we must turn to Plato and Aristotle.

III

The first and most persistent question that Plato set himself with regard to poetry was the question of truth: how is the truth of poetry related to the truth of ordinary everyday life, or to scientific truth, and from what source does the poet gain his knowledge and his authority? In the *Ion*, Plato plays ironically with the claims of poets and rhapsodes to inspiration from external sources, using ideas familiar from the mystical cults: "madness," "enthusiasm," and a "divine dispensation" ($\theta\epsilon\acute{\iota}\alpha\ \mu o\hat{\iota}\rho\alpha$). Ion, the rhapsode, is at last allowed to take refuge in the claim that he, like the poets, is inspired. Shallow creature that he is, he proves an easy victim of the Socratic or Platonic irony. But this does not mean that Plato has given up the traditional Greek view that the poet is inspired by some external influence. He does indeed believe that it is futile to go to the poets for certain kinds of practical information; but he is ironically showing that Ion has no understanding of the nature of another kind of knowledge, which we may call poetic truth, and of the way in which poets attain to it.

The *Meno*, together with its doctrine of "recollection" of absolute knowledge held in a previous existence, includes a provisional acceptance of "right opinion" for many practical uses. Theoretically inferior to "knowledge," "right opinion" is often as effective in practice and is the method of statesmen, interpreters of oracles, seers, and "all poetic persons": they are all divinely inspired.[12] Note here that Plato in his doctrine of "recollection" is hinting at a standard of absolute truth never to be fully attained in this life. At the same time, he is now placing poetic inspiration and knowledge of practical things, which were mutually opposed in the *Ion*, in the same category, and is now contrasting them with the hypothetical absolute knowledge. Actual statesmen and poets, unscientific and unable to deduce truth rationally from a cause, succeed only through makeshifts and happy accidents or the "grace of God," as we might say. Again there is irony, but only to the extent that the actual always falls short of the ideal or the absolute; yet at this stage the claim of poetry to express truth is in peril.

And now the theory of poetry is caught up in the developing doctrine which becomes central in the Platonic philosophy: the doctrine of "ideas," eternal and immutable, imperfectly expressed in the world of phenomena, whether in conduct or in art or in cognition. The doctrine appears in different contexts in the *Symposium*, the *Phaedo*, the *Republic*, and the *Phaedrus*, and is elsewhere subjected to criticism or modification. In the *Symposium*, Plato describes not so much recollection of an absolute as the love of beauty, passing by prescribed ascending steps from single beautiful bodies to all beautiful bodies, from bodies to souls and practices and laws, till the lover contemplates "the vast sea of beauty," the goal of all his striving, and in turn begets images in its likeness.[13] The aesthetic idealism of the *Symposium* has its counterpart in the intellectual idealism of the *Phaedo*, where the dualism of soul and body points to a reality attainable only by the philosophic soul that has been purified of bodily impediments and that may grasp by pure thought the intelligible universal principles. It is only by using sense perceptions of particular things that we can pass beyond them to the eternal principles, but the eternal principles stand absolutely in their own right. The perception of beauty is here only one of several types of experience; but beautiful things are beautiful "by reason of beauty." [14]

Later, in the *Phaedrus*, Plato returns to the problem, in the course of his discussion of the conditions of a philosophical rhetoric, based on a supposed vision of absolute truth in which the Many are ranged under the One, particulars being organically related to the whole.[15] Again the notion of poetic "madness" is revived and distinguished from other forms of madness; [16] poetry can not be produced by mere art, the pedantic following of rules, without the madness of the Muses. But that this is not merely the traditional theory of irresponsible inspiration appears from the mythical account that follows. Stripped of the mythical imagery, Plato's account means that the experience of individual objects of sense may in theory lead to the direct contemplation of the "ideas"; actually, the process is rarely if ever achieved, hence the depreciation of the poets. Furthermore, though the account of the vision of reality is in general terms and mentions "beauty, wisdom, goodness, and the like," [17] it goes on to restrict the channel of recapture to one concept: that of earthly beauty,[18] because it is in the beauties of our sensible world that the supernal vision shines most brightly and is most palpable and most readily incites us to the recollection of real beauty.[19] Actual poetry, then, and the attitude of the "imitators" who are content to tarry with mere images without pressing on to reality, Plato disparages; but he leaves room for what may be called a philosophic poetry.[20] The doctrine of ideas is not an obstacle to the passage of the mind from the world of sense to truth; it is rather a bridge, and inspiration by a god has given place to inspiration by the vision of the ideas.

So far the criticism of poetry by Plato has been concerned chiefly with the problem of poetic truth. But the Socratic quest for truth was intimately interwoven with the quest for moral goodness. When Plato undertook in the earlier dialogues, and above all in the central *Republic,* written probably earlier than the *Phaedrus,* to define the several virtues, he was bound to reckon with the poets, the traditional educators of Greece. He quoted them freely, sometimes in approval, sometimes in sharp disagreement. In the second and third books of the *Republic,*[21] as his sketch of social development proceeds from primitive village life to a complex state, he takes over the traditional education in poetry as conducive to the formation of the kind of character that his future rulers should have; it is at least a foundation on which the higher education may rest. Though myths may be literally untrue, they may convey truth. But it immediately appears that the myths of Homer and Hesiod must suffer expurgation in the interest of morals; for neither gods nor men must be represented as acting unworthily, and allegorical interpretation of the myths is rejected. God is to be represented always as he is: as good, as the cause only of good, as unchanging, as never deceiving. Heroes must not be shown as cowardly or as fearing death. Finally, it is affirmed provisionally, subject to the exact definition of justice still to be discovered, that the poets should not be allowed to represent wicked men as prospering and just men as wretched.[22] Whether Greek tragedy, as we know it, could be tolerated on this last principle may be gravely doubted. But it should be observed that to this point, the criticism of poetry has been concerned with its subject matter and has been based on ethical grounds, as was that of Xenophanes. It has not been held that poetry is incapable of representing, or, as Plato would say, of "imitating," gods and men truly. What he has censured is not fiction as such, or imitation as such, but bad imitation, that is, the imitation of untrue and unworthy objects, or of worthy objects in an unworthy manner.

In what follows,[23] it turns out almost immediately that Plato is not here prepared to accept or to reject poetry simply on the ground that it is more or less imitative,[24] but rather is inquiring what effect imitative poetry has on the mind and character of the public. Much, therefore, in the contemporary theater, though pleasant and appealing, Plato will not accept; the poet who insists on imitating everything in his poems is to be treated with courtesy, but is to be exiled.[25] The exile of tragedy is qualified; and even comedy, if produced in a proper spirit of jesting, is to be tolerated.[26]

The discussion, then, has continued to be concerned with ethical questions. And we must particularly observe that Plato has not yet raised at all any question whether it is possible for poetic imitation to give any grasp of truth. It is assumed that poetry may imitate good character or may imitate bad character; to that extent it appears that it may deal with universals. In theory, at least, there is a form or type of character and of speech[27] which not only can be imitated but should be imitated. As Plato proceeds [28] to discuss musical "modes" and sculpture, he gives further support to the conception. Music both expresses character and influences character. The young who are surrounded by noble works of sculpture and architecture and music receive, like a breeze from a healthful region, an effluence of every good thing, and are insensibly brought into harmony with the beauty of reason. The future guardians thus learn to recognize the essential "forms" of virtue and their "images" in every context. This is not a complete theory of imitation, nor does it depend on the fully developed doctrine of "ideas"; but it distinctly implies that there is room for a poetry which uses "images" of reality. Later, in the fifth book, the philosopher, who loves the vision of truth, is distinguished from the "lover of sights and sounds," the dreamer who takes the semblance for the reality, and who therefore lingers in the realm of opinion and relativity and the senses.[29]

The sixth and seventh books of the *Republic* are still more deeply involved in metaphysics and the theory of knowledge, and include as the culmination of the training of the future guardians the study of dialectic and the "ideas" and the ultimate "Idea of the Good." This idea, nowhere formulated in detail, but only adumbrated in imaginative language, is affirmed to be the cause of all being and all goodness. And Plato nowhere suggests that he or any man can fully attain to the vision of it; absolute knowledge is only a goal, the hypothetical limit of an endless quest.

At the beginning of the tenth book, however, Socrates expresses gratification at the legislation that has been passed with regard to poetry, namely, "the exclusion of poetry so far as it is imitative." [30] If we recall that in the earlier discussion imitative poetry was not excluded as such, but only the imitation of what is morally bad, or of worthy objects in an unworthy manner, we have reason to hold that there is a discrepancy. Our misgivings increase as we observe in the sequel the example of imitation that is chosen. Whereas Plato has previously entertained the possibility that poetry may imitate ethical ideas, here he deliberately uses the illustration of the painter who copies the bed which the carpenter has made, itself a copy of the ideal bed conceived by the designer; obviously the painting is several removes from reality.[31] Furthermore, such imitation of sensible objects may be confused by simple persons with the objects themselves; poets and painters have not the knowledge of many things that technical experts have; and they appeal to the irrational part of the soul that can see only appearances, and that finds pleasure in emotional excitement; such poetry "feeds and waters passions that should be dried up." [32]

This last charge, that poetry stirs us to the indulgence of emotions, should be considered with Plato's treatment of pleasure in the *Philebus*, in which he distinguishes between "impure" pleasures—those which are only the temporary relief of pain, whether physical or, as in drama and indeed in life itself, spiritual—and "pure" pleasures, which are not thus conditioned, and which, moreover, exemplify the principles of measure or limit, as in health, astronomy, music, and all ordered beauty.[33] Though Plato both in the *Republic* and in the *Philebus* is hostile to the fleeting and impure kind of pleasure, which is a sort of purging of painful emotions, Plato provides the germs of a theory of catharsis for Aristotle. But to return to the *Republic*, in the passage dealing with imitation and emotion Plato concluded that only an austere poetry can be admitted to his state, "hymns and praises of famous men"; for if the Muse of pleasure be admitted, the place of law and of universally accepted reason will be usurped by the standards of pleasure and pain. In short, there has always been a quarrel between philosophy and poetry, and the former judgment of exile passed against poetry is justified by the nature of poetry.[34]

Why has Plato so deliberately and, as it must appear, so unfairly sought to damage the cause of poetry? Can he be in earnest? He himself gives us a clue to help us out of our perplexity. He who listens to poetry should, fearing for the safety of the city "which is within him," be on his guard against her seductions.[35] The very phrase has just been used of that city which is an ideal that cannot be realized.[36] Plato, then, tells us as plainly as words can tell us that *poetry as it is* is being brought into opposition with an *ideal of philosophy* such as he admits is unattainable. It is precisely because he is so deeply in earnest about the paramount claim of the philosophic ideal, and because he also feels so keenly the power of poetry and the fleeting world of the senses, that he points the contrast by dramatically, almost comically, confronting the absolute philosophy with the temporal and specious and inconclusive poetry of familiar experience. Poetry is, poetry must always be, like opinion, in some degree a makeshift. This is not the time for Plato to remember all that he has said, or for us to recall what he was to say in the *Phaedrus,* about the contact of poetry with the ideal world; or, on the other hand, his frequent admissions that dialectic and the Idea of the Good are only ideals of the philosophic imagination; or, again, his remarks about the practical value of "right opinion." If we have the reality, the poet as an imitator is of course superfluous. But we need not outdo Plato and suppose his exile of poetry from an imagined Paradise to be his last word in literary criticism; it must be read rather as a dramatic gesture, as a bit of satire on the accepted educators of Hellas. Nor should we forget that when, as an old man, and in a more realistic mood, Plato returned in the *Laws* to the consideration of politics, he reopened the question of poetry. In his "second-best state," a state not beyond the hope of realization, he provides for the regulation of the poets, who are to express the character of good men; [37] moreover, he finds it possible to admit tragedy and, with certain restrictions, even comedy, which is useful as exhibiting kinds of character to be avoided. [38] For the legislator, too, is a creative poet and will not brook rival poets, [39] unless they are chastened and willing to assist his enterprise.

Plato's view of poetry is not complete, nor will it satisfy all people. It lacks historical perspective, for example, in its treatment of Homer and of drama. Many will regret its strong negations: its willingness to resort to censorship and regulation in the interest of morality and a healthy social organism; the austerity of its canons and the danger of a dull uniformity in the poetry to be tolerated. (*Laws* 665c suggests, however, that variety, within limits, is to be encouraged; the question is how variety is possible.)

On the positive side, Plato provides a valid approach to the eternal antithesis between the realm of sense phenomena and the realm of ideas. The Parable of the Cave [40] may be read as

satire on the plight of the average movie-goer and the average
novel reader, who take the world of the film and the novel as
a truthful representation of life. Plato invites us to turn away
from sense phenomena and to contemplate the realities which
any particular story only imperfectly approximates; he is fond
of pointing to the ideas as the models to which the artist should
"look." [41] He even insists that the ideas can never be fully realized.[42] Literature, in other words, must not be content to present
realistic pictures of the surface of things; it must see beneath
the surface the true significance of things, of human and cosmic
forces, and above all of moral law. At one point Plato has provisionally laid down the principle that poets must not be allowed
to represent wicked men as prospering and just men as
wretched.[43] That is, they must not violate what has been called
the principle of "poetic justice," the notion that poetry should
show forth the vindication of the virtuous and the punishment
of the vicious. Plato himself admits, of course, that in the world
as we know it the wicked often do prosper and the just do suffer, at least in the immediate and material sense; his point therefore is concerned with a long-range view that penetrates beneath
the surface and reckons with spiritual good and evil.

The poet, then, deals not merely with particular facts, but also
with ideal truth, with universals. But the universals of poetry
are not the universals of science, conceptual products of the
logical method. As the Idea of Good regulates the moral life, so
the ideas to which the poet "looks" are the regulative principles
that give meaning and consistency to the multifarious and conflicting phenomena of the world about him. There is room, for
example, in Plato's view, for the free creative activity of the poet
in the selection and arrangement of his materials.

Moreover, Plato provides at least the materials for a theory of
the imagination, and some indication of the means by which it
may make itself felt in practice. Whenever he undertakes to
express the relation of the world of sense to the world of ideas,
and especially to express the role of the Idea of the Good, he
finds himself forced to resort to image, metaphor, simile, myth; [44]
the details, the concrete symbols, he will not dare affirm to
be true, but that "something like this" is true or probable, he

will insist.[45] Music, metaphor, myth do not so much state as suggest the character of attitude or mood that he would capture.
They represent a lacuna in the scientific understanding.

From his predecessors Plato took such terms as εἰκών, "image,"
and φαντασία, "appearance," and their cognates, with no philosophical implications; but at first he contrasted such "images"
disparagingly with "reality."[46] Yet a "phantasy" (φαντασία) is at
least a fact, as a mental phenomenon, such as a dream, and may
even be subject to control.[47] "Images" are still inferior to the
truth revealed by the pure reason, as the figure of the Divided
Line is intended to show, but they may supply the suggestions
or "steps" by which the reason will proceed to the truth.[48] The
Parable of the Cave, to be sure, and the renewed discussion of
art in the tenth book of the *Republic,* both maintaining the
sovereignty of the "ideas," set a low value, as we have seen, on
the image-making or imitative activity of artists;[49] their creations may be not merely imitations, but imitations of mere appearances.[50] This is the rejection of naturalism, and more especially of relativism, in art. Furthermore, the *Theaetetus* (for
example, 161de) and the *Sophist* (for example, 233c; 235d;
236ac) refute the sophistic art as the attempt to substitute not
merely "appearances," but particularly subjective "appearances,"
for reality. This development implies, however, a distinction between true and false "phantasies," between "imagination" and
"fancy." The subjective, false kind of "imitation" or "image-
making" is rejected; but the true is a kind of creation, as in the
divine act of creation, of the universe and other images (a point
further developed in the *Timaeus*), or of our dreams and our
poetic inspirations, and also, as it would seem, in human artistic
creations. On the latter point, Plato is not so explicit in the
Sophist as in the theory of imitation of the *Laws,* in which music
is called "imaginative" (εἰκαστική),[51] or indeed in Plato's own
practice; for he calls his description of a state "the truest tragedy."[52] And elsewhere in his later dialogues, Plato is willing to
recognize the part played by sensation, mental images, memory,
and the recall of past experience, each of which may be either
true or false, and may also give a true or a false basis for future
action or feeling or thought.[53] This recognition was to become

the source of a part of the Aristotelian and the Stoic views of the imagination.

The psychology of the *Sophist* and the *Philebus* is supplemented by the theory of dreams of the *Timaeus*,[54] which distinguishes grades of truthfulness; some visions are divinely sent, not to our reasons, but to the parts of our natures most concerned with desires and passions, when these are duly regulated. The *Phaedrus* myth, too, unfolding the doctrine of divine madness, of lover or of poet, describes the process by which the soul may rise from the perception of concrete images of beauty to the pure form of beauty itself. Thus Plato's early distrust of the imagination (phantasies) came to be replaced by a view that actually claimed for some images a divine origin and that linked imagination with inspiration by God or by the Ideas. It remained for Dio Chrysostom to advocate the expression in visible form of what is invisible;[55] for Philostratus to prefer imagination to imitation, the unseen to the seen;[56] and for Plotinus to abandon imitation altogether in favor of the creative imagination.[57]

In Plato's insistence on the division of labor in artistic as in economic activities, and also in the fact that Greek writers had always tended to be specialists in particular genres, we have the fundamental basis of the doctrine of literary forms, each with its own specific nature and laws, which require propriety ($\tau\grave{o}$ $\pi\rho\acute{\epsilon}\pi o\nu$, decorum) in the adaptation of means to ends. The doctrine will reappear constantly, explicitly or implicitly, for better or for worse, in most subsequent critical theory. Aristotle will define the different species of poetry and their specific requirements; Cicero will trace the conception of the ideal orator directly to Plato's "ideas";[58] Horace will take the literary forms for granted and lay down precepts for successful writing in the various kinds. And all will assume that not only the "imitation" of life but the imitation of extant masterpieces of art in the various kinds is a means of achieving success. Nevertheless, so far as Plato's "ideas" are objects of intuition rather than logical concepts, so far as the "literary forms" represent a generalization of norms from actual practice rather than absolute laws, and so far as the poet has freedom in the selection of images and symbols for the expression of truth, so far does Plato tolerate or rather encourage poetry.

The value of Plato's criticism of poetry, then, consists not so much in its strong negations, or even in specific principles of aesthetic appreciation, as in the bridge that it provides between poetry and philosophy. Plato urges us to consider every work not merely as beautiful in itself but as the vehicle of abiding truth. So far as its imitation of our world is a means to this end, so far is it to be welcomed, and the ancient conflict between philosophy and poetry may cease. But how few poems, or works of art in any kind, will deserve Plato's cordial acceptance!

IV

The philosophy of Aristotle in its most characteristic phases springs from the philosophy of Plato, but develops in special directions; and Aristotle is often at pains to emphasize the points of disagreement rather than the fundamental agreement. The *Poetics* does not mention Plato, but it is none the less in part a polemic against certain tendencies in the Platonic attitude. Plato has considered poetry against a background of moral reform and has judged it severely; he has considered it as "imitation," and though he has admitted, nay insisted on, its ideal possibilities, he has contrasted its actual performance with the hypothetical possibilities of philosophy and has found mere "imitation" wanting. In the *Gorgias*[59] and in the *Republic* and in the *Philebus* (in his discussion of "pure" and "impure" pleasures), he has accused poetry, along with other activities, of catering to mere pleasure and to emotional orgies without measure or control.

Aristotle accepts Plato's challenge. As usual, his sympathies are nearer than Plato's to average human nature; and in poetry, as in all else, he looks for development and the flowering of potentialities. He boldly accepts the current conception of "imitation," but deepens it; by implication he accepts the proposition that the aim of poetry is to give pleasure, but defines more carefully the kind of pleasure that is proper to all serious art, and offers an explanation of the special function of tragedy in arousing and releasing emotion. He admits that tragedy presents moral problems, but attempts to distinguish among the varieties of tragic plots those which satisfy the moral sense. He is the first critic who deals with the artistic problems of dramatic construction, and one of the first to be interested in the elements and varieties of "style." The *Poetics*, then, is the earliest "Art of Poetry," and the earliest "Defense" or "Apology" for poetry. Incidentally, it is the first study of poetry that attempts, however imperfectly, to introduce literary history and the rudiments of grammar.

The *Poetics*, like the *Rhetoric*, is intended to help form the principles of the poet or the speaker, and incidentally to assist the critic. These principles in the nature of things will not claim the absolute validity of scientific laws, but rather of generalizations based on observation of human nature and human documents. The plan of the *Poetics* seems not to have included much discussion of lyric poetry; moreover, the treatment of comedy was inadequate, unless it was resumed in a lost second book of which traces are preserved in the later document known as the *Tractatus Coislinianus*. What we have in the extant book, on this assumption, is a "torso." Even within the pages that have been preserved, there are anomalies in the use of terms, differences of method and inconsistencies in the thought, digressions and a frequent lack of orderly arrangement, which have suggested that what we have was written at different times or has been subjected to interpolations. It is possible to distinguish early sections, in which the author is attacking Platonic problems and using Platonic methods, from other sections that consider different problems and use different methods. Moreover, the partly polemical character of the work seems to have limited its scope, so that many problems of artistic technique, more fully explored even by Aristophanes, are neglected, to say nothing of the fact that Aristotle almost completely fails to deal with the thought, the content, and the magical appeal of poetry as such.

I have said that Aristotle deepens the current conception of "imitation" ($\mu\ell\mu\eta\sigma\iota\varsigma$). The term, to be sure, is not very satisfactory, since it may easily beg all the questions at issue. Drama, epic, in fact, all the arts, must start with certain materials and shape them in some way for some use or effect. Poetry deals particularly with men, above all with men in action, by impersonation or by report of their needs or words or feelings. At its lowest level this is mimicry, photographic recording, or reënactment, resulting to some extent in an illusion that the actual object is before us; at its highest level it is creation, the representation of something not actual, but possible, and in a sense (Plato's sense, and Aristotle's) something more real than actual objects, because universally true. Aristotle admits that the artist, working in a world of appearances, imitates things not as they really are, but as they appear.

In fact, Aristotle recognizes three distinct possible objects of imitation: "things as they were or are, things as they are said or thought to be, or things as they ought to be." [60] The last of these categories corresponds to what Plato said the artist should imitate; [61] in a word, the artist who uses concrete images to express such truth "idealizes" his subject matter. The phrase "things as they ought to be" sounds as if a moral judgment were involved. But that is not necessarily the case. Elsewhere Aristotle suggests that it is the function of art to complete the imperfections of purposive Nature. For "Art imitates Nature"; [62] and Nature is purposive, but not always successful in her efforts.[63] Art, however, can succeed when Nature fails, by representing what Nature, through the impediments of "necessity" or "matter," can seldom perfectly achieve—the ideal or the universal. Poetry is therefore contrasted by Aristotle with history; and it is interesting to note that it is in the context of his discussion of unity of plot and of "probability or necessity" that he makes the comparison. In this perception of the universality of poetic truth, based not so much on a scientific generalization or mathematical average of individual facts as on the law of "probability" and the inner consistency of persons acting in accordance with their natures in a well constructed work of art, Aristotle has found his reconciliation of Plato's "ancient quarrel between poetry and philosophy."

I have said that Aristotle believes that the aim of poetry is to give pleasure, but that he defines the kind of pleasure proper to serious art. Not only is pleasure in imitation and harmony and rhythm universal and natural and instructive,[64] but it is pointed out that objects which in themselves are viewed with pain, when realistically represented are contemplated with delight, through the intellectual, or philosophical, pleasure of recognition. Thus natural instincts lead from improvisations to poetry and its sub-divisions: so tragedy developed till it reached "its natural form" and stopped.[65] This conception of the "natural form" ($\varphi\acute{v}\sigma\iota\varsigma$) of a work of art, with its Aristotelian implication of the fulfillment of an end ($\tau\acute{\epsilon}\lambda o\varsigma$', is fraught with significance. It implies that certain works, to be cited, represent the *ne plus ultra* of an art, and that from them may be derived a definition of the genre. Whether Aristotle's famous definition of tragedy, which follows shortly,[66] is actually derived from the works cited, or whether again it is (as is stated) in all respects deduced from the principles laid down, remains to be seen. For tragedy, at least, it involves the doctrine of literary forms.

The beauty of tragedy depends not only on the orderly arrangement of its parts, especially on its organic unity, but also on its magnitude, or scale, neither too large nor too small,[67] as well as on its embellishments of language and music. Parts of the famous definition of tragedy, as Aristotle remarks, are derived from his previous analysis; not so the requirement of completeness (developed in the idea of unity in chapters 7, 8, and 9), nor that of catharsis, which Aristotle had probably broached in his dialogue *On the Poets* and which he briefly discusses in the *Politics*,[68] with an offhand reference to the Poetics for "clearer discussion." But in its present form the *Poetics* tells no more. The problem arises from Plato's distinction in the *Philebus* between "pure" and "impure" pleasures. Whether Aristotle is using merely a medical metaphor, and the catharsis of pity and fear implies only the ridding from our systems of painful emotions, leaving us temporarily relieved, as most recent scholars have held, or whether he is concerned with an artistic matter, the reduction of the emotions to a symmetry or due proportion, or whether he means that our emotions are purified, and a permanent elevation of taste and character is achieved, is a question that may be endlessly discussed. Aristotle believes that the function of poetry is to provide an emotional release. This, then, is the answer to Plato's puritanical objection to the art that caters to mere enjoyment. It revives the ancient claim of the Homeric bard that poetry brings delight; but more, to Plato's complaint that poetry "feeds and waters the passions that should be dried up," and to his demand that poetry, if tolerated, should be "useful" as well as pleasant,[69] Aristotle replies that it is good that these emotions should exist, should find their proper objects, and should so become not merely painful but the source of pleasure. Thus poetry is useful.

At the same time, Aristotle is fully aware of the close relation between pleasure and the moral life; and, in one of the rare cases in which he goes out of his way to express agreement with Plato, he declares that right education consists in being led from childhood to feel pleasure or pain at the proper objects.[70] And here it is important to notice that, in spite of his acceptance of pleasure as the end of art, and of his criticism of art from the point of view of aesthetic enjoyment rather than moral instruction, Aristotle does incidentally consider tragedy from an ethical point of view. This he does by asking "what the poet is to aim at, and what to avoid, in constructing his plots, and what are the conditions on which the tragic effect depends."[71] And his answer deals not only with matters of technique, but above all with kinds of plot, of tragic hero, and with the two emotions, pity and fear, that he has said should be subjected to catharsis. Spreading before us all the theoretically possible kinds of plot, Aristotle discovers by a process of elimination the one kind of plot, and of tragic hero, that satisfies the emotional and moral demands of tragedy. Passing over the rejected kinds, we may merely notice that Aristotle, alike in his brief reference to "undeserved suffering,"[72] which does evoke the desired pity, and in his disparagement of "double plots" with opposite outcomes for the good and the bad characters, as also in his commendation of the "unhappy endings" of Euripides, indicates his disagreement with the principle of "poetic justice." There remains the tragedy of a kind of hero who is called "intermediate" (δ $\mu\epsilon\tau\alpha\xi\acute{u}$): that of "a man, not preëminently virtuous and just, whose misfortune, however, is brought about not by vice or depravity, but by some error [$\delta\iota'\dot{\alpha}\mu\alpha\rho\tau\acute{\iota}\alpha\nu$ $\tau\iota\nu\acute{\alpha}$]; one of those men who is highly renowned and prosperous, like Oedipus, Thyestes, and illustrious men of such families." [73] Presently the character of the ideal tragic hero is qualified as being "either such as we have described, or better rather than worse" (in conformity with principles laid down previously, in chapter 2, and justified later, in 26); and the error is called "a great error." [74] Moreover, the further classification of tragic plots, mostly drawn from "a few houses" and developed in "the right way" (καλῶς), so as to elicit the pleasure proper to tragedy, continues to turn on questions of moral sentiment.[75] And foremost among the requirements of character in the tragic hero (already described as "not preëminently virtuous and just," or "better rather than worse" than that) is that he be "good" (χρηστός, 1454a17; ἐπιεικής, 1454b13), or "better than ordinary" (βελτίων, 1454b11), as well as consistently drawn.

Now what is to be made of Aristotle's interest in the moral nature of tragedy, and in particular of his conception of the character of the tragic hero and his *hamartia*? Does it interpret correctly the actual trend or "nature" of the Greek tragedies that he knew, or that we know? Is it of value for tragedy more generally? The tragic hero, he holds, suffers because of some *hamartia*. Does that imply that he is morally culpable? The word *hamartia* and its cognates, to be sure, bear many shades of meaning, from simply "missing the mark" and intellectual error to moral lapses, but seldom to sinfulness of will. In the *Ethics* Aristotle recognizes various grades of moral responsibility. I think there can be no doubt that in the *Poetics* he attributes some moral culpability to the hero's act. To that extent, in a just universe, suffering must be deserved. Yet Aristotle's explicit reference to the tragic pity occasioned by "undeserved suffering" [76] and his preference for "unhappy endings" indicate that he finds the essence of tragedy in suffering that is not proportionate to *hamartia,* but arising from the collision of the hero's act with forces too great for him. In such a case we shall not have a theodicy, justifying the ways of god to man, but we may have the spectacle of suffering not wholly deserved but heroically met; not divine justice, but an exalted humanism.

Writing two or three generations after the greatest period of tragedy, Aristotle looks back to the three great poets and selects what suits his conceptions, and now and then cites the practice

of lesser dramatists of his own day. Of the three, he refers most
often and with greatest admiration to Sophocles. Aeschylus he
almost ignores (and indeed his plays were little performed in
the lifetime of Aristotle), and Euripides (whose popularity was
mostly posthumous) he cites chiefly for matters of technique.
Yet it might be argued, paradoxically enough, that the Aristotelian idea of *hamartia* fits the ignored Aeschylean heroes—for
example, the philanthropic Prometheus, who made the "mistake"
of defying the "new tyrant Zeus"; [77] or, better, Agamemnon, with
his more obvious crime. For it is Aeschylus who sought to achieve
a theodicy, and who may be said almost to have created the conception of a Zeus who began as arbitrary power (*Prometheus
Bound*) and developed into a god of justice and mercy (*Sup-
pliants, Persians, Prometheus Unbound, Oresteia*).

But the idea of *hamartia* simply will not fit Sophocles, for all
the frequent use of the term that is made in his plays. The tragedy of *Ajax* is the tragedy of a man whose very virtues, whose
arete, cannot be contained in the social frame, so that he must
perforce leave this life; Athene can save his honor, but not his
life. Antigone, too, finds that she can fulfill herself only at the
cost of her personal happiness and of her life. There is no
hamartia here, unless in a narrow sense; and if there is a sin
against heaven in the *Antigone*, it is Creon's. But the gods in
Sophocles are not agents of justice; either they represent, like
Homer's Athene, the projection of great human powers, or they
are the symbol of forces indifferent to man. Thus, at the end of
the bitter *Trachiniae*, after loving Deïanira has "erred, meaning
well," [78] and brought ruin to her erring husband and to herself,
we are told that "in all these things there is naught but Zeus." [79]
In other words, these things had to be. Certainly it was in one
sense Oedipus who, through flaws of character and judgment,
brought about his own downfall; yet sheer chance, and the
oracle of Apollo, the external and indifferent and timeless rati-
fication of the things that are, must as certainly be held responsible. In the last plays, the *Philoctetes*, and the *Oedipus at
Colonus*, the suffering heroes are represented as all but blame-
less and as achieving final glory. This is humanism, the triumph
of an internal conception of life, not really a theodicy.

If *hamartia* will not explain Sophocles, still less will it explain Euripides. The early *Hippolytus* and the late *Bacchae* show the terrible vengeance of offended and jealous divinities, who represent human propensities. And the sufferings of Phaedra and Hippolytus and Pentheus are out of all proportion to any moral offense. The other plays of Euripides cry out even more against the cruelty and unworthiness of the traditional gods who make havoc of human lives and show moral dignity only in some of the human characters. The "unhappy endings," however contrived, at least make Euripides for Aristotle "the most tragic" of the dramatists by the test of actual stage production,[80] and his conflicting remark about happy endings or incidents [81] must be somehow minimized.

The Greek tragedies that we possess, still more the larger number known to Aristotle, vary too much to be reduced, even by an Aristotle, to a formula descriptive of tragedy that has achieved its "natural form." If the notion of *hamartia*, for example, is at all valid, the fluid meanings of the word require different applications for different plays. What is true of *hamartia*, which I have discussed by no means exhaustively, is true also of other ideas, which I cannot develop here (catharsis, the so-called "unities," the comparison of tragedy and epic). The methods of Aristotle (observation of materials, classification by *diaeresis*, definition, historical sketches, comparisons of genres), which are so fruitful in his other works, are in the *Poetics* less carefully coördinated. The result is that, although the work abounds in germinal ideas deserving of the closest study, it nevertheless must be used with caution even for the interpretation of Greek drama, and must, of course, be used with even greater caution for the study of later drama and of poetry generally. The misuse of Aristotle by later critics and poets is one of the curiosities of criticism and may not be reviewed here. Yet we may remark that the doctrine of "literary forms," inherited by Aristotle from Plato, is a *damnosa hereditas*.

Since Aristotle's historical sketch of early drama is defective, his method of defining tragedy as it ideally should be, even if based on actual plays, has little room for a truly historic understanding of the newer trends. Certain plays, both of the earlier and of the later periods, which we should count among the greatest, or at least among the most interesting, he passes over without comment. In fact, the whole theory of genres, convenient for purposes of classification, suffers from its tendency to assume that it is enough to extract from a definition a complete picture of the creative arts. It tends to suggest that free creation and the evolution of new forms is impossible, simply because they are not easily predictable, and tends to divert attention from the imitation of "the universal in accordance with probability or necessity" to the imitation of existing works of art. For one whose thought in other fields often stresses growth and development, Aristotle's thought in the *Poetics* is surprisingly circumscribed; it takes some ingenuity to apply his principles to modern literature, with its new forms, except for certain very general principles, such as unity, universality, consistency. There are a few hints, however, of the possible existence of intermediate or mixed or "nameless" genres and styles (for example, 1, 7–9: 1447a20–b23, which might recognize the novel).

The modern reader of Aristotle may be troubled, too, by what may seem to be an excessive preoccupation with intellectual principles; we have been prepared to find a generous recognition of emotional experience, and we are invited (except for the recognition of catharsis) to consider order, form, necessity, probability, the proper kind of plot and hero, and the like. The reason, however, is in part that Aristotle is answering Plato's strictures on poetry and his elevation of philosophic truth as the final norm. Furthermore, it is largely by principles of logical construction (rather, for example, than in lyric poetry or in recourse to external nature) that he believes that painful experience can be organized in such a fashion as to convey a beautiful and satisfying effect; and these principles he indeed finds confirmed in the practice and in the effect of the actual masterpieces of drama that best exemplify the ideal possibilities of tragedy.

Some of Aristotle's omissions can be supplied by the reader. If there is no mention of the classic moral antithesis of *hybris* and *nemesis,* nor of fate, the conception of the tragic "error" (*hamartia*) and of the "necessary" consequence of the action to a large extent takes their place. If he says nothing of tragic "irony," his description of the "reversal of fortune" (*peripeteia*) nearly covers the idea.[82]

More serious is the neglect of lyric poetry, and indeed of all that is most personal and dependent on the individual's attitude toward life—the attitude of a Lucretius or a Wordsworth. The specific content (moral ideas and problems) even of tragedy is neglected in favor of its form and universal quality. Aristotle's concentration on "man in action" has prevented him, and many of the Greeks whom he faithfully criticizes, from reckoning fully with external nature.

The chief concern of most of the later critics of antiquity, and of many modern critics, was to be "style" (λέξις). Aristotle, both in the *Poetics* and in the *Rhetoric*, initiates the interest, though without the elaborate classification of styles that was soon to emerge. A good deal of the discussion in the *Poetics* deals with grammatical distinctions; the rest is concerned chiefly with diction, or the choice of words. "The perfection of diction is to be clear without being mean." [83] The choice of familiar words makes for clearness; distinction is achieved by the use of various strange words or forms and deviations from ordinary usage, and above all by the use of metaphor, a device on which, both in the *Poetics* and in the *Rhetoric*, Aristotle spends considerable attention.[84] In all attempts to secure distinction, it is important to observe propriety (πρεπόντως χρῆσθαι); [85] this stipulation agrees with Aristotle's constant regard for propriety and consistency in other matters—in plot construction, in character delineation, in the choice of proper subjects for the arousing of the proper kind of pleasure—and the *Rhetoric* will develop further the principle of propriety. "But the greatest thing by far is to be a master of metaphor." [86] This is both a true and a very important statement, for which many of Aristotle's other omissions may be forgiven. Yet he does not press further, as he might have done, the point that all poetry as such is metaphorical, in so far as it uses concrete materials to express universal truth. In fact, Aristotle nowhere attempts, except in piecemeal fashion, to define poetry as such, with its specific qualities and functions.

Nor should we seek in Aristotle much light on the nature of

poetic imagination. In the *Poetics* he seems to avoid the terms
(φαντασία, εἰκασία) that Plato had employed to indicate the
images or appearances which he had at first distrusted and finally
accepted, with safeguards, as god-given vehicles of inspiration.
The reason is not far to seek. Aristotle's whole empirical attitude
is opposed to the severance between the world of the senses and
the world of universals; for him both phenomena and concepts
are phases in a single system, and form and matter are united in
reality. Thus, in the *Poetics* he does not connect "imitation" with
"images" or "phantasies"; imitation, or representation, is of the
universal in reality. But in his psychology (best set forth in the
De Anima) and in his ethical system he recognizes φαντασίαι
as sense-drawn impressions, on which judgments true or false
may depend, leading to action; remembered, as weakened "present sensations," distinguishable from their original objects, they
affect emotion and conduct and provide matter for thought. Memory is "the permanence of an image regarded as the copy of the
thing it images." [87] That means that Aristotle has no room for any
theory of the imagination as divinely inspired, or for prophetic
dreams. Dreams, in fact, are to be dealt with like any phenomena
of the waking consciousness. The images employed by the artist
are to be contemplated for the pleasure that they may give; they
are valuable so far as they serve to indicate nature's trends and
purposes, and to this extent cease to be merely imitative and become the vehicles of universal truth.

Yet there is in Aristotle just a hint of the traditional idea of
poetic inspiration; that comes when he is discussing the dramatist's
visualization of the action while working out his play and his emotional sympathy with his characters. "Hence it is that poetry demands a man with a special gift for it, or else one with a touch
of madness in him; the former can easily assume the required
mood, and the latter may be actually beside himself with emotion." [88] Here, for a brief moment, Aristotle seems to hover on
the verge of accepting Pindar's claim for the genius of exceptional
natural endowments, or Plato's plea for poetic madness and ecstasy. And once more, in commending metaphor as "the greatest
thing by far," he continues, "this is the one thing that cannot be
learned from others; and it is also a sign of genius, for to make

good metaphors implies an eye for resemblances." [89] The hint is tantalizing in its brevity and is not developed into a theory of the poetic "imagination"; that conception was still to come, from other hands. Finally, there is the remark, apropos of the discussion of the irrational, or improbable (τὸ ἄλογον), in epic: "Homer more than any other has taught the rest of us the art of telling lies the right way." [90] His point here is a special one; but it could be generalized, in the light of the subsequent remark on "convincing impossibilities," [91] into a reply to Solon's innuendo that "the poets feign many a thing," and to Plato's distrust of the imitation of "appearances"; it is a recognition of the element of illusion, of the concrete representation of the impalpable, or the idealization of the actual, that enters into all but the most obvious forms of art.

v

Most critics after Aristotle are concerned with oratory, but deal with poetry as well as with prose, sometimes almost equally; for prose, it was realized, could "charm" and "lead the soul," as even Plato had urged; [92] and poetry was often regarded as rhetoric, with some kind of "persuasion" as its end. Thus, examples of the various styles, to illustrate the principles of order, rhythm, and diction, are drawn almost indifferently from the orators and the poets. In their quest for passages worthy of imitation in the various "styles," such critics as Dionysius of Halicarnassus, Demetrius, and "Longinus" are laying the foundations of the theory of "classicism." Theophrastus, with his eye for words that are "naturally beautiful," Hermogenes, with his quest for the qualities (ἰδέαι) of style to be found in various works of literature, and the critics just named, alike look chiefly for aesthetic principles in the lesser members of a work, thus making amends for Aristotle's predominant interest in the structure of works in the large.

The last, and, with the exception of Aristotle, the greatest, of the major Greek critics is the anonymous author of the essay *On the Sublime* (περὶ Ὕψους), whom we must resign ourselves to calling "Longinus" (no longer confusing him, however, with the Cassius Longinus of history). He writes in an age of literary decadence, which he associates [93] with a subtle moral decline. His theme is nothing less than the effect of great literature on the soul. No other ancient critic gives such stimulating and refreshing reading. Less conventional than his predecessors, he realizes that literature is not created by observing rules, but is the expression of greatness of spirit; yet he provides little of the advice on the structure of speeches, or of other literary forms in the large, that one finds in other treatises on rhetoric or poetics. "Composition" σύνθεσις) for Longinus, as for Dionysius, seems to mean almost wholly the mutual adjustment of the smaller members of a passage, rather than the development, for example, of a tragic action with its necessary outcome and its moral content.

Longinus therefore serves to complement, not to replace Aristotle. Though his criticism is almost wholly aesthetic, and though he is interested in problems of expression, he is not content, like the rhetoricians, to seek "persuasion," [94] but seeks rather to discover what produces "ecstasy." He is not concerned with the traditional classifications, nor in developing the characteristics of any one "style"; rather, he wishes to inquire into the sources and effects of all great literature. With Aristotle, he seems to agree that the end of art is emotional satisfaction; yet his specific demand, that it achieve ecstasy, has an even greater affinity with Plato's doctrine of inspiration. Though he makes certain concessions to the Stoics, who would save some myths by allegorical interpretation,[95] his ethical concern is with the moral roots of great literature. He is an independent, therefore, and belongs to no previous school of criticism; oddly enough, he exerted no influence in antiquity, was not rediscovered until the Renaissance, and exercised his greatest influence in the pre-Romantic period.

To call the subject in English "The Sublime," using a Latin equivalent of the Greek (τὸ ὕψος), may be convenient, if it does not encourage us to take a too limited view of the term; and "sublime" has for us rather special suggestions of the magnificent and awesome and morally uplifting. Elevation, indeed, the Greek word distinctly denotes; but it is an elevation shared by writers in verse and prose alike, as different as Homer and Demosthenes, as Sappho and Thucydides, and the many others whom our author cites. The common quality of them all is a nobility derived from character as well as from the art of the several writers; the test of its presence is its power to arouse ecstasy in readers and hearers. It is "a certain distinction and excellence in expression" (ἀκρότης καὶ ἐξοχή τις λόγων).[96] "The effect of elevated language [τὰ ὑπερφυᾶ] upon an audience is not persuasion but ecstasy"; that is, it stirs the soul out of itself, as poetry and music have been held by Greeks of previous ages to stir the soul.[97] It must be admitted that Longinus does not define his subject more precisely. The term "sublimity" (ὕψος) is itself a metaphor, as is at least one of its alternatives, the "supernatural" (ὑπερφυής),[98] and as are the various terms used to describe its effect (ἔκστασις, ἔκπληξις).

Quite Platonic, or Socratic, is the inquiry "whether there is such a thing as an art of the sublime or lofty," or whether it comes not by teaching and only by "nature." Longinus answers it prudently: nature comes first, but needs art to guide it, sometimes to "curb" it.[99] If, in the central part of the essay,[100] the emphasis seems to be on art, Longinus nevertheless tells us roundly enough that the rules are not enough, that the faultily faultless artist is inferior to the genius whose faults we willingly overlook.[101] "Beautiful words"[102] and the skillful arrangement of them,[103] and metaphors,[104] and the "figures"[105] are all very well, are, in fact, important aids to the total effect; but art must be concealed if it is to be effective, so that it will seem to be the natural expression of feeling.[106]

It would not be difficult to show that the reliance of Longinus on nature, "curbed" by art, goes back to Plato, whose characteristic images and ideas are often suggested, particularly the images in which nature, inspiration, and imagination are given preference over the petty refinements of art. Two long digressions, containing the very heart of our author's belief, are full of Plato. Thus, in the contrasts between Lysias and Plato, and between Hypereides and Demosthenes,[107] it is the Bacchic frenzy and lack of sobriety of Plato's language[108] and the god-given power of Demosthenes[109] which he prefers to the grace of Lysias and the sobriety[110] of Hypereides. The admiration of greatness in nature is itself a gift of nature: a remark made with an eye on Plato and the other "peers of the gods" who aimed in their writing at the greatest, despising mere accuracy[111]—that accuracy which is

the province of art.[112] In the other digression,[113] the epilogue on the
decline of eloquence, we have a fuller treatment of a point made
in an earlier passage quoted from Plato,[114] namely, the relation
between all decline and men's failure to "look up" (ἀναβλέπειν)
toward things better than themselves. Not only in these Platonic
preliminaries and digressions, but in the central portion of the
essay, Longinus shows that he has only a general concern with
"propriety" (τὸ πρέπον), the great preoccupation of the critics from
Aristotle on, and no concern at all with "the styles." His emphasis
is rather on effectiveness, expressiveness, the striking or exciting.

Akin to this emphasis is his remarkable (and Platonic) conception of the imagination, which is closely related to the notion
of inspiration. "Images" (φαντασίαι) contribute greatly to dignity,
elevation, and power; some use this term, images, of actual
mental pictures (εἰδωλοποιΐας αὐτάς). For the term imagination
(φαντασία) is applied in general to an idea which enters the mind
from any source and gives birth to speech. But at the present
time the word has come to be used chiefly in cases where, by
reason of enthusiasm and passion, you seem to see what you
describe and to bring it before the eyes of your audience." [115]
This is something more than the visualizing of a projected scene
that Aristotle commends to the playwright; [116] the reference to
"mental images" reminds one of Stoic psychology; but the suggestion of "enthusiasm" and the phrase "which enters the mind
from any source" is nearer to the older view of inspiration from
external sources which Plato had to some extent entertained.
Again, when Demosthenes uttered his sudden oath "by those who
risked their lives at Marathon," he was "as though suddenly inspired by heaven, and as it were frenzied by Phoebus." [117] In thus
raising, if not finally settling, the question of the artist's selection
of "images" or "figures," our author carries forward the older
view of inspiration by connecting the image-making faculty with
it and with passion.

The magnificent homage of Longinus to the grandeur of the
cosmos and to the human mind that is born to love it [118] is worthy
of Lucretius and Wordsworth, and, we may add, of Plato. In
Plato's *Symposium* [119] the love of individual physical beauties
leads to the love of intellectual beauty; and in his *Phaedrus* [120] the

souls that soar to the vault of heaven behold "the things beyond," on which *feeds* the divine intelligence, and are carried around in the revolution of the spheres. Here it is difficult to distinguish the love of beauty from the purely intellectual or dialectical process. And Longinus, who has observed that the "sublime" may exist in "a bare idea," also holds that great thoughts "lift" the soul and leave it with "more *food for thought* than the mere words at first suggest." [121] Behind Longinus stands Plato; and later there will be Spinoza's "intellectual love of God."

How can one endowed with some natural gifts make progress in literature? By acquaintance with the "sublime" in great litera- ture, a matter which implies maturity of judgment,[122] but which is powerfully assisted by the possibility of referring to works which by common consent are not of merely ephemeral appeal, but have met the test of time: in a word, what we call "the classics." [123] Here is a new interpretation of "universality" as a literary ideal; the test of literature is its universal appeal to all sorts and conditions of men, the *consensus gentium.* Noteworthy is the inclusion, among the "classics" that illustrate "nobility of soul," of the Bible.[124] It follows that the novice will learn some- thing by imitating and emulating his predecessors, the exemplars of greatness. We may note that here a new depth of meaning is given to the use of the old word "imitation"; not the imitation by the artist of models in the "real" world, or even in the realm of "ideas," but the imitation of previous works of art, which to be sure might on Platonic and Aristotelian principles be justified on the ground that such great works had successfully embodied the ideal potentialities and significance of their material.[125] Neverthe- less, this is not a merely literal imitation, no mere plagiarism, how- ever much neoclassic theory was to encourage such an attitude; it is, on the contrary, a process of orientation toward the original and still living sources of inspiration that have called forth the existing great works and that may again call forth new works.[126]

For Longinus the final test of literature is the effect that it pro- duces on hearers and readers; this is the test that he applies to the Greek "classics." He is unique as a critic in not stopping short with analysis and classification and the labeling of beauties of style. But his special glory comes from his realization that the magic of literature is not the sum of its ingredients, but is something over and above the "figures" and the other artifices of style. There must be an intimate marriage of form and matter, and there must be the glow of personality. So the "sublime," or greatness of utterance, is the echo of greatness of character [127] and evokes a like greatness in its audience: "deep calleth unto deep."

VI

One would therefore be false to the principles of the best Greek critics, above all to the spirit of Longinus, who should attempt to lay down definitive rules for poetry. With them we may recognize the idealizing possibilities of art, its function in affording pleasure while controlling emotion, its need of subordinating detail to the demands of an ordered and concentrated whole, its adaptability in form and style to different human requirements. But that is only the beginning. What remains to do is to return from theory to the practice that came before theory, to the Greek poets themselves; and then to turn to the poets of later ages whom the Greeks could not know, but whose practice in countless ways verifies and enriches their theory and practice, and to the later theory that will supplement earlier theory. This open-minded and informed experience of good art in all ages, in fact, is what is meant by "classicism."

Notes

1. I have assumed that the reader of this essay is already somewhat familiar with at least the more famous critical texts and editions, whether in the Greek or in English, and with standard modern works. I have therefore refrained as far as possible from lengthy quotation and from reference to contemporary controversy, and content myself with the mention of the following modern articles which are probably better known to classical students than to students of modern criticism. Many other excellent recent articles I am obliged to pass over without reference, simply for lack of space.

I have dealt with some of the matters discussed above in "Plato's View of Poetry," *Harvard Studies in Classical Philology*, XXIX (1918), 1–75; "The Spirit of Comedy in Plato," *H.S.C.P.*, XXXI (1920), 63–123; *Moira* (Cambridge: Harvard University Press, 1944), esp. pp. 89–219; and "Aristotle on Metaphor," *Classical Weekly*, XXXIX (1946), 94 ff. J. Tate, in "Imitation in Plato," *Classical Quarterly*, XXII (1928), 16–23, and in "Plato and Imitation," *C.Q.*, XXVI (1932), 161–169, incidentally takes issue with my emphasis on the discrepancy between Plato's treatment of poetry in *Rep.* II–III and the treatment in *Rep.* X, and with my explanation of it; I remain unconvinced by his argument on this point, which is, however, not essential to his excellent discussion. R. K. Hack, in "The Doctrine of Literary Forms," *H.S.C.P.*, XXVII (1916), 1–65, seems to me sound in his scholarship, but unfair to the idealizing tendency of certain forms of art. H. D. F. Kitto, in *Greek Tragedy, A Literary Study* (London: Methuen, 1939), pp. 102–114, emphasizing the dramatic rather than the ethical aspect of Aeschylean and Sophoclean art, reaches a quite different conclusion with regard to *hamartia* from that suggested above (pp. 39 ff.). Useful in their several ways are M. W. Bundy, "The Theory of Imagination in Classical and Mediaeval Thought," *University of Illinois Studies in Language and Literature*, XII (1927), 2–3; F. Solmsen, "The Origins and Methods of Aristotle's *Poetics*," *C.Q.*, XXIX (1935), 190–201; G. F. Else, "Aristotle on the Beauty of Tragedy," *H.S.C.P.*, XLIX (1938), 179–204; H. Kuhn, "The True Tragedy," *H.S.C.P.*, LII (1941), 1–40; LIII (1942), 37–88; and L. A. Post, "Aristotle and Meander," *Transactions of the American Philological Association*, LXIX (1938), 1–42. With P. W. Harsh, " Ἁμαρτία Again," *T.A.P.A.*, LXXVI (1945), 47–58, I agree that Aristotle attributes some degree of moral culpability to the tragic hero; but I hold that Aristotle's generalization is not relevant to many of the extant tragedies.

2. *Od.* 17.518–521.

3. *Ibid.*, 1.337–352.

4. Hesiod, *Theog.* 27f.

5. Solon, 21, Diehl.

6. *Rep.* 607.

7. *Ol.* 1.28–34.

8. *Nem.* 7.20–24.

9. *Ol.* 9.100–104; cf. *Ol.* 2.86–88; *Nem.* 3.40–42.

10. *Glory of the Athenians*, 348c.

11. *Frogs*, 1009 f.: δεξιότητος καὶ νουθεσίας, κτλ.

12. *Meno* 98ac; 99cd.

13. *Symp.* 210a–212a.

14. *Phaedo*, 100c–e; cf. 75a–d.

15. *Phaedrus* 249bc; 265cff–266b; 277 bc.

16. *Ibid.*, 243eff; 265a.

17. *Ibid.*, 246de; cf. 247d.

18. *Ibid.*, 249d.

19. *Ibid.*, 250a–e.

20. *Ibid.*, 277e–278d.

21. *Rep.* 367e–392b.

22. *Ibid.*, 392ac; cf. 364b.

23. *Ibid.*, 392dff.

24. *Ibid.*, 394d.

25. *Ibid.*, 395b–398b.

26. *Ibid.*, 396de.

27. *Ibid.*, 396bc; 398b; 401bc.

28. *Ibid.*, 398c–403c.

29. *Ibid.*, 475e–476b.

30. *Ibid.*, 595a.

31. *Ibid.*, 599a.

32. *Ibid.*, 606d; cf. 605c–606c.

33. *Philebus* 31d–52c; cf. 25c–26b, and the *Timaeus*, for the ordered perfection of the cosmos.

34. *Rep.* 606e–607b.

35. *Ibid.*, 608ab.

36. *Ibid.*, 591e; cf. 592ab.

37. *Laws* 653ff; 660a; cf. 801c; 802a.

38. *Ibid.*, 816de; 935dff.

39. *Ibid.*, 817ad.

40. *Rep.* 514a–521c.

41. *Ibid.*, 596b; *Gorg.* 503e.

42. *Rep.* 472b–473b deals with justice, but with an illustration from painting; *n.b.* 472d: οἷον ἂν εἴη ὁ κάλλιστος ἄνθρωπος, a phrase foreshadowing Aristotle's remark about poetic universality, *Poet.* 1451b5, οἷα ἂν γένοιτο, as contrasted with historic fact; see above, p. 36.

43. *Rep.* 392b; see above, p. 27.

44. *Rep.* 506d; cf. 332b, 413b; *Theaet.* 149c; *Polit.* 277d; *Phaedrus* 262c.

45. *Phaedo* 108d, 114d; *Rep.* 533c.

46. *Cratylus* 423d–424a, 439a; cf. 386e; *Symp.* 211a; *Rep.* 380d, 381e.
47. *Rep.* 571e–572a.
48. *Ibid.*, 509d–511d; cf. *Symp.* 211c.
49. *Rep.* 514e; 596e.
50. *Ibid.*, 598b.
51. *Laws* 668a.
52. *Ibid.*, 817b.
53. *Phileb.* 38c–40d.
54. *Tim.* 71a–72b.
55. Essay XII, 59.
56. *Apoll. Tyan.* VI, 19.
57. *Enneads* I, 6.
58. *Orator* 10–12; 75.
59. *Gorg.* 501e–502d.
60. *Poet.* 25, 1: 1460b10f, οἷα εἶναι δεῖ; cf. 1451b5, οἷα ἂν γένοιτο.
61. *Rep.* 472d; see above, p. 31.
62. *Phys.* II, 2: 194a21.
63. *Pol.* I, 6; 1255b2–4.
64. *Poet.* 4, 1–5: 1448b4–19; cf. *Met.* I, 1: 981b17ff; *Pol.* VIII, 5: 1339b11–1340a6.
65. *Poet.* 4, 12: 1449a9–15.
66. *Ibid.*, 6, 2: 1449b24–28.
67. *Ibid.*, 7, 4–8: 1450b35–1451a15.
68. *Pol.* VIII, 7: 1341b32–1342a16; cf. 1341a21–23.
69. *Rep.* 607d8: ὠφελίμη.
70. *E.N.* II, 3: 1104b8–13; cf. *Rep.* 401e; *Laws* 653a.
71. *Poet.* 13, 1: 1452b28–30.
72. *Ibid.*, 13, 2: 1453a4.
73. *Ibid.*, 13, 2: 1453a7–12.
74. *Ibid.*, 13, 3–4: 1453a7–17.
75. *Ibid.*, 14, 3–9: 1453b11–1454a15.
76. *Ibid.*, 13, 2: 1453a4.
77. Cf. *P.V.* 9, 260, 266.
78. *Trach.* 1136.
79. *Ibid.*, 1278.
80. *Poet*, 13, 6: 1453a24–30.
81. *Ibid.*, 14, 9: 1454a4–9.
82. *Ibid.*, 11, 1: 1452a22–29.
83. *Ibid.*, 22, 1: 1458a18; cf. *Rhet.* III, 2, 1–2; and III, 2, 5, on the illusion produced by poetry

through the selection of words from common speech, as by Euripides.
84. *Poet.* 22, 3: 1458a31–34; 21, 4–8: 1457b7–34; *Rhet.* III, 2, 6–13.
85. *Poet.* 22, 9: 1459a3–4.
86. *Ibid.*, 22, 9: 1459a5–8.
87. *De Memoria* 451a15.
88. *Poet.* 17, 2: 1455a32–34; cf. *Rhet.* III, 7, 11: 1408b: "poetry is a thing inspired."
89. *Poet.* 22, 9: 1459a6–9.
90. *Ibid.*, 24, 9: 1460a18f.
91. *Ibid.*, 24, 10: 1460a26; 25, 17: 1461b11–12.
92. *Phaedrus* 261a; 271cd.
93. *On the Sublime* 44.
94. *Ibid.*, 1, 4: 39, 1–3.
95. *Ibid.*, 9, 7.
96. *Ibid.*, 1, 3.
97. *Ibid.*, 1, 4: ἔκστασις; in the next sentence, ἔκπληξις, and cf. 15, 2; for persuasion contrasted with music, cf. 39.
98. *Ibid.*, 1, 4; 9, 4; 16, 2.
99. *Ibid.*, 2; cf. 36, 3–4.
100. *Ibid.*, 9–40.
101. *Ibid.*, 33–36.
102. *Ibid.*, 30.
103. *Ibid.*, 39–40.
104. *Ibid.*, 32; 37.
105. *Ibid.*, 16–29.
106. *Ibid.*, 17; 22.
107. *Ibid.*, 32, 8–36.
108. *Ibid.*, 32, 7.
109. *Ibid.*, 34, 4.
110. *Ibid.*, 34, 4.
111. *Ibid.*, 35.
112. *Ibid.*, 36, 3.
113. *Ibid.*, 44.
114. *Ibid.*, 13, 1.
115. *Ibid.*, 15, 1. The verb παριστάμενον here used has its counterpart in the noun used earlier where, in Platonic language, Longinus urges that we "make our souls pregnant, so to say, with noble inspiration" (παράστημα, 15, 1; and cf. 16, 2).
116. *Poet.* 17.

117. *On the Sublime* 16, 2; cf. 13, 2.
118. *Ibid.*, 35, 2–3.
119. *Symp.* 210a–211c.
120. *Phaedrus* 247c–250e.
121. *On the Sublime* 7, 2–3.
122. *Ibid.*, 6.

123. *Ibid.*, 7, 3–4.
124. *Ibid.*, 9, 9.
125. See also above, p. 33.
126. *On the Sublime* 13, 2, recalling the doctrine of inspiration contained in Plato's *Ion.*
127. *Ibid.*, 9, 2.

NOTES
ON CONVENTION

Harry Levin

I

The history of criticism may seem at times to be something of a logomachy. This is perhaps because it faces the problem of dealing, in a fixed and limited set of terms, with a complicated and endlessly changing body of phenomena. Inevitably, when older schools are questioned and new movements arise, they engage in controversies over words; catchwords are attacked, slogans bandied, and neologisms deployed with the unflagging energy of language itself. Thus the same word means different things to differing critics. To cite the obvious instance, "romanticism," Irving Babbitt's poison, is Jacques Barzun's pap. It follows, not that the concept is meaningless, but that it is both broader and subtler than the endeavors of its interpreters to pin it down. To compile its multiple meanings and balance contradictory interpretations has therefore proved highly enlightening; but we need not stop, as Professor Lovejoy would, with an irreducible plurality of definitions. No single formulation or simple pattern may cover, to anything but a rough approximation, a process so organic and continuous. But the common emphasis of the various romanticists on organism and continuity, as Professor Wellek reminds us, is in itself a clinching illustration of the attitudes they shared.

As for the classicists, it is mainly when viewed from a retrospective distance that they seem so consistent, so unanimous, indeed so urbane. We have only to glance at any of the commentaries on Aristotle's *Poetics* to realize how vast an area of verbal argument has been glossed over by their principles. Both adjectives, "classical" and "romantic," serving as a pair of labels, do little more than distinguish each from the other. Yet each is associated with a train of characteristic words, whose development may be historically traced and whose significance may be critically analyzed. Literary discourse acquires precision and perspective in the measure that it gains control over such words. It is charted by such landmarks as the sudden arrival of "originality," the gradual retirement of "imitation," the strategic vicissitudes of "imagination." Comparable changes have been taking place in our critical vocabulary during the century that separates the romantic period from our own day. Our failure to register them explicitly, to test them and prove them, to examine the circumstances that prompt them and the intentions they convey, may well be one of the sources of present confusion.

Contemporary criticism is nothing if not word-conscious. Yet we may observe, more regretfully than reproachfully, that our critics are not so semantically strict with themselves as they are with other writers. Mr. Empson has taught them to perpetrate, as well as to discriminate, ambiguities. Mr. Ransom has provided them with "texture"—a word which, though it sounds concrete and craftsmanlike, leaves a good many impressionistic loopholes. Mr. Burke has concocted an eclectic diction, heavily fraught with italics and hedged with quotation-marks; by tinkering with terminologies, he has produced some very ingenious gadgets and some rather clumsy contraptions. Mr. Richards, having translated *katharsis* into the language of modern psychotherapy, has acknowledged the inadequacy of his translation. Repentance, it must be added, has carried him all the way back to Plato and the Bible. How far from them, for all our wishful talk about apparatus and method, can we be said to have come? Can we specify the impact of experience, on a reader or a writer, by opaquely referring to sensibility? Do we know more about what goes on, between one mind and the other, when we call it tension? Are opposites to be logically reconciled by the easy device of ambivalence? Though we shy away from value-judgments like "great" and "good," we are always bestowing the accolade of "distinguished"—distinguished from what?

In default of immediate and positive answers to these questions, we need not conclude that criticism has been moving backwards or standing still. We need merely remember that, since its

latest vantage point is for better or worse our own, we are in no
position to draw conclusions. We can gauge directions, however,
by projecting a curve which is based on a series of *loci critici* from
the recent and remoter past. In pursuing one particular idea,
together with the term that denotes it, we can hardly pretend to
be definitive; for it has been the nature of that idea to evade
definition, to take things for granted, to presuppose tacit acceptance. Nor can we be exhaustive in a matter which gathers importance with current aesthetic discussion. We can take a few
soundings and cut across categories, since the term "convention,"
which occurs in post-romantic contexts, has neoclassical associations. Since it not only facilitates the processes but establishes
the motifs of art, it transcends the question-begging dichotomy
of form and content. Since it depends upon the relationship between author and public, it opens up a viable channel to historians of style and taste. But like all words that come to be
widely used, it stands in increasing danger of obfuscation. The
following examples and comments are set down in the hope of
illustrating its utility and of possibly contributing toward its
clarification.

II

Our starting point, then, is its currency today. This can be
demonstrated *a fortiori* by reference to *Life,* a periodical more
conscientiously devoted to photographic sensation than to verbal
nicety. A recent editorial, campaigning for a more eupeptic brand
of American fiction, attacks what it chooses to call "the slumming
convention." [1] It thereby echoes, as we shall see, the earlier coun-
terattack against naturalism: the accusation that, in revolting
against genteel conventions, the naturalists simply introduced
hard-boiled ones. The significant, though questionable, implication is that *Life's* millions of readers—or rather, whatever proportion of its spectators can be counted upon to read its editorials—
would appreciate the force of that paradox. Further examples
could be multiplied by browsing at random through little maga-
zines and scholarly journals. The most suggestive text that casu-
ally presents itself is a sentence from a review of a current novel

in a popular weekly, by a critic whose usual writing is equally notable for common sense and responsible employment of the King's English. "Every novelist has his own conventions," writes George Orwell in *The New Yorker*, "and, just as in an E. M. Forster novel there is a strong tendency for the characters to die suddenly without sufficient cause, so in a Graham Greene novel there is a tendency for people to go to bed together almost at sight and with no apparent pleasure to either party." [2]

Our first reaction is provoked by the final clause. Nothing could be farther from what convention implies, when we speak of it in ordinary conversation, than the twofold tendency that Mr. Orwell ascribes to Mr. Greene's characters. Clearly there are conventions and conventions, and the kinds invoked here conform more closely to literary impulse than to social habit. It is precisely their departure from what he regards as a social norm to which Mr. Orwell takes exception, not so much on the grounds of propriety as of probability. In the past it has more commonly been propriety, the other kind of convention, which has rendered a novelist's treatment of sexual relationships improbable. In the one case personal vagaries, in the other moral constraints, exaggerate or distort a basic pattern of human behavior. But exaggeration or distortion may inhere in the medium: it was thus conventional, in early romances, for heroes and heroines to die of love. This is not to say, as Mr. Orwell says of Mr. Forster's characters, that those deaths are inadequately motivated—nor that they are required by poetic justice in expiation of a fate which was worse, nor that they are gratuitous sacrifices on the altar of tragedy or desperate stratagems for terminating a story. We must ask not what motivates the characters, but what the situations express; for when the means of expression is inadequate or incomplete, the materials must be oversimplified, the effects externalized.

But when Messrs. Forster and Greene, with all their technical adroitness and psychological sophistication, stray beyond the credulity of their readers, is it relevant to appeal to the license of convention? The novel began, with *Don Quixote*, by ridiculing the conventions of romance. We like to think that modern novelists are unconstrainedly expressive, informal to the point of amorphousness, "lawless" in André Gide's phrasing. To be reminded that they observe laws of their own is therefore to admit that artistic media are never quite free from some degree of formality. To add, with Mr. Orwell, that certain conventions are peculiar to certain writers is to give the term an unconventional twist. Few words have been more loosely construed in latter-day criticism than "myth," as applied to the efforts of single individuals to promulgate their unique imaginative constructions. A private convention, like a prefabricated myth, is a contradiction in terms; neither, after all, can be unilateral; just as genuine myths presuppose beliefs, so conventions rely on prior awareness and widespread acceptance. The former are warranted by a body of ideological assumptions, the latter shaped by a series of material conditions; and tradition is another name for the mechanism by which both are assimilated, organized, transmitted. The artist who lives in an untraditional epoch, like Blake at best, can only create pseudo-myths. And the very refusal of critics like Mr. Orwell to accept a pattern of fictional behavior, the reader's disagreement with the writer's premise, relegates it to the category of pseudo-convention.

Now where the reader's sense of actuality corresponds with the writer's account of it, no special agreement between them is necessary. So sensitive a relationship, however, can all too easily be strained by either party. Originality, at the other extreme from conventionality, has very often manifested itself through unwillingness to abide by the preconditions and presuppositions to which the public clings. Critics, more often than not, have approached that conflict from the traditional side. They are therefore being somewhat inconsistent when they use the term "convention" pejoratively. The point at which they ordinarily apply it is wherever literature would seem to diverge from life. Such a divergence, when exemplified by the pastoral, was professedly unrealistic. But when writing which professes to be realistic is termed conventional, the problem of defining convention is augmented by the problem of agreeing on a definition of reality. This is not to be discovered, according to the editors of *Life*, in disillusioned novels of slums or wars. Yet what attests, more spectacularly than the Luce publications, that journalism and photography can be conventionalized? Alerted against the pseudo-conventions

of our contemporaries, we hesitate to identify works of the past
with the realities of their respective periods. It may be that the
Greeks had as brusque a notion of courtship as Graham Greene.
On the hypothesis that they did, John Dennis tried to prove that
love was conventionally slighted because it could not be realistically represented in classical tragedy.[3]

If mere technique were directly correlated with real experience, the concept of convention would never have been called
into being. It traces its origin to imperfection—not to the fault of
the craftsman, but to the limitation of the craft. Since art never
imitates nature quite perfectly, there must be a margin of error:
an allowance for unnaturalness, a residue of artificiality. Though
this may result from numerous causes and appear in innumerable
guises, it has two related and recognizable phases: it stereotypes
life and it humanizes technique. The first phase includes stock
characters, standardized scenes, recurrent themes—an example
which subsumes them all is the *commedia dell'arte;* another,
closer at hand, the detective story. The second phase is harder to
discuss, and in greater need of discussion, because it involves
devices of presentation, modes of stylization, restrictions of form.
Formal terms have an ambiguous way of associating themselves
with their incidental content. Thus "genre" begins by designating
an artistic type, or perhaps a style, and ends by characterizing a
type of painting wherein the subject is more important than the
style. Yet the adaptation of any subject matter to the requirements
of craftsmanship must, to some extent, enlist the aid of convention.
And every convention, however formalized, occupies a plane
where the discrepancies between matter and manner can be
circumvented; it upholds a covenant through which technical
factors and human variables, in the most literal meaning of the
word, come together.

III

From the Latin roots for "coming together" to the modern instances just cited, the word "convention" has a long and varied
semantic history which can barely be outlined here. Though its
connection with literary criticism is of fairly recent date, it prob-

ably owes its wide European circulation to Roman law. Conventions as quasi-parliamentary bodies, empowered to call the king himself to account, played a decisive part in seventeenth-century England and eighteenth-century France. Conventions as non-political treaties, deeply rooted in the theory and practice of international relations, continue to operate in such matters as copyright. Over the centuries the area of connotation has broadened to cover a range of extralegal, socio-cultural applications: to extend the contractual principle, in short, into many different fields of human activity. This is the general significance that critics have been attempting to specialize for the purposes of aesthetics. It is not accidental that convention was clearly discerned in the plastic arts before it began to figure in discussions of literature. And, like so many of our critical terms, it was well established in French before it appeared in English. *C'est convenu.* For those whose frame of reference is Anglo-American, however, the *New English Dictionary* is the immediate authority to be consulted. The fact that, among the many meanings it records, the one we seek is only vaguely comprehended, does little to lessen the need for fuller discussion.

The first of two major categories, into which the definition breaks down, is devoted to "the action of convening" in its political and diplomatic aspects. The second, which more especially interests us, is concerned with "agreement, conventional usage." Ten subsidiary definitions are elaborated in roughly historical order, of which only the last two make any reference to the arts (an eleventh disposes of compounds). This is the ninth: "General agreement or consent, deliberate or implicit, as constituting the origin and foundation of any custom, institutions, opinion, etc., or as embodied in any accepted usage, standard of behavior, method of artistic treatment, or the like." The tenth follows: "In a bad sense: Accepted usage become artificial and formal, and felt to be repressive of the natural in conduct or art: conventionalism." This last variant, now obsolescent, is illustrated below with a quotation significantly chosen from Harriet Martineau's *Society in America* (1837). "The incubus of conventionalism" was apparently the English feminist's phrase for a state of mind which our native satirists would subsequently particularize. What is most significant is that no form of the word seems to have been employed in a nontechnical sense before the later years of the eighteenth century. It would then seem that the wave of individualism and the cult of nature associated with Rousseau, along with the concomitant distrust of etiquette and customary observance, helped to make men more explicitly conscious of social convention.

By failing to distinguish between social and artistic convention, the Oxford lexicographers have somewhat confused the chronology. Out of the romantic protest against everything conventional, the critical usage emerged; hence its initial coloring was bound to be pejorative. The single literary citation that appears in the *NED* is late enough to observe historical neutrality. The year is 1879, the writer Matthew Arnold: "The Germans . . . were bent . . . on throwing off literary conventions, imitation of all sorts, and on being original." Here "imitation" and "original" are historically related to the issue he is describing; but presumably Arnold, a hundred years after the event, is pioneering in English when he links them with the continuance or rejection of convention. Not until we compare the cited fragment with the text of Arnold's essay, "A French Critic on Goethe," do we appreciate how directly the term has been imported from the Continent.[4] The *points suspensifs* conceal the pertinent fact that Arnold was virtually paraphrasing Edmond Scherer's account of the *Sturm und Drang:* "Il s'agissait de s'affranchir des conventions classiques, spécialement de l'imitation de la France," Scherer had written in 1872, and had gone on—followed by Arnold—to discuss the substitution of romantic for classical models.[5] Possibly Scherer's background gave him a cosmopolitan insight; very likely he was prompted on this occasion by his subject, Goethe. We shall find that, though the Germans implicitly grasped the idea of convention, they never quite assimilated the key-word.

The priority of the French can readily be documented, coinciding as it did with the adoption of the term into art criticism. Thus *convention* has no place in Lacombe's *Dictionnaire portatif des beaux-arts* (1759), but is fully discussed with respect to painting in Watelet and Levesque's *Dictionnaire des arts de peinture, sculpture, et gravure* (1792). This is at least fifty years in advance

of England, where it is ignored by Elmes' *Dictionary of the Fine
Arts* (1826), and only the adjectival form is touched upon by
Fairholt's *Dictionary of Terms in Art* (1854). By this time, its
meaning had been more authoritatively stated in Ruskin's *Stones
of Venice* (1851), as instanced by the *NED:* "Representation is
said to be conventional either when a confessedly inadequate imitation is accepted in default of a better, or when imitation is not
attempted at all, and it is agreed that other modes of representation, those by figures or by symbols, shall be its substitute and
equivalent." These chary remarks are borne out by Ruskin's application of the term. Since nature was his aesthetic ideal, under
whose auspices he placed even Giotto, convention was destined
to become his *bête noire.* He even lectured on "The Deteriorative
Power of Conventional Art over Nature" (1859), and argued—
from his own low estimate of Oriental art—that the Orient had
produced no great civilization.[6] He did not seem to be aware
of how richly convention was typified in his venerated Gothic.
It remained for another generation, schooled in the neater sym-
metries of Renaissance and Baroque, to give the term a sympathetic inflection.[7]

In contrast to the English, who habitually take a vitalistic attitude toward artistic creation, the French have never hesitated
to stress its mechanical details. Turning to them, we can also
expect a sharper formulation of the problem at hand. In France,
where the Convention made revolutionary history, the word itself
seems peculiarly at home; and the special denotation that concerns us occupies an important place in the standard definition.
"Accorde tacite pour admettre certaines fictions ou certains pro-
cédés. La peinture, le théâtre offrent plusieurs conventions." This
is Littré (1863), who amplifies—logically, if not chronologically—
by indicating certain nuances: "Manière fausse de certains ar-
tistes. Dessin, couleur de convention." Now it happens that the
official admission of words into the French language can be more
or less accurately dated, because of the surveillance exercised by
the Academy and the periodic revision and republication of its
dictionaries. In the fifth edition of the *Dictionnaire de l'Académie*
(1811), as in previous editions, *convention* is broadly defined
without mention of its artistic or literary implications. In the sixth

(1835), after reprinting the same generalities, some new illustrations are added: "Dans l'architecture il y a des ornements de convention. Dans beaucoup de pièces de théâtre, les paysans parlent un langage de convention. La comédie italienne a plusieurs personnages de convention."

Hence the date of acceptance coincides with the heyday of romanticism. On the other hand, the French Academy embodies the very spirit of convention—we cannot yet say the letter—so thoroughly that, even in this case, we must allow for a lag. We are justified in supposing that the new sense of the old word would never have received academic recognition had it not been introduced by more unconventional minds a generation or two before. We encounter it earliest in the criticism of that prescient thinker, versatile writer, and dramatic innovator, Diderot. In the second dialogue of his *Paradoxe sur le comédien*, expatiating on the differences between nature and art, the first speaker criticizes the monstrous unreality of theatrical characters.[8]

LE SECOND.   Mais pourquoi ne révoltent-ils pas au théâtre?
LE PREMIER.   C'est qu'ils y sont de convention. C'est une formule donnée par le vieil Eschyle; c'est un protocole de trois mille ans.
LE SECOND.   Et ce protocole a-t-il encore longtemps à durer?
LE PREMIER.   Je l'ignore. Tout ce que je sais, c'est qu'on s'en écarte à mesure qu'on s'approche de son siècle et son pays.

But this passage is more prophetic than influential: written around 1770, it was not actually published until 1830. And though it anticipates nineteenth-century usage, it retains a tentative and metaphorical tone, as if Diderot were deliberately transferring the expression from law or diplomacy to the theater. The alternative, *protocole*, as his editor points out, is elsewhere utilized in his writings on art. His attitude is intermediate, both recognizing and questioning the authority of convention, regarding it as one of those encrustations of the past which progressive enlightenment might confidently be expected to eliminate.

A work of much larger scope and influence, Madame de Staël's *De la littérature* (1800), was an agent of transition in this respect as in so many others. Contrasting the artificial grandeur of Racine's protagonists with the primordial simplicity of the Greek tragic heroes, the Swiss intermediary declared: "Tous les poètes ont peint ainsi les caractères, avant que de certaines habitudes monarchiques et chevaleresques nous eussent donné d'une nature de convention." [9] The final turn of phrase—which was perforce omitted from the contemporary English translation—is almost a contradiction in terms. In a later chapter it attains the status of an axiom: "La nature de convention, au théâtre, est inséparable de l'aristocratie des rangs dans le gouvernement: vous ne pouvez soutenir l'une sans l'autre." Here it is worthy of note that the anonymous translator, seeking an English equivalent for *convention,* was obliged to render it by "conformity." Madame de Staël may be said to have carried the nonconformism of Rousseau from social institutions to literary genres. She believed that literature was perfectible; that works of the imagination, by repudiating all contrivance and acknowledging no limit, became the unimpeded vehicles of philosophy and sensibility. Convention, which for Diderot was a gentlemen's agreement, had for her become a universal oppression; it was she who equated the *ancien régime* in politics with neoclassicism in the arts. It was Stendhal who turned her fundamental antithesis between Latin and Germanic writers into propaganda for the emergent romantic drama.

Not less ahead of its own time, not less paradoxical than Diderot's posthumous dialogue, Stendhal's *Racine et Shakespeare* was engendered in the controversy over the English Shakespeareans performing at Paris. It dismissed not only the classical unities and the rules of the French Academicians, but the "exigencies" and "necessities" of the stage itself, with a sweeping pun: "*habitude profondément enracinée.*" [10] But, with the legal metaphor that Diderot had used to explain the excesses of theatricality, the same set phrase that Madame de Staël had attached to the tyranny of custom, Stendhal, in the classical mood that led him to recommend the Civil Code, counseled respect for language— "*qui est une chose de convention,*" he added, in a footnote to the second of these two pamphlets (1825). In an unpublished essay, comparing the Italian language with French, he had already developed that penetrating insight: "Une langue est une convention; il faut que plusieurs millions d'hommes conviennent . . ." However arrant his individualism, he accepted the obligation to reach an understanding with his fellow men. He would be regarded, by the posterity he addressed, as more of a realist than a romanticist; in the long run *Racine et Shakespeare* foreshadows the naturalists by conceiving the proscenium as an invisible fourth wall. Its naturalistic prediction that verse would yield to prose was soon to be parried by the arch-romantic Hugo; and Hugo's preface to *Cromwell*, without naming convention, would show an appreciation of its role. Though Stendhal realized that the stuff of the theater was illusory, he held that the greatest playwrights offered their audiences moments "d'illusion parfaite." In defining that illusion, ironically enough, he had recourse to Dr. Johnson's apology for Shakespeare. Still more ironically, he did not realize how he was thereby redefining convention: "l'imagination du spectateur se prête avec facilité aux suppositions du poète."

IV

Although the very name conveys a suggestion of the transient, the pretentious, and the superficial, convention has—as Stendhal glimpsed—an underlying purport which, instead of setting up barriers, draws men together. Since words are not the same as things, communication depends upon arbitrarily substituting the one for the other; each art, each genre exists by a prearrangement of available signs, a shared vocabulary of symbols; and what is true of verbal expression is even truer of the plastic arts, where the medium is more concrete, the representation more selective, the limitation—as Lessing demonstrated—narrower. When three dimensions are expressed by two, when the whole spectrum is reduced to black and white, when floral designs subserve architectural needs, when the human figure bends to the conformation of ivory or jade—when, in a word, the picture or sculpture challenges a visual comparison with its object, it soon exposes the process of conventionalization. Conventions are less evident in literature, as long as they are still working; they are seldom recognized until they have been nearly outgrown. Thus the invocation to the muse, which fulfilled a functional purpose as long as the epic was oral, survived as a conventional ornament of the literary epic. The recognition of convention, we have seen, historically coincided with its repudiation. Paradoxically, it was discovered by romanticists and realists who flouted it; while classicists and neo-classicists, who had embraced it, had done so unconsciously.

It was more or less assumed that conventions were survivals which, with the aesthetic emancipation of mankind, would wither away. Some cultures were more conventional than others, to be sure, but they were commonly regarded as primitive or backward. The hypercivilized French were exceptional, for convention was the pivot around which their development revolved; they were at once its exemplars and its critics. Inevitably, when they rejected it, they turned for guidance to their nonconformist neighbors, the English, and to the notorious unconventionality of Shakespeare. Because the drama is plastic as well as literary, because it is both the most social and the most technical of forms, because it brings real and artificial components into such striking juxtaposition, it provided an arena in which the critical issue could be fought out. Pleading for the Shakespearean mode, in the preface to *Cromwell* (1827), Hugo undertook to distinguish: "d'indiquer quelle est la limite infranchissable qui . . . sépare la réalité selon l'art de la réalité selon la nature." [11] Stendhal's refusal to make this distinction had led him to attack dramatic verse: when the Cid speaks in prose, Hugo answered, why should not logic and realism equally compel him to speak in Spanish? Art cannot give us *la chose même* except by resorting to artifice; the theater has its trick mirrors, its optical illusions; the playwright, like the painter, manipulates techniques and calculates impressions. As for the unities: "L'unité d'ensemble est la loi de perspective du théâtre."

Convention thereby repeated the ancient principle of *ut pictura poesis*. The next step was for dramatic criticism to set forth its own version of the laws of perspective. This was very largely the contribution of Francisque Sarcey, the shrewd and popular critic of *Le Temps*, whom forty years of play reviewing equipped with a technician's point of view and a highly professional concern for the "well-made play." During the summer of 1876, when the theatrical season had fallen off, Sarcey devoted his weekly column to sketching an "Essai d'une esthétique de théâtre," which later served as the introduction to his collected reviews. His point of departure was the basic condition the artist must face: in

painting the flatness of the canvas, in drama the presence of the
audience. Consideration for the latter explained those asides,
soliloquies, and other conventions which differentiate what happens on the stage from the way it might happen in actual life.

Il ne faudrait pas donc simplement affirmer que le théâtre est la
représentation de la vie humaine. Ce serait une définition plus exacte
de dire: que l'art dramatique est l'ensemble des conventions uni-
verselles ou locales, éternelles ou temporaires, à l'aide desquelles, en
représentant la vie humaine sur un théâtre, on donne à un public
l'illusion de la vérité.[12]

Frankly considering the dramatist an illusionist, Sarcey used
tricherie synonymously with *convention*. Earlier and elsewhere he
had pointed out that sentiments could be just as conventional
as actions. Consistently, as an exponent of the single impression,
he justified the classical separation of tragedy and comedy. Few
unwritten books have as tantalizing a sound as his projected history of theatrical conventions.

In popularizing the term, Sarcey eliminated its disparaging
overtones and increased its usefulness for matter-of-fact description. Hereafter the younger Dumas, even while attacking social
conventions, could freely acknowledge his dependence on theatrical ones; and could defend himself, in the preface to *L'Etrangère*
(1879), by describing all art as "une convention perpétuelle." [13]
Meanwhile the naturalistic school was assaulting tradition, and
soon the Théâtre Libre would attempt to replace the *pièce bien
faite* by the *tranche de vie*. Stanislavsky, reversing Diderot's paradox, would teach his actors to identify themselves emotionally
with their roles, and would preach that convention (*uslovnost'*)
was the very opposite of truth (*pravda*) and the very epitome
of everything the Moscow Art Theater sought to avoid.[14] The
pros and contras are cogently stated by the literary historian,
Charles-Marie Des Granges, in a pair of articles suggestively entitled *Les conventions du théâtre naturaliste* (1904). He observes
that the naturalists were primarily novelists, impatient with the
technicalities of a stricter medium. "Zola et ses collaborateurs,
en prétendant chasser certains conventions, en ont acclimaté
d'autres." [15] Whereas the old ones had been aristocratic and sentimental, the new ones were lurid and proletarian. Yet, "con-

vention pour convention," Des Granges concedes that naturalism
has accomplished for its time the valued function of recalling the
theater to the source of art, nature.

Tolstoy, whose career was an emphatic protest against the unnatural, was able to render grand opera ridiculous by merely
taking its conventions literally. Wagner, one of the targets of
What is Art?, was being quite as literal when he installed the
most realistic and up-to-date stage machinery at Bayreuth.
Though Ibsen was praised and blamed for coming so danger-
ously close to reality, his meanings have subsequently been pursued to the plane of symbolism: Nora Helmer's tarantella has
become a rite of liberation for her sex, and Eilert Lovborg, with
vine leaves in his hair, is hailed as a reincarnation of Dionysus
himself. Are the butlers and telephones and expository ruses of
drawing-room comedy any less conventional than the choruses
and messengers and *confidantes* of a statelier drama? If what the
modern playgoer contemplates is a room with the fourth wall
removed, why must its furniture always be facing that wall, and
its occupants take such pains to balance each other? Does convention really tend, with the progress of art, to undergo technological obsolescence? Or does each succeeding period reënact its
peculiar conventions? Clearly some compromise is called for,
such as Sarcey's distinction between the permanent and the
ephemeral. Differences of degree, as between France and England, and between the eighteenth and nineteenth centuries, were
noted by Henry James. Something could be said, he wrote from
London in 1877, for that quality which the theater had been losing: "there was at least a certain method in its madness; it had
its own ideal, its own foolish logic and consistency." [16]

The extent to which their respective traditions have lasted may
be reckoned by contrasting the grand manner of the Comédie
Française with the casual understatement of the British stage
today. Critics like Stendhal and historians like Taine, believing
that this contrast is inherent in the difference between blank
verse and the rhymed alexandrine, assume that it has always
prevailed. Even Bernard Shaw, that unconventional master of
convention, accepts it and plays upon it in his preface to *Over-
ruled* (1912). A self-conscious series of parodies (for example,

The Critic) and burlesques (the Savoy operettas), conventionaliz-
ing the conventional as it were, characteristically reveals the English distaste for any kind of histrionic distortion. The fact that
Shakespeare's audiences included the middle class, while Racine
addressed himself to courtly circles, may help to account for the
comparative realism of the Elizabethans. Again, Restoration drama
was aristocratic, and took place—according to Lamb's well-known
essay (1822)—in an artificial world of make-believe.[17] Lamb had
a keen perception of stage illusion, of the "tacit understanding"
between actor and audience, of "the barrenness of the imaginative faculty in the productions of modern art." But the gap between reality as he knew it and imagination as embodied in Shakespeare evoked an especially British paradox—that the greatest
dramas ought not to be performed. Lamb therefore transposed
them to narrative and anthologized their purple passages. His
dramatic essays, as collected by Percy Fitzgerald, frequently hint
at convention: "that symbol of the emotion which passes current
in the theater for it." In his own person Fitzgerald, a play re-
viewer rather than an armchair critic, contributed a practical
volume called *Shakespearean Representation: Its Laws and Limits*
(1908). In *The World behind the Scenes* (1881), he pioneered
by laying bare the conditions, the tricks, and the "conventionali-
ties" of the English stage.[18]

Taine's *Histoire de la littérature anglaise* (1863–1867) was a
naturalistic sequel to the romantic manifestoes of Hugo and Stendhal; the subject attracted him because it seemed free from the
neoclassicism that shackled French literature; like all too many
commentators—and unlike his classmate, Sarcey—he equated
Shakespearean drama with life itself; and because he was looking for documents rather than models, he confounded theatrical
tradition with historical truth. Thus, forgetting that feminine
roles were played by boys, Taine naïvely inferred that Elizabethan women had had a certain masculinity.[19] Actually, it could
be maintained that Shakespeare's plays are more conventional
than Racine's, since they take so much more for granted and
incarnate so many traditions. At all events, their twentieth-
century interpreters have tried to reconstruct the vast and complicated framework of convention within which Shakespeare oper-

ated. Though he ignored the *liaison des scènes,* he observed what has been called "the law of re-entry": he carefully synchronized exits and entrances with changes of scene. Since neither he nor his fellow playwrights bothered to formulate the rules they worked by, it has been the helpful task of such scholars as W. J. Lawrence to sift the antiquarian and textual evidence.[20] More recently these findings have been utilized for critical purposes in such books as Miss M. C. Bradbrook's *Themes and Conventions of Elizabethan Tragedy.*[21] E. E. Stoll, in analyzing Shakespearean characterization, has followed the lines laid down by Sarcey's analysis of Molière; and although Shakespeare's characters transcend the conventions in which they were cast, Professor Stoll's method has proved an effective counterweight to the tenuous psychologizing of the romanticists.[22]

French criticism made convention a weapon for offensive and defensive use in contemporary polemics. Anglo-American scholarship made it an instrument for the reinterpretation of great works composed in obsolete forms. It was made the basis of an invidious and iconoclastic comparison by William Archer in *The Old Drama and the New* (1923). Translator of Ibsen, colleague of Shaw, spokesman for a modernism which has since become somewhat dated, Archer endeavored on behalf of these allegiances to debunk the Elizabethan and Restoration dramatists. Drama comprised two elements, he declared: "faithful imitation" and "wilful exaggeration." [23] Its evolution, from Webster to Galsworthy, was a gradual "purification"; extraneous matter, lyrical and operatic, had been—in Archer's slippery phrase—"sloughed off"; and the theater had progressed from a maximum to an "irreducible minimum" of conventions. To this T. S. Eliot, in "a preface to an unwritten book" (1924), retorted: "Mr. Archer confuses faults with conventions." [24] Eliot found it easy to reconcile Archer's attitude with Lamb's, since both consented to a divorce between drama and poetry. But where the Elizabethans were too conventional for Archer, they were too realistic for Eliot: only one English play, *Everyman,* escaped the disintegrating force of "unlimited realism" and came "within the limitations of art." That exception may throw some light on the limitations of *Murder in the Cathedral* and *The Family Reunion.* In his subsequent "Dia-

logue on Dramatic Poetry," Eliot relates this doctrine to his other
orthodoxies by deploring our modern lack of social and moral, as
well as artistic, conventions.[25]

V

Thus far we have been concerned with explicit enunciations
and clear adumbrations of our term. To look beyond the term is
to pursue an idea so comprehensive and ubiquitous that, in full
justice to it, the history of criticism ought some day to be re-
written. All that these sketchy paragraphs can do is to indicate
certain points which are connected by the word, certain gaps
which are filled in by the concept, once it has been enunciated.
Probably that connection was first established by Sarcey's more
erudite and imaginative fellow critic, Jules Lemaître, when, in
1888, he pointed out that what Corneille called "*fictions du
théâtre*" were known to latter-day writers as *conventions*.[26] Conventions, of course, are implicit in any critical system; but not
until the romantic movement, which honored them more in the
breach than in the observance, was it necessary to name them;
classical critics merely referred to "the rules." The change in terminology is significant because it emphasizes the difference between compulsory enforcement and voluntary acceptance. It
parallels the transition in political thought from natural law to
the Rousseauistic doctrine of social contract. Classicism itself,
with its codes and academies, its judgments and legislations, is—
as Irving Babbitt put it—"a great convention." [27] What need was
there to designate the basis on which so widely accepted a body
of principles rested? Adherence to custom or violation of propriety could, in the specific instance, be dealt with under the
heading of *decorum*. Yet literature is increasingly conscious of its
own exigencies and, long before it recognized convention, it made
use of a cognate expression: *les convenances*.

We may say without drastically simplifying the classicists that,
in balancing the rival claims of talent and technique, of subject
and medium, of the living and the literary elements in a work,
they exhibit either a Longinian or a Horatian emphasis. Clearly
convention is on the side of the latter, with its norm of *usus*, its

catalogue of *colores*. Aristotle, who was broad enough to comprehend both positions, attributed aesthetic experience to the
interplay of two fundamental instincts: *mimesis* and *harmonia*
(1448b). As a philosopher, he was primarily interested in the
problem of imitation—that is, in the external relationship of art
to nature—and this preoccupation is reflected at length in the
thinking of other critics. None the less the *Poetics*, in some detail,
goes into the internal relations of artistic form, describes the
physical conditions under which genres developed, and even pre-
scribes appropriate meters, stylistic techniques, scenic practices,
and so forth. With practical injunctions, rather than theoretical
formulations, ancient rhetoric and medieval *dictamen* paid their
respects to convention. But convention excludes invention, which
sooner or later reasserts the claims of the other side: the real
thing, the "nameless grace," the *je ne sais quoi* that is never quite
conveyed by the descriptive and prescriptive tradition of the *Ars
Poetica*. Hence the neoclassical rediscovery of the "sublime,"
which in its turn was tamed by the romanticists. Sublimity was
brought down to the conventional plane that beauty occupied in
Burke's antithesis, while the "grotesque" supplied that inventive
element which Hugo found characteristic of modern realism.

The classical ideal, as formulated by Longinus and others
(193r), was posited on the perfect correspondence of nature and
art. To the extent that this ideal had been realized, conventions
had been allowed to pass unnoticed. As long as the artist had
treated probable subjects and overcome the inherent difficulties
of his medium, there could have been no question of artificiality:
artificiale, for the critics of the Italian Renaissance, meant simply
artistic. Rhyme ideally corresponded with reason, according to
Boileau, and Pope made little distinction between copying models
and imitating nature. But neoclassicism, by overinsisting upon the
rules, went from "nature methodized" to denatured method; and
thereupon romanticism drew its heavy line between the artificial
and the natural. When Thomas Campion attacked the irration-
ality of rhyme, when Dryden condemned a dramatic personage
for stepping out of his role, their term of reproach had been "inartificial." [28] Naturalistic critics, pledged to eliminate artifice from
the arts, would have left off the privative prefix. In the actual in-

stances the criticized fault was more cogently defended, on the grounds of convention, than it could later have been; for meanwhile the body of opinion on which judgment hinged, no longer coming together, was falling apart; and the old consensus, its basis in common sense, was breaking down into disputed tastes and subjective impressions. It grew accordingly harder to evaluate, by any objective canons of correctness or probability, how closely a given representation approximated the object represented. The distance that now revealed itself between them was the province of convention.

If art and nature were anywhere united, Friedrich von Schlegel declared, it was in the theater.[29] Yet the drama of Elizabethan England and of Spain's Golden Age, which proved so convincing to romantic generations, had been severely censured by contemporaries for its lack of verisimilitude.[30] To the Platonic charge that poets were liars, much echoed in the Renaissance, apologists like Sidney replied by differentiating poetic from literal truth, and by according the poet "libertie . . . to frame the Historie to the most Tragicall conveniencie." [31] Toward the plays of his age, however, Sidney took as censorious a view as Cervantes took of Lope de Vega, or as the French Academy would take of the *Cid.* Corneille, like Ben Jonson, was caught in a midway position between a heritage of indigenous conventions and the superimposition of classical rules.[32] He regarded the dogma of the three unities as an effort to repudiate the persisting convention (or fiction) of the simultaneous scene. The Italian promulgator of that dogma, Lodovico Castelvetro, bore witness to the development of the proscenium, the adaptation of perspective to the stage, and the use of scenery to create a pictorial illusion. Castelvetro really took nothing for granted; if he sanctioned verse, his reasons were strictly functional: because he believed it carried better than prose.[33] He believed that spectators, having literally accepted the setting as one particular place, should never be asked to consider it another; and, above all, that the time they spent in the theater should actually coincide with the timing of the dramatic action. Seldom can such positive recommendations as the unities of time and place have been founded on such negative considerations as an unwillingness to try the faith of the audience.

Classical precept, with Horace, had warned against straining credulity by melodramatic improbabilities: "quod ostendis mihi hic, incredulus odi" (188). The neoclassical unities articulated a rational and realistic program for avoiding possible confusions and arbitrary discontinuities. But, while predicating a mentally immobile spectator, they demanded from him an incredible agility in following the crowded events of an "artificial day." The multiple scene that Sidney ridiculed, where Europe confronted Asia across the same stage, was scarcely any more conventional than the situation Dryden looked askance at, where a farfetched succession of public events had to take place in the king's bedchamber. Dryden's *Essay of Dramatic Poesy* is an equable study in opposing conventions: ancients against moderns, French against English, Elizabethan against Restoration, rhyme against blank verse. In his *Defence of the Essay* Dryden pushed his arguments much further. "Bare imitation" should be heightened by artifice; playwrights, like painters, should avoid "too near a resemblance"; in so far as drama was fiction rather than truth, it should be judged by imagination rather than reason.[34] In appealing "to every man's imagination," Dryden paved the way for Dr. Johnson's preface to Shakespeare, with its decisive appeal "from criticism to nature." [35] If nothing more immutable than "the laws which custom had prescribed" kept tragedy and comedy apart, Johnson saw no objection to their intermingling. And, if the spectator could once imagine himself in another time and place—"Delusion, if delusion be admitted, has no certain limitation." Unity was just as conventional as multiplicity. When Johnson spoke of delusion rather than illusion, he kicked the stone; he reminded audiences that, under any circumstances, the stage was a stage and the players were merely players. To transcend the unrealities of art required that deliberate effort which Coleridge would call for: "that willing suspension of disbelief . . . which constitutes poetic faith." [36]

None but the most naïve, like Partridge at the play, could mistake the reproduction for the reality. Connoisseurs could feel, with the Abbé du Bos, that their awareness of form brought higher satisfactions: "que l'art de l'imitation intéresse plus que le sujet même de l'imitation . . . Que le plaisir que nous avons au

théâtre n'est point produit par l'illusion." [37] Artists, encouraged
by Sir Joshua Reynolds, could make "professed" or "allowed deviations from nature," and thereby perfect "the natural imperfection of things." [38] Art could be nature's master instead of its
slave; and convention could be the hallmark of artistry, instead
of the sign of imperfect mastery. These were the changing conceptions that came to a head when Schiller, uniting Greek with
Shakespearean tragedy, revived the chorus in *Die Braut von
Messina* (1803), and justified his experiment with a prefatory
note which—in essence—was a plea for convention. Schiller reconciled this with the quest for freedom by envisaging reality as a
constraining force and imagination as "eine gewisse Befreiung
von den Schranken des Wirklichen." [39] Since art realized its ideal
by idealizing the real, he maintained, the artist should scorn
illusion and oppose naturalism.

> Der bildenden Kunst gibt man zwar notdürftig, doch mehr aus kon-
> ventionellen als aus inneren Gründen, eine gewisse Idealität zu; aber
> von der Poesie und von der dramatischen ins besondere verlangt man
> I l l u s i o n, die, wenn sie auch wirklich zu leisten wäre, immer nur
> ein armseliger Gauklerbetrug sein würde. Alles Aussere bei einer dra-
> matischen Vorstellung steht diesem Begriff entgegen—alles ist nur
> ein Symbol des Wirklichen.

This passage links our original semantic inquiry with the broader
questions we have since encountered. The word *konventionel* is
here employed, in the more traditional and superficial sense, on
the very occasion when a more dynamic and profound idea of
convention is being put forward. The French derivation of the
word is underlined by its context; the German equivalent, *Über-
einkunft* or *Vertrag*, seems to have been a neglected possibility;
in recent Shakespearean scholarship *Konvention* is virtually in-
terchangeable with *Stilform*. [40] It is perhaps worth noting that,
where the American translation of *Die Geburt der Tragödie*
speaks of "conventions," Nietzsche has used the more general
term, *Wesen*. [41] Nietzsche, however, echoing Schiller and her-
alding Wagner, lifted the whole subject to a high plane of generality when he asserted: ". . . es sei nicht genug, dass man das nur
als eine poetische Freiheit dulde, was doch das Wesen aller
Poesie sei."

VI

The foregoing definitions could be supplemented, and the applications could be multiplied indefinitely, but already they range from one extreme to the other: from limit to license. At one extreme, we make allowance for technical faults, crude materials, restrictive conditions. At the other, we become aware of willful irregularities, self-conscious liberties, specialized virtuosities. Between these poles of under- and over-development comes a central phase where the disparity between art and nature seems to disappear, where difficulty has been overcome and mannerism has not yet set in. Such, in rough outline, is the history of most artistic genres—for example, of Western painting from the Italian Primitives to the School of Paris. Frequently, too, the career of a great artist falls into such a pattern. Goethe described the part that convention plays in the apprenticeship of genius when he wrote: "In der Beschränkung zeigt sich erst der Meister." If genius is distinguished by originality, convention is what originality is distinguished from. "Invention"—the old rhetorical term for "imagination"—may be the most exact antonym for our term; and we may well agree that convention without invention would be undesirable; but we seldom realize that the converse is quite unthinkable. We are still the heirs of the romanticists, and our basic unit of aesthetic discussion is still personality. Our literary history is largely collective biography; and though stylistic criticism has taken some promising steps, it still conceives its subject too exclusively in terms of personal expression. Convention, more broadly conceived, is collective style. Whereas new movements are propelled by individual talents, the vehicle of convention is tradition.

We live, however, in what Thomas Mann has lately called "a time of broken-down conventions" (*zerstörten Konventionen*).[42] This is at least as true of society at large as it is of literature; our critics, social as well as literary, register a growing fear of disintegration on every plane. Some of them look upon civilization itself, in Irving Babbitt's phrase, as "a great convention," whose survival depends upon the revival of old-fashioned doctrines and

outmoded institutions.[43] Their critique of naturalism, in philosophy, scientific experiment, and the arts, has retroactively extended
through the Enlightenment to the Renaissance. Over that period
they rightly discern a consistent and accelerating tendency to cast
off conventions in every genre and approach the goal of literal
reproduction. The accumulation of technique, and indeed of technology, made it possible to reproduce directly things which here-
tofore had been conventionally rendered. Perspective and the
unities, as we have seen, converted the spectator of a dramatic
performance into the witness of an actual event. But each medium,
though it be more fluid than the last, has its limitations. If not
with the discovery of the silent film, then surely with the introduction of sound, art might be said to have completed its illusion
of reality. And if our films are unimaginative in their use of
music, perhaps it is because they are afraid of spoiling the illusion. Hence any burst of song must be realistically motivated;
there can be no hint of the operatic, unless perchance the scenario
includes a visit to the opera. Such thoroughgoing literalness, which
finds its usual theme in the life-story of a composer, is destined to
be defeated by convention; for the truth turns out to be rather
uneventful and must therefore be twisted into conformity with
the conventional standards of Hollywood entertainment.

The film is more successful in its mechanical aspects which, like
all smoothly operating conventions, are seldom discussed; audiences more or less consciously understand that lapses of time and
changes of place are betokened by certain tricks of cutting; and
the association we make between moving lips on the screen
and words which emerge from the public address system is convention at its purest. When Daguerre developed photography, it
discouraged painters from competing with reality and encouraged
a keener sense of the peculiarities and potentialities of canvas and
pigment. Similarly, the cinema released the drama from its sub-
servience to the claims of realism: the dramaturgy of Bertolt
Brecht is a striking, but by no means unique, return to the for-
malities of an earlier or more exotic stage. In 1916 W. B. Yeats
announced that he was going to Asia for a more distant, a more
aristocratic, a more symbolic form.[44] In admiration for the Jap-

anese *Noh* plays, Ezra Pound went so paradoxically far as to repudiate "Western convention of plot." [45] Granted that every culture has its own conventions, it was precisely the strictness of Japan's that attracted such Bohemian westerners as Lafcadio Hearn; but though a writer can reject his native convention, he cannot arbitrarily and eclectically choose another, as Pound's later *Cantos* demonstrate. On the way conventions are formed and break down, an authoritative light has been thrown by John Livingston Lowes' *Convention and Revolt in Poetry* (1919). Professor Lowes, the accomplished interpreter of both Chaucer and Coleridge, was equally sympathetic to the manifestoes of Imagism then resounding. Knowing that "revolt is perennial," he welcomed "the new poetry" as the sort of reaction that had occurred before and would occur again—for he also knew that conventions, though differing in detail, were similar in behavior. [46]

His cyclical interpretation of poetic trends seems to have been richly corroborated a generation afterward. Today, when Amy Lowell is no longer "the most modern of the moderns" and *vers libre* is more quaint than revolutionary, her nephew writes in metaphysical strophes and other young poets outvie each other in sestinas and pantoums. While the *avant-garde* fights a rear guard action, the experiments of the 1920's are assimilated by slick middlebrow periodicals; and while documentary journalism proves to be stranger than fiction, serious novelists once again feel free to abandon the realistic for the historical and legendary, the mythical and fantastic. Walt Whitman, for whom convention was incompatible with democracy, inevitably failed in his program to "express the inexpressible," since expressibility presupposes the replacement of a vague emotion by a concrete image —a symbolic process which is also conventional, if and when the symbolism is accepted. Convention, as Paul Valéry redefined it, is a mysterious difference between impression and expression. [47] When Thomas Campion proposed—on behalf of a stricter convention—to liberate English poetry from the shackles of rhyme, Samuel Daniel opposed him on the basis of tradition, custom, and example. When Valéry defended those voluntary chains, "les exigences d'une stricte prosodie," he did not assume that reason accorded with rhyme. He argued in 1920 that language naturally offered too little resistance; that it must be artificially framed by rules; that art, after all, is a game in which man seeks to satisfy "un instinct de l'artificiel." The Aristotelian instinct of "harmony," so long subordinated to "imitation," has thus been reasserting itself. By turning Aristotle upside down, and maintaining that nature imitated art, Oscar Wilde overstated the case for convention; but he reëmphasized its primary importance and its subsequent neglect.

With the decline of the nineteenth-century view that the secrets of nature had all but yielded themselves to the human mind, it appeared that all knowledge—even science—reposed on no greater certainty than convention. The truth, it now appeared, was less likely to be biological than mathematical. The eminent mathematician, Henri Poincaré, who considered Euclidean geometry "une sorte de convention de langage," adapted this concept to scientific method.[48] The result was a positivistic distinction between the framework of man's assumptions and the structure of the universe: the so-called laws of nature, if not arbitrary, were conventional. Meanwhile, at the opposite pole, Benedetto Croce has polemicized against convention from his well-known anti-empirical point of view. Hesitating over the term, Croce writes: "But if these are to be conventions, something must exist which is no convention, but is itself the author of convention. This is the spiritual activity of man." [49] And this is the kind of thinking that leads to idealism in philosophy and intuitionism in aesthetics; that begs the questions Poincaré's empiricism has faced and sets critics off on a futile quest for the inexpressible. To merge the arts with all the intangibles that enter into the spiritual activity of man, to overlook the work in favor of the author, is to forego our best opportunity for understanding what expression is and how it functions. Technicalities, however limited, help us more than generalities—particularly when they concern the relations of technique with history and society. Our socio-historical approach needs to be balanced—not canceled out—by methods of formal analysis; we could do much worse than borrow a leaf from the books of Viktor Shklovsky and the Russian formalist school.[50] Without questioning the ultimate importance of whatever lies

beyond, we may humbly remember that there are no short cuts
to it, and that conventions are avenues which lead from us to it,
if not from it to us.

Notes

1. "Editorial: Fiction in the U.S.," *Life*, August 16, 1948, p. 24.
2. George Orwell, "The Sanctified Sinner," *The New Yorker*, July 17, 1948, p. 62.
3. John Dennis, "The Impartial Critick," in *Critical Essays of the Seventeenth Century*, ed. J. E. Spingarn (Oxford, 1909), II, 151.
4. Matthew Arnold, *Mixed Essays* (London, 1879), p. 284.
5. Edmond Scherer, *Etudes de littérature contemporaine* (Paris, 1882), VI, 334.
6. John Ruskin, *The Two Paths*, in *Works*, ed. E. T. Cook and Alexander Wedderburn (London, 1905), XVI, 259, 288.
7. Geoffrey Scott, *The Architecture of Humanism* (London, 1924), p. 72.
8. Denis Diderot, *Paradoxe sur le comédien*, ed. Ernest Dupuy (Paris, 1902), p. 104.
9. Madame de Staël, *De la littérature*, in *Oeuvres* (Brussels, 1830), IV, 75, 350. Cf. Madame de Staël, *A Treatise on Ancient and Modern Literature* (London, 1803), I, 109; II, 182.
10. Stendhal, *Racine et Shakespeare*, ed. Pierre Martino (Paris, 1925), I, 9, 144, 17, 14; II, 41.
11. Victor Hugo, *Oeuvres* (Paris, 1896), I, xlii, xxxv.
12. Francisque Sarcey, *Quarante ans du théâtre* (Paris, 1900), I, 132, 197, 134. Selections have appeared in English as *A Theory of the Theatre* (New York, 1916), tr. Glenn Hughes and ed. Brander Matthews, who contributes a well-informed appraisal.
13. Alexandre Dumas *fils*, *Théâtre complet* (Paris, 1879), VI, 179.
14. K. S. Stanislavsky, *Rabota aktera nad soboy* (Moscow, 1938), p. 499. This manuscript, written over a considerable period of years, was first published in an abridged English translation by E. R. Hapgood, *An Actor Prepares* (New York, 1936); cf. p. 249.
15. C. M. Des Granges, "Les conventions du théâtre naturaliste," *Le Correspondant*, LXXVII (May 10, 1904), 505, 499; (May 25, 1904) 658, 678.
16. Henry James, *The Scenic Art*, ed. Allan Wade (New Brunswick: Rutgers University Press, 1948), p. 93.
17. Charles Lamb, *The Art of the Stage*, ed. Percy Fitzgerald (London, 1885), pp. 48, 30, 11.
18. Percy Fitzgerald, *The World behind the Scenes* (London, 1881), pp. 3, 202, 204.
19. Harry Levin, "Literature as an Institution," in *The Novelist as Thinker*, ed. Balachandra Rajan (London: Dennis Dobson, 1947), pp. 140ff.
20. W. J. Lawrence, *Shakespeare's Workshop* (Boston, 1928), p. 17.
21. M. C. Bradbrook, *Themes and Conventions of Elizabethan Tragedy* (London, 1935), pp. 4f.

22. E. E. Stoll, *Art and Artifice in Shakespeare* (Cambridge, England, 1933), p. 49; *Shakespeare Studies* (New York, 1927), pp. 336, 433.

23. William Archer, *The Old Drama and the New* (New York, 1923), pp. 5, 16, 33. See also the same author's *Play-Making* (Boston, 1912), p. 398.

24. T. S. Eliot, *Selected Essays* (New York, 1932), pp. 93, 41.

25. On the variance between social and theatrical conventions, see George Santayana, "A Contrast with Spanish Drama," in *Soliloquies in England and Later Soliloquies* (New York, 1922), pp. 149ff.

26. Jules Lemaître, *Corneille et la poétique d'Aristote* (Paris, 1888), pp. 67, 68.

27. Irving Babbitt, *Rousseau and Romanticism* (Boston, 1919), pp. 10, 136, 389.

28. G. Gregory Smith (ed.), *Elizabethan Critical Essays* (Oxford, 1904), II, 327.

29. Friedrich Schlegel, "Über die Grenzen des Schönen," in *Sämmtliche Werke* (Vienna, 1822), V, 157.

30. For the social and cultural implications of this attitude, see Karl Vossler, "El tiempo y el lugar en la poesía dramática," in *Formas literarias en los pueblos románicos* (Buenos Aires, 1944), pp. 76, 77.

31. Sir Philip Sidney, *The Defence of Poesie*, ed. Albert Feuillerat (Cambridge, England, 1923), p. 39.

32. G. R. Kernodle, *From Art to Theater: Form and Convention in the Renaissance* (Chicago: University of Chicago Press, 1944), pp. 4, 176, 201ff.

33. H. B. Charlton, *Castelvetro's Theory of Poetry* (Manchester, 1913), pp. 33, 84, 86.

34. W. P. Ker (ed.), *Essays of John Dryden* (Oxford, 1900), pp. 49, 113, 114, 127.

35. Samuel Johnson (ed.), *The Plays of William Shakespeare* (London, 1765), I, xiv, xiii, xxvi.

36. This celebrated formulation from the *Biographia Literaria* seems to be adumbrated in Coleridge's notes on *The Tempest*, as well as in his fragmentary remarks on dramatic illusion. See T. M. Raysor (ed.), *Coleridge's Shakespearean Criticism* (Cambridge, Mass., 1930), I, 131, 199ff; especially the jotting on page 220, which is Coleridgean in its cryptic suggestiveness, as well as in its Germanic inspiration: "Apply the phrase and illustration of perspective (*perspectivische*) to the stage."

37. J. B. du Bos, *Réflexions critiques sur la poésie et sur la peinture* (Paris, 1755), pp. 69, 453.

38. Sir Joshua Reynolds, *Discourses*, ed. Edmund Gosse (London, 1888), pp. 242, 247.

39. Conrad Hofer (ed.), *Schillers sämmtliche Werke* (Berlin, n.d.), XVIII, 271, 278, 274.

40. Wolfgang Clemen, "Shakespeares erste Dramen," *Geistige Welt* (January 1947), I, 4. Ernst Kaun, *Konventionelles in den Elisabethanischen Sonnetten* (Greifswald, 1915), p. 8, still employs the adjective in a somewhat less technical sense.

41. Friedrich Nietzsche, *Die Geburt der Tragödie* (Leipzig, 1895), p. 53. Cf. *Ecce Homo* and *The Birth of Tragedy*, tr. C. P. Fadiman (New York, n.d.), p. 206.

42. Thomas Mann, *Doktor Faustus* (Stockholm, 1947), p. 294.

43. *Ibid.,* p. 387. See also T. E. Hulme, *Speculations* (New York, 1924), p. 121.

44. Richard Ellmann, *Yeats: The Man and the Masks* (New York: Macmillan, 1948), p. 214.

45. Ernest Fenollosa and Ezra Pound, *"Noh," or Accomplishment: A Study in the Classical Stage of Japan* (New York, 1917), p. 17.

46. J. L. Lowes, *Convention and Revolt in Poetry* (Boston, 1919), pp. 3, 137, 55, 92, 127. Lowes may well have derived his antithesis from the article of Francis B. Gummere, "Originality and Convention in Literature," *Quarterly Review,* CCCVI (January 1906), 26ff. But Gummere instanced Lowes's earlier Chaucerian studies for examples of convention at work (p. 34). Gummere, in his turn, was reviewing Leslie Stephen's *Literature and Society in the Eighteenth Century,* and expounding its defense of convention against the rival claims of invention, in the light of his own concern for the communal elements of poetry. He was also concerned with relating this problem to the social and political theories of Gabriel Tarde and Walter Bagehot.

47. Paul Valéry, *Variété* (Paris, 1924), 57, 63, 59. There are further animadversions on the relation between poetic and scientific convention in *Variété II* (Paris, 1930), p. 156.

48. Henri Poincaré, *La Science et l'hypothèse* (Paris, 1903), pp. 111, 134. See also W. V. Quine, "Truth by Convention," in *Philosophical Essays for Alfred North Whitehead* (New York, 1936), pp. 90ff.

49. Benedetto Croce, *Æsthetic,* tr. Douglas Ainslie (London, 1922), p. 31.

50. Their point of departure is evident from the following statement translated from Viktor Shklovsky, *Khod Konya* (Berlin, 1923), p. 9: "There are many reasons for the oddity of the knight's move, and the major one is the convention of art. I write about the conventions of art."

OTTO LUDWIG'S
SHAKESPEAREAN CRITICISM

Alfred Schwarz

I

The critical treatment of Shakespeare in Germany during the century following his reception and final acceptance took a varied course; it ranged from neoclassic suspicion to romantic bardolatry. At first Shakespearean criticism was occasional, fragmentary, and largely appreciative in character. Except for Eschenburg, whose volume *Ueber W. Shakspeare* (1787) summarized all that was known at that time about the poet and his work, no one attempted to consider Shakespeare from a full, critical view until A. W. von Schlegel's monumental *Vorlesungen über dramatische Kunst und Litteratur* (1809). With the first truly adequate translation of Shakespeare's plays, that of Schlegel and Tieck, the Germans finally mastered the form, content, and poetry of the dramas, in short, all but the subtlest effects which are not transferable. Naturally, the need was soon felt for an informative, comprehensive treatment of Shakespeare's life and work, a task which surprisingly enough no English writer had as yet undertaken; therefore, about the middle of the nineteenth century such studies as that of Gervinus, treating the development of Shakespeare's art, began to appear.

In contrast with the tendency of his contemporaries to comprehend the whole figure of Shakespeare and his work, Otto Ludwig[1] concentrated in detail on Shakespeare's dramatic technique. The reason for the subsequent neglect of his *Shakespeare-Studien,* which were first posthumously edited by Moritz Heydrich, is not difficult to find. It is the loose form of the book that discourages study; for Ludwig left a series of notebooks which contain short essays and notes, written in diary form over a period of nearly twenty-five years. Besides the first editor, who simply arranged the great mass of material in chronological order, Adolf Stern, in his edition of the collected writings in 1891,[2] and more recently Professor Léon Mis [3] have tried to reduce these day-by-day jottings to some surveyable order. Since Ludwig presumably wrote his observations on the spur of the moment, for his own use, and with no thought of publication, many points are often repeated, some are expanded in detail, and some perceptibly deepened.

The unity of purpose behind all these entries holds them together. They reflect the dramatist's desire to search for the formula of a tragic art which would, as it were, restore contemporary drama to health. Ludwig speaks of the serious influence on the drama of the current philosophical trend. Excessive reflection destroys all ingenuous instincts, he complains, all artlessness and naturalness. Philosophical systems mislead the poet; for, if he starts from preconceptions, he is unable to accept the natural course of affairs. Let him commence with tangible reality and with human nature as he finds them. "What we Germans chiefly lack is a developed power of moral judgment. Schiller also confused it. He takes motifs and effects from Shakespeare, but he does not plant them with their roots to let them grow organically; he introduces them quite mechanically and arabesque-like." [4] In short, Ludwig thought that the existing state of the drama justified his *Studien*. Only a true reëvaluation of the tragic art, its place, its purpose, and its dramatic laws could point the way out of a regrettable situation.

The technique of drama is that part of the art which can be taught and learned; therein lies the motive for Ludwig's preoccupation with Shakespeare. From him the German dramatist wanted to learn, and he spared no effort to analyze with unusual care the finest points of Shakespeare's dramaturgy.[5] He called his studies at one time a dramatic self-education. But only after he had completed his own dramatic work and found it unequal to his ideal, did Ludwig spend the bulk of his time on his critical studies. This is not the place to consider the much-discussed question whether his critical work obstructed his creative work or not, and what part his tragic illness played in this shift from creative production to the searching analysis of dramatic composition. The fact remains that in his notebooks only plans, fragments, and re-

visions of plays are interspersed among the critical notes. He himself never profited from his findings. He never put into practice
the results of years of critical labor.

Ludwig's *Shakespeare-Studien* are then the record of a practicing dramatist's inquiry into tragic dramaturgy; and finding in
Shakespeare's all the desirable qualities, he drew examples chiefly
from it and evaluated contemporary drama by Shakespearean
standards. It is the short critical observations on Shakespeare
that are of interest here. Even though an exclusive emphasis on
Ludwig's Shakespearean criticism may distort the intent of the
Studien as a whole, yet to draw forth the part that concerns
Shakespeare alone may direct attention to much valuable comment, which, lying embedded within a more abstract study, has
hitherto been largely neglected.

The method and character of Ludwig's critical studies betray
his similarity to another playwright-critic, Lessing. Not unlike
him, Ludwig explores the nature and the conditions of dramatic
art, but more fully if not more systematically. In the short essay,
entitled "Die dramatischen Aufgaben der Zeit: Mein Wille und
Weg," he speaks of Lessing in terms of the highest praise for having first pointed out that Shakespeare, and not the *tragédie
classique*, should be the model of German drama. But Lessing,
he thought, lacked a deeper understanding of the tragic in Shakespeare.[6] Therefore, in his own studies Ludwig devotes a great deal
of space to the exploration of the nature of tragedy, to the analysis
of tragic passion, guilt, and suffering—in short, to all the elements
which make up what he calls the "ideal nexus" in tragedy.

Continuing and expanding in detail where Lessing had made
the first suggestions about the meaning of Shakespeare for modern
German drama, Ludwig tried to find what in Shakespeare's technique made his drama so eminently appealing. Being a dramatist
as well as a sharp-sighted critic, he remained at all times close to
practical considerations. His approach may be called inductive;
for he subjected to minute scrutiny various dramatic devices of
Shakespeare's technique, as they appear in the great plays, and
from these comprehensible facts he formulated the laws and principles (the "dramatic aphorisms," as Stern calls them) which are
the basis of his ideal tragedy.

Ludwig's observations on Shakespeare, which were rather a
means to the larger design of his dramatic studies than an end in
themselves, are so varied and rich in detail that the following bare
abstract of them must necessarily omit all but the most representative principles and only hint at the sensitivity of the playwright-
critic to the finest points of Shakespeare's dramatic art. The poet
Coleridge could respond better than anyone to Shakespeare's
poetic genius; through a comparable fellow-feeling, the dramatist
Ludwig understood the subtlest devices of Shakespeare's dramaturgy. Therein perhaps lies his chief merit, and therefor he de-
serves a recognized place in the literature of Shakespearean
criticism.

II

Ludwig started from the sound premise that Shakespeare's best
dramatic writing is effective and appealing. To see what makes the
dramas great, he examined the nature of Shakespearean tragedy
as a whole, as well as its component parts and the details of
execution.

Three persons, he pointed out, are actively concerned in a
dramatic work of art: the poet, the actor, and the spectator. It is
the poet's job to combine efforts with the actor in order to create
the desired effect in the spectator. He must not only produce his
intended impression, but also keep any undesired impressions out
of the play; for example, if on the stage a subordinate part, no
matter how well acted, deflects interest from the leading part, the
dramatist is somewhere at fault.[7] "I know only one dramatic poet,"
he writes ardently, "in whose work the central idea and purpose
is omnipresent, whose dramatic composition arises exclusively
from that idea, and with the semblance of a natural, self-accom-
plishing process; therefore, I cannot understand why Shakespeare's composition should not be considered exemplary."[8] In
most other dramatists he sees the means obstruct the desired end,
one impression erase the next, and consequently produce a false or
undramatic effect.

The final test of dramatic composition is the actual production
in the theater, where the work of the poet and of the actor fuse

so that the subject matter, drawn from real life, disembodied and endued with thought and meaning (that is, *vergeistigt*) by the poet, may be reëmbodied by the actor. And, if the poet has the living actor in mind as he writes, he will not degrade him to the role of reciter. Contrary to the "lyrical" drama of Schiller, for instance, the script of a Shakespearean play supplies often little more than the import of a role which the actor must supplement with his physical presence and personality.

The central idea, the intended effect, is at all times before Shakespeare's eyes; he subordinates the purpose of every speech to the purpose of the character as a whole, and the character to the intended effect of the entire drama. The core of a character which makes him appear the same in different situations is the *idea* of that character. Ludwig points out that though *Richard III* is a loosely constructed play, its unity lies in the single idea of the main character, in the role of Richard, in the exhaustive representation of such a nature. Thus, each of Shakespeare's great dramas is an organic entity, for every part bears reference to the dominating idea which animates the entire action.[9]

The total effect is, then, the most important unity to be observed. This is an inner, ideal unity, out of which grows the external unity of action. The circumstances of the tragic fall may vary, yet the typically calamitous course of tragic passion (*Leidenschaft*) is generally the same. In *Macbeth*, for example, this inner connection, the so-called ideal nexus, is clearly the main consideration and purpose: the connection between the hero's character, his tragic passion, and the incurred guilt which leads to an internal affliction and an external catastrophe. Ludwig carefully distinguishes this simple, ideal nexus, which is borne by and developed through the tragic hero, from the so-called pragmatic nexus of the plot. Resting on the basis of this tragic sequence, the drama provides the all-important feeling of tragic necessity, for the outcome does not depend on the accidents of the plot, but is clearly anticipated throughout the play.

In Lessing's *Emilia Galotti* and Schiller's *Kabale und Liebe* the catastrophe could have been conceivably avoided; but so important and strong is the ideal tragic nexus in Shakespeare that the actual catastrophe becomes a mere formality, a foregone conclusion. The dramatic interest rests in anticipation. Though the causal connection of the fable must satisfy the understanding, it ought never to come unduly to the fore. The machinery must be simple and hidden; the exercise of judgment must be submerged in the theater, because the playwright appeals primarily to the imagination, not to the reflective faculty, to gain his desired total effect. Shakespeare knows how to paralyze the understanding and to stimulate the imagination through artistic illusion.

To this end he has in his tragedies separated the pathos, the tragic nexus itself, from the event, the poetry from the prose, so to speak. The former is presented in the "play-scenes" (*Spiel-szenen*) and belongs to the main characters; the latter is relegated to definite scenes of exposition, matter generally for subsidiary characters, intermingled with a minimum of pathos or with none. Such disposal is prejudicial neither to the understanding of the continuity of the events, nor to the unity of the tragic passion.

In an entry entitled "Artistic Illusion" Ludwig touches in general terms on the role that the imagination plays in Shakespeare's drama. On the whole there is no other poet who remains so true to life, yet whose details often operate in the realm of the imagination. Hence his use of symbolism, the artistic device by which, when naturalistic reproduction is out of the question, the poet says, "This means that"; for example, the scene in which Richard woos Anne. The admirable fact is that such scenes convince although not a single word is true to nature. The reason for this is that the whole presentation is of a symbolic character, that it never aspires to a commonplace, realistic deception, but only to artistic illusion.[10]

And again, under "Poetic Realism": The more shut off from common reality the drama is through richness and depth of thought, and through the plastic fullness of expression, the more daringly it may epitomize, and the more ideal may be the treatment of time and place. Naturally, the poet cannot use action and characters as they are in real life, of which they are but part; he must invest them with totality. Shakespeare and Goethe have done this. Both have detached actions and characters from their connections in reality and have again made an entirety out of them. Both, in this respect, are ideal.[11]

Writing about *Richard III*, Ludwig penetrates at once to some of the dramaturgic difficulties faced by Shakespeare and to his admirable solution of them. "Again I am reading *Richard III*," he begins in his personal manner, "and am once more astonished at the art with which Shakespeare knows how to make everything possible." It is amazing what a mass of subject matter is here compressed, and with what wisdom Shakespeare avoids all disadvantages attendant on that condition. First, the lack of clarity. But we know his device of joining all that belongs together in an easily comprehensible order. The greater, then, is the danger of unnatural swiftness of action. The ideal treatment of time secures him against that; in no other play are the events more forcefully compressed, and nowhere else is time treated so ideally. There is no yesterday, no tomorrow, no clock, no calendar, only past, present, and future. The danger of dryness and barrenness, which attends on swiftness and compression, he meets and balances through his dialogue, which is poetically rich and full of ease. The fullness of thought in his dialogue avoids still another evil: the painful impression which would be inevitable were the subject immediately comprehended.[12]

In short, "dramatic-artistic composition" is first of all the construction of effects, the plan according to which the interplay of sensations within the spectator must run its course; the excellence of composition does not depend primarily on the arrangement of external facts and events, satisfactory to the understanding, but on the choice and disposition of them according to the demands of the predetermined total effect to be gained.[13]

III

Most instructive for his own purposes were Ludwig's investigations of Shakespeare's treatment of character, tragic passion, guilt and punishment. Again and again he returned to consider details concerning these important elements of tragedy. The course of the entire drama must be that of a typical case, which the poet spots in his source—novel, chronicle, or real life—and, lifting it out, as it were, brings it, in its artistic entirety, complete with beginning and end, before our eyes. Shakespeare motivates the possibility of the guilt not through an individual peculiarity of the character, but rather through a tragic trait or passion which every man knows, and the power of which, to a greater or lesser degree, every man feels. Each Shakespearean hero stands for a class; one could speak of Hamlets and Macbeths. Character, guilt, and the resulting fate in Shakespeare are at all times typical.[14] "The subject of Greek tragedy is an idealized anecdote; that of Shakespearean tragedy, an individualized type." [15]

The situation in tragedy awakens an impulse, sets a task, which is too great for the character and stands opposed to his very being. This incongruity between a given task and the capability of accomplishing it is the basis for a struggle which results in suffering and physical destruction. Brutus undertakes a task, dictated by his impulse toward freedom, a task which contradicts his mild nature; and he perishes by it, sparing Antony. Similarly, Lear's suffering springs from the conflict between his nature and the position into which he has put himself.[16] In *Coriolanus*, also, there is inconsistency between the hero's nature and the task which his piety dictates. Nor can Hamlet's human impulse overcome his individual natural disposition. A tragic struggle arises when an external moving force demands decisiveness from a deliberative individual nature. And in Othello, the conflict lies between unbelief and an individual disposition toward simplicity and credulity, between suspicion and a most trusting soul.[17]

Shakespeare likes to force a position on his hero which allows of the greatest contrast with his nature. Every inch a king, the born commander must beg; the sorrowful and sad fool must jest. The gentle nature must use force. The more striking the contrast between that which the task demands of the hero and the inadequacy of his nature, and the more compressed in time and place the representation of this contradictory relationship, the more dramatic, in proportion, is the tragedy. It is distinctly impressed on us how Coriolanus is supposed to act in order to win over the raging mob; in a short scene his mother acts out the correct way before him. Yet in all his speeches, even in those that express his determination to be, to speak, and to act according to his mother's advice, how clearly apparent it is that he cannot be, speak, and act in this fashion—that he cannot be, but only appear to want to be, thus! And what drastic contrast, as an illustration, between his actual behavior before the people a few minutes later and his previous determination! [18]

Important for Ludwig's distinction between Shakespearean and contemporary tragedy is his insistence on the fact that tragic passion does not represent a right, a moral momentum against wrong, but a human impulse, a strong, natural moving force which struggles with the more powerful and imperturbable course of the world. The subject, then, of Shakespeare's character-tragedy is the course of a passion which he wishes to paint as it rises from the slightest predisposition to the point where it destroys the character who is its bearer. With reference to his own time, Ludwig complains that tragedy, through its misuse as a vehicle for polemic tendencies which paralyze the effects that it ought to have as tragedy, has deviated from its natural and artistic purpose. Brutus and Cassius nowhere assert that freedom represents a moral or human right; it appears rather as the object of their passionate desire. In *Macbeth* the conscience does not win because it is right, but because it is strong. The character knows the power that proves to be his ruin; consciously he undertakes the risk.

The tragic hero becomes impressive through this consciousness, and through his rebellious and energetic presumption. At the same time, he is the object of our pity because his tragic passion drives him unrelentingly on. He is at once free and helpless. Since, despite his sense of responsibility and self-determination, he inclines toward the part of will, freedom and necessity are curiously combined in Shakespeare's heroes. In tragic passion these two sides of human nature meet; for this reason it is the central motive of the true tragedy.[19]

Here Ludwig has analyzed and articulated a set of facts about Shakespearean tragedy which is the basis of our never diminishing interest in the tragic heroes: we see them at all times in a double aspect. They seem free, yet we know they are bound. They seem great and imposing, yet we know they are the playthings of fate. And it is true that in human passion the two are reconciled, for it is the basis both of heroic action and of the resulting ruin.

So far Ludwig's analysis is acceptable, but he goes on to advance a theory with which it is more difficult to agree. Still speak-

ing of the tragic flaw, the passion, in the hero, he says in substance: the defect of a single natural trait, the disharmony and
struggle within the hero, Shakespeare did not arbitrarily determine to be the fundamental condition of tragedy, nor did he in-
vent it and use it as an artistic device; on the contrary, he saw this
basic fault in human nature and in history as the last discoverable
ground for the fate of men, and transferred it to his art only because he wished to found his tragedy on reality.[20]

This statement implies a naturalistic identification of Shakespeare's stage with real life; but tragedy seldom occurs in the
world of men. It is a contrived art form, which has only its roots
in real life. To see the tragic trait, this basic fault, in human
nature, as Ludwig says, is possible; yet to describe it as the last
discoverable ground for the fate of men is to confuse Shakespeare's practice in the great tragedies with ordinary, everyday
life. In his source the dramatist recognizes a potential tragedy,
but the tragic nexus of passion, guilt, suffering, and punishment
is his own invention; it has no counterpart in reality.[21]

No passion (*Leidenschaft*), Ludwig says elsewhere, manifests
itself in continuous emotionality (*Affekt*); each passion is but a
strong inclination in one direction, which may have its ebb and
flow. Quietly and continuously possessing a character, it breaks
out into flame at each obstruction and crossing.[22] Accordingly,
Richard II, Hamlet, Lear are temperamental men; Macbeth,
Coriolanus, Richard III, Othello, passionate men. With the former
small motives prevail, with the latter great ones. Temperamental
men have no purpose which they wish to attain; on the contrary,
their nature contradicts purpose. Their life is no stream which
rolls powerfully in one direction, but rather a mosaic of provoca-
tions and temperamental outbreaks.[23]

It is of great importance, in fact, that a character be not always seen manifesting the individual tragic trait of which he is
possessed. He must also be shown in the intimate situations of
daily life. Only when we see more than one side of the character
can we believe in him as a living person. That is what lends convincing reality to Shakespeare's characters and leaves us with the
feeling in the end that we have known them intimately. We see
Hamlet not only in action, in the narrowest sense, but also indif-

ferently in contact with other men, his typical manner and judgments in various situations; we see the sum of his existence.[24]
Gesprächsmimen is the technical term which Ludwig uses to describe the general character traits that thus round out the individual figure and add credibility to it; they are such attributes as
are typical of sex, age, rank, nationality, and occupation. Though
they are universal in kind, yet they help to individualize the character and make him convincing.

Furthermore, the total being of a character, that is, his full
physiognomy, cannot be better made visible than by showing it
from all sides, in relation to others. Thus, Hamlet turns a different
part of his face to each of the other characters: to himself, the
full face; to Horatio, perhaps something of his profile; and to the
rest, more or less of his face.[25]

The character of Hamlet does not fare well in Ludwig's judgment. His view of him is unromantic to the point of injustice.
Though he confesses that the hero's mental superiority sustains the
play, he regards Hamlet as a weakling, a sullen coward toward
the King, though courageous and ruthless toward women, a
treacherous assassin (stabbing through the arras or murdering
by another hand), worth nothing in action, yet a vain genius in
speech and reflection, whose chief pleasure it is to hear himself
speak, reflect, and affect wit; he is even a weak intriguer. What
is it then, asks Ludwig, that we like so much in him—especially
since he constantly examines his own weakness? It is nothing but
the theatrical fullness of the role, the wealth of tones, and the
frightful pressure of the situation, which make us feel that he who
succumbs to it is not likely to be a complete weakling. The character represented is weak, but the representation itself is full of
strength and at all times provokes our sensibility and occupies
our mind.[26]

IV

Ludwig's examination of Shakespeare's composition and dramatic dialogue led him to the realization of a principle which
seems to be common to both. He shows that in the tragedies the
action as such is as simple as possible, but that quite artfully the

playwright lends it the illusion of ampleness and richness. The situation is large and simple, but expanded and worked out in exhaustive detail. Ludwig greatly admires the way in which Shakespeare thus fixes and exploits the impression of each scene, and imprints it on the heart and memory of the audience.

It is evident that the essential substance of such a scene must always be slender and easily understandable. In *Lear,* for example, the action itself is reduced to its main points; thereby room is made for whole scenes which are almost entirely detail; and in those rests the content. In this detail the characters "live out" their nature, and the situation is fully explored. Without such pausing for detail, the scenes advancing the action would succeed one another too rapidly, as in a camera obscura which lets the pictures move along without pause so that the spectator has no chance to familiarize himself with any: impressions, but no impression.[27]

As with the scenic structure, so with the dialogue. It is a striking fact, Ludwig writes, that all the speeches in Shakespeare's drama that he has hitherto examined, among them the longest and liveliest, which appear to be whole series of independent sentences, can be reduced to single, short sentences, simply by ignoring the punctuation and by discarding parenthetical matter. Such a short sentence, as it stands, would be complete in itself and would contain the essence of that which Shakespeare wants to say by means of the elaborate and artificial structures from which it has been condensed.

Choosing a speech of Othello, Ludwig exemplifies the process of reducing it to its essentials. The details of this analysis are interesting and worthy of consideration, since here, as in many other cases, the critic examined and articulated facts about Shakespeare's technique which through repeated reading of the text we may have subconsciously suspected, but never objectively realized. The process of enriching and expanding the dialogue by means of substantial and intricate parentheses Ludwig regards as the emancipation of the dialogue from the form of a catechism, and as a method of indirect treatment and "retardation" as well.[28]

He ventures the opinion that perhaps Shakespeare first dramatized each scene simply and concisely, with as few speeches as possible, each speech with brief sentences, in which he retained only the essential substance of the scene. Then he might have gradually expanded certain parts, but without adding anything that was not already contained in the original version. And, in the form of a cautious rhetorical question, Ludwig suggests the possibility that Shakespeare's general composition of a drama may have gone through a similar development, that is, a gradual expansion and enrichment through detail of a simple course of events, again without deviating from the slender essentials of the original dramatic action and the intended total effect.[29]

The result of such composition is a kind of artificial and intended absence of construction. It brings about a paradox which, according to Ludwig, mainly characterizes Shakespeare: a definite purpose concealed under apparent aimlessness, a premeditated semblance in his plays of the lack of all premeditation. This peculiarity of Shakespeare's composition has not gone unnoticed. Maurice Morgann's celebrated essay on the dramatic character of Falstaff contains a similar reference to Shakespeare's "cunning" concealed under a "careless air"—"All the incidents, all the parts, look like chance, whilst we feel and are sensible that the whole is design." [30] Morgann senses that Shakespeare aims at a total impression and that he achieves it "with so much ease, that he never betrays his own exertions." Ludwig's theory of expansion and retardation by parenthesis, by the addition of what he calls the "typical appurtenances" of real life, typical gestures in action and conversation, explains how Shakespeare so successfully achieves perfect naturalness in his drama.

v

This review of Ludwig's *Shakespeare-Studien* is necessarily far from adequate, not only because of the considerable quantity and diversity of his criticism, but also because of the intentional emphasis here on those portions which pertain immediately to Shakespearean drama. The systematic collection and formulation of the countless short essays and notes on a larger scale would result in a miniature encyclopedia of dramaturgy, more orderly, but definitely less readable than the original, since it would lose the spontaneity of Ludwig's remarks and his enthusiastic man-

ner, which reflects at times sudden insight, at other times a sharp
and uncompromising critique of himself and other modern dramatists, at all times profound admiration for Shakespeare's mastery.

On this last account Ludwig has been most often criticized.
His idolization of Shakespeare, it has been said, blinded him to
the possibility of any other kind of tragedy, which in the theater
may be equally appealing. Such pronouncements as "I realize
more and more that the Shakespearean form is indispensable to
the most perfect tragedy, that it is no license but law," [31] have
persuaded some of Ludwig's reviewers that the critic indeed suf-
fered from a bad case of Shakespearomania. That view is exag-
gerated.

True, Ludwig leaves little doubt in his reader's mind that he
deems Shakespeare to have been the greatest man of the theater.
He limits his idea of good tragedy largely to the Shakespearean
type of character-drama, constantly recurs to the same few plays,
and in those he often sees only what he wants to see. Yet Ludwig's
unbounded admiration for Shakespeare was not blind reverence
for an accepted dramatic genius, but the tested conviction of a
practicing artist; he always presented good reasons and detailed
explanations for his one-sided preference. He did not declare
Shakespeare to be the norm and automatically condemn all other
drama; rather did he find in Shakespeare the nearest realization
of his ideal tragedy; and then he judged the *tragédie classique*,
the German classics, and finally his own work by the unassailable
Shakespearean standard.

He was not always consistent, however, about whether he expected his studies, intended for himself and possibly for the contemporary drama, to have significance beyond the limits of dramatic craftsmanship. On the one hand, he speaks of undertaking
to explore only that part of drama which can be taught and
learned, the technical part; on the other hand, in the sections on
the nature of the tragic art, he hints unmistakably that modern
drama has also in this respect a safe model to follow. Ludwig's
fault in the *Shakespeare-Studien*, if one may speak of a fault in
what amounts to a private, dramaturgical diary, lies not so much
in his exclusive preference for Shakespeare, nor in his sharply discriminating comparisons of the types of tragedy—after all, in his

personal quest for a worthy tragic art, he had to compare and choose. It lies in the fact that, though he recognized the plight of contemporary tragedy, he failed to see that the temper of his time, the public mind, had a large share in shaping modern tragedy into what it was, and that the mere transplantation of Shakespeare's dramatic art to the contemporary theater, its "original adaptation" as he called it, could never succeed in renovating the art form.

"What we Germans chiefly lack is a developed power of moral judgment," he had written. The connection between the moral health of the nation and its tragic art loomed large in Ludwig's mind. The state of the drama today bears out his apprehensions of one hundred years ago. At that time he blamed the preconceptions of a dominant philosophical idealism for the confusion of the true sense of moral justice as exemplified in the "naïve" [32] Shakespearean tragedy. The tragic struggle in Shakespeare, he pointed out, is a struggle between elementary forces, between the basic conditions of human nature, and is naturally independent of philosophy and religion. On the side of the elementary, the immediately perceptible and sensible, stand the Greeks, Shakespeare, and Goethe; on the side of philosophical reflection, Schiller and the French classicists. The work of the latter has sprung forth from a certain philosophy or convention, and can be comprehended and enjoyed only within that frame of reference.[33]

Today the veritable absence, on a national scale, of an active and consistent sense of morality makes an original tragic art modeled on Shakespeare again extremely unlikely. Sound moral judgment is not so much the result as the necessary basis of this type of tragedy, which uses typical and known character traits and magnifies them for us. Little Macbeths, Hamlets, and Othellos still exist everywhere; but the post-Shakespearean stage took refuge in philosophy and comedy from that inexorable exercise of judgment, Shakespearean tragedy.

That Ludwig's motive for performing this critical labor was perhaps a little unrealistic detracts in no way from its merits and its undoubted value. The *Shakespeare-Studien* constitute an important résumé of dramatic essentials, which, for all their one-sidedness, are not only instructive, but also stimulating to anyone interested in the drama. Representing as he does the rare and fortunate combination of a successful practitioner and a philosopher of the drama, Ludwig was enabled, with a wider perspective than his famous forerunner Lessing, to probe deeply in the half-neglected field of dramatic composition. His informal manner makes the *Studien* an attractive book; he speaks extempore, as if in leisurely conversation across the room; and the informality of his tone should not obscure the clarity of his perception or the originality of his contribution.

Notes

1. Ludwig (1813–1865) is better known as a dramatist (*Der Erbförster,* 1850; *Die Makkabäer,* 1853) and novelist (*Zwischen Himmel und Erde,* 1856) than as a dramatic theorist. Only recently Eric Bentley in *The Playwright as Thinker* (New York: Harcourt, Brace, 1946), p. 83, has called attention to Ludwig's importance as a philosopher of drama.

2. *Otto Ludwigs gesammelte Schriften* (Leipzig, 1891). Volumes V and VI of this edition contain the *Studien* and Volume V is referred to without any further designation throughout this discussion. Translations are mine.

3. *Les Etudes sur Shakespeare* (2nd ed.; Paris, 1929).

4. Pages 238–39.

5. Complaining mainly about the want of discipline (*Zuchtlosigkeit*) in the existing drama, Ludwig's contemporary Gustav Freytag, in *Die Technik des Dramas,* also maintained that the reaffirmation of the essential dramatic principles was not only justified, but desirable, and that it certainly did not mean death to free artistic creativeness, especially when these principles depended entirely on the actual practice of the greatest dramatists. Certain dramatic rules were always valid.

6. Page 45.

7. Pages 158–59.

8. Page 160.

9. Pages 262–63, 217.

10. Pages 271–72.

11. Page 108.

12. Pages 219–20.

13. Pages 265–66. This is reminiscent of Lessing's dictum that the only unpardonable fault of a tragic poet is to leave us cold; provided he interests us (that is, achieves his impression), he may do as he likes with the little mechanical rules.

14. Page 123. Compare Dr. Johnson's similar observations in the *Preface to Shakespeare* (1765): "His [Shakespeare's] persons act and speak by the influence of those general passions and principles by which all minds are agitated. . . . In the writings of other poets a character is too often an individual; in those of *Shakespeare* it is commonly a species."

15. Page 84.

16.   Idle old man,
    That still would manage those authorities
    That he hath given away!
                         (*Lear*, I, iii, 16–18)
    17. Pages 175–177. In character-comedy such a contradiction is also a most effective method.
    18. Pages 69–70. Professor Stoll, in *Art and Artifice in Shakespeare* (Cambridge, England, 1933), similarly emphasizes the great value of contrast for dramatic effect, even though the postulated situation be an improbable fiction. It matters more than fidelity to life that the situation be artistically effective that it can be exhausted for all its tragic content. And reminiscent of Ludwig's remarks on the central significance of the total impression, the whole matters more than any part, emotional illusion more than verisimilitude, dramatic and poetic structure more than character and plot. The immediate impression on the audience of the rapidly played drama is important, and simplification, contrast, and concentration are the dramatist's tools.
    19. In *Shakespeare und kein Ende* Goethe had likewise recognized this reconciliation of freedom and necessity in Shakespeare's tragic heroes: "Niemand hat vielleicht herrlicher als er die erste grosse Verknüpfung des Wollens und Sollens im individuellen Charakter dargestellt."
    20. Pages 171–72.
    21. See Lily B. Campbell's *Shakespeare's Tragic Heroes Slaves of Passion* (Cambridge, England, 1930), chapter ii, for a discussion of the Renaissance conception of tragedy as an effective method of teaching, by *exempla* and imitation, the result of loose and ungoverned passions.
    22. Pages 74–75.
    23. Pages 180–81.
    24. Pages 65–66.
    25. Compare L. L. Schücking's full treatment of characterization in *Character Problems in Shakespeare's Plays* (New York, 1922).
    26. Pages 249–50. Professor Kittredge points to Fortinbras' closing speech as a sufficient answer to those critics who regard Hamlet as a weak creature.
    27. Page 100.
    28. Compare Strindberg's related remarks on dramatic dialogue, a generation later, in the preface to *Miss Julie*.
    29. Pages 153–155.
    30. D. Nichol Smith (ed.), *Eighteenth Century Essays on Shakespeare* (Glasgow, 1903), p. 250.
    31. Page 228.
    32. In Schiller's special sense.
    33. Pages 173–175.

EDWARDS · LOCKE · AND THE RHETORIC OF SENSATION

Perry Miller

I

"Tell me, Hylas," demands the interlocutor in Bishop Berkeley's *Three Dialogues*, the Socratic Philonous who is the transparent disguise for Berkeley himself, "hath every one a liberty to change the current proper signification attached to a common name in any language?" Can he call fire water, or trees men? The hapless Hylas, who perfectly embodies the received, enlightened, respectable opinion of 1713, is bound to answer in only one way, bound to fall into Philonous' trap, for Hylas is, inevitably, a reader of John Locke. Of course not, he replies, such conduct would not be rational because "common custom is the standard of propriety in language." [1]

Neither Berkeley nor his alter ego had any intention—indeed they were not capable—of refuting Locke. Men of the early eighteenth century were not so much the beneficiaries of Locke, they were his prisoners. Try as he might, Berkeley could not transcend the *Essay Concerning Human Understanding;* he could only alter a few emphases and enlarge the method. So, being resolved to deny the existence of "an absolute external world," not only did he have to commence with the sensational psychology, not only did he have to borrow Locke's method even while extending the critique to primary as well as secondary qualities, but he had, still more unavoidably, to accept Locke's third book, the treatise on the nature of language, and then try to bend it to his own devices. He had to prove upon sound Lockean principles that even Locke, by persisting in his belief in material substance, was, despite his own Book III, entangled in "the embarras and delusion of Words." [2]

For two or three generations after 1690 practically all the

theorizing upon language attempted by English or colonial American writers, and much of that on the Continent, was a re-working or reinterpretation of Locke. Vast differences slowly began to emerge, but the starting points remained, into what we call the romantic era, those of Book III; perhaps these are still the tacit assumptions even of schools that are hostile to the Lockean temper. Yet Locke's own motive for devoting a section to language (he says that he had not intended such a discussion, but that as he proceeded he found "so near a connexion" of words, which interpose themselves between the understanding and truth, with knowledge that he could not escape the challenge) [3] was simple: he blamed theological disputatiousness, the word-spinning of "schoolmen," for the commotions of Europe. If words could be reduced to what in fact they are, mere sounds, which "in their first original, and their appropriated use" do not stand for clear or distinct ideas, then the "disputing natural and moral philosophers of these latter ages" could be silenced and the soft voice of reason at last be heard.[4] "The multiplication and obstinacy of disputes, which have so laid waste the intellectual world, is owing to nothing more than to this ill-use of words." [5] More than any other influence, except perhaps sheer exhaustion, Locke's treatise brought about that cessation from acrimonious theological pamphleteering with which English Protestantism greeted the new century. But John Locke, who died in 1704, did not live long enough to see that, whereas his downright and common-sensical doctrine delivered men from the wrangling of theologians, it raised up as many problems as it solved and condemned mankind to a new, and almost as bad-tempered, warfare of rhetoricians.

After a century of it, human endurance weakened, and the reexamination of Locke became a revulsion, identifying him and all his commentators with an era declared to have been dead to the things it knew not and wed to "musty laws lined out with wretched rule." Only in our own day, when one may safely suggest that the romantic denunciation was possibly excessive, can it be perceived that the Lockean analysis actually posed the very terms in which the romantic counterrevolution was phrased, and that, with all its fatal limitations, it was still a heroic effort to come to grips with the problem of language. To the extent that our own conception of speech has become less transcendental, and the Coleridgean and Emersonian belief that the word may become one with the thing no longer seems so plausible, we find ourselves, to some extent, facing once more the issues posed by the third book of the *Essay Concerning Human Understanding*.

Locke's treatise exerted so profound an influence on the eighteenth century not only because of his felicity in phrasing the doctrine, but because the doctrine itself was the culmination and synthesis of a development that had been gathering way for a century. It was, one might say, the final recognition and acceptance of the consequences for philology of the scientific revolution. The essence of Locke's theory is that language, like government, is artificial; it rests upon contract, and neither vocabulary nor syntax have any inherent or organic rationale. By themselves, words are only noises, having no transcendental or preternatural correspondence with what they name; there is no "natural connexion . . . between particular articulate sounds and certain ideas," and a specific word serves as the sensible mark of a particular idea only "by a perfect voluntary imposition." [6] Meaning is arbitrary, the result of social convention. And therefore—to Locke's adherents this was the liberating discovery—words are *separable* from things. They are related to reality according to nothing more than their conscious designation by society, and no utterance can convey meaning to anyone who does not accept, who is too boorish or too eccentric to accept, the manners of society.

Behind this formulation lay the long effort of the partisans of nature to achieve, against the futilities of the scholastics and the pretensions of sectaries, what they fondly expected would be the serenity of a universal and sane truth, a truth which would have the further advantage of utility in mechanics and accounting. By making words their target, they executed a flank attack on theologians. "Words," said Bacon, setting the theme his followers were assiduously to enlarge, "as a Tartar's bow, do shoot back upon the understandings of the wisest, and mightily entangle and pervert the judgment." Verbiage is the enemy, which makes it impossible for men "to follow and as it were to hound nature in her wanderings." [7] By the middle of the seventeenth century, the chorus was swelling: the "guardians and tutors" of mankind, said Cowley, have withheld him from nature's endless treasure by distracting him with painted scenes, but Bacon at last has turned his mind from words, "which are but Pictures of the Thought," to things, "the Mind's right object"; he who now would make "an exact Piece" must disregard the images of fancy, and

> before his sight must place
> The Natural and Living Face;
> The real Object must command
> Each Judgment of his Eye, and Motion of his Hand.[8]

The manifesto of the Royal Society, Bishop Sprat's *History* of 1667, was studied with condemnations of "notional wandrings," "imaginary ideas of conceptions," demonstrations "onely fitted for talk," and proudly asserted that the aim of the Society was "to separate the knowledge of Nature, from the colours of Rhetorick, the devices of Fancy, or the delightful deceit of Fables." [9] In Locke, therefore, Sprat's ideal of style, freed from the domination of colors, devices, and deceits, maintaining "an inviolable correspondence between the hand and the brain," received at last a psychological and physiological justification. Locke proved by the nature of things that when men "set their thoughts more on words than things," they are employing terms learned "before the ideas are known for which they stand," and therefore could not possibly know what was being talked about.[10] Fortified by his authority, the doctrines of the separableness of words from objects and of the artificial origin of language became the dominant stereotypes of the eighteenth century. Gathering up the platitudes of the new criticism, Alexander Pope declared in 1711,

> Words are like leaves; and where they most abound,
> Much fruit of sense beneath is rarely found.[11]

Typical spokesmen, like Adam Smith in 1759, declared that the names of objects are merely "assigned," [12] and Hugh Blair in 1783 epitomized the whole theory in a sentence: "Words, as we now employ them, taken in general, may be considered as symbols, not as imitations; as arbitrary, or instituted, not natural signs of ideas." [13]

Hence Berkeley, who may be said to inaugurate a minority report in the "age of reason," executed a strategic maneuver when, far from calling in question the fundamental premises of Locke, as a Cambridge Platonist might or as Leibniz did, he accepted entirely the analysis of language and then proceeded to argue that from it followed consequences utterly opposite to the comfortable assurances of Locke and the popularizers of Newton. Granted that language is a social convention, as arbitrary as one wished, had not Locke, by the rigor of his own logic, been forced to assert that the correspondence was arranged not between the word and a material object, but between the word and an idea in a man's head? Locke's "new way of reasoning by ideas" had to see words as simply impacts on the senses which were artificially linked with other impacts derived from objects; what men experienced as gold they called "gold," but properly speaking, the word applied to the experience, not to the material. Locke could not see why anyone should be disturbed over this consideration. As he worked out his psychology, he found that the basic components of thought were "simple ideas," which did come directly into the mind from concrete objects; hence the elements of speech, the vocabulary of basic English, so to speak, would be attached to those mental entities "only to be got by those impressions objects themselves make on our minds, by the proper inlets appointed to each sort." [14] Since all men possess the same inlets, they would get the same impressions; gold would be experienced as gold, and the word "gold," though in itself simply a vibration of the ether, would stand securely for one, and only for one, thing. This was an adequate basis for coherent society—or for "the comfort and advantage of society," [15] which was all Locke wanted. The social compact and the rights of property rested firmly on the assurance, given by psychology, that a man can make articulate signs "stand as marks for the ideas within his mind." [16]

There was one slight danger to guard against. Even Cowley, naïvely assuming that the real object could directly command the judgment, had still confessed, although in parentheses, that we do "perversely" draw our thoughts sometimes from words. Sociable creature though he was, Locke was obliged to perceive that the process of attaching words to ideas might be reversible. A name is normally affixed to the idea derived from experience, but in the temporal order of experience the name may come first and so excite the idea, or some idea, before the object has even been met. By custom and education, Locke agreed, words are indeed assumed to stand for the things; the connection between "certain sounds and the ideas they stand for" becomes, by constant use, so intimate "that the names heard, almost as readily excite certain ideas as if the objects themselves, which are apt to produce them, did actually affect the senses." Obviously, children learn many words before they know the things, and adult discourse, consisting largely of general terms, actually requires that speakers do not perpetually have in mind, or put into words, all the component ideas, let alone the myriad sensations, that enter into an "abstract idea." [17] If they did, they would be bores!

Locke had no intention of augmenting boredom. In fact, by the mechanics of his psychology, an elision of detail was imminently to be expected: "ideas become general, by separating from them the circumstances of time and place, and any other ideas that may determine them to this or that particular existence." [18] The principle of separation, which accounts for the origin of language in general, also operates within language; thus a generalized name—honor, truth, regeneration, grace, matter—becomes affixed to this or that abstract idea. So far, so good; but did not Locke run the danger, at the end of his subtlety, of introducing by the back door the very "imaginary ideas of conceptions" he and the scientists had expelled by the front? Was he admitting, after all, that there are some words, the very words over which the wars had been fought, from which men might legitimately, instead of perversely, draw their thoughts?

Locke's answer was emphatically no. He protected his argument against this objection by his ingenious distinction between simple ideas and all the forms of complex ideas: mixed modes, relations, and substances. Simple ideas are the hard pellets of sensation, the irreducible atoms of impression, out of which complex ideas are built; simple ideas—this is the heart of Locke's conception—can be given a name only by those who have first had the sensation. No word alone can impart a simple idea, and therefore such ideas "are not capable of any definition"; "all the words in the world, made use of to explain or define any of their names, will never be able to produce in us the idea it stands for." He who has never tasted "pine apple" cannot get, from any number of words, "the true idea of the relish of that celebrated and delicious fruit." [19] This was Locke's major contribution to the Enlightenment, his weapon against enthusiasm, incantation, and priestcraft, his guarantee against perversity. The primary alphabet of thought simply cannot be taken from words; words can only be attached subsequently, by public agreement, to indubitable shocks of sense. This was the way to achieve what Sprat had defined as the goal of the Royal Society, the correspondence of hand and brain, the way—once and for all—to emancipate the solid knowledge of nature from the frivolous and discordant colors of rhetoric.

Thereafter the sailing was clear. Complex ideas are mechanical compositions of simple, made not from new or unitary sensations but by "putting together those which the mind had before." They are wholly, completely "voluntary," "put together in the mind, independent from any original patterns in nature." Complex ideas do not need to correspond to real conjunctions of simple ideas in nature; they are "always suited to the end for which abstract ideas are made"—which is to say, for counters in civilized conversation—and as long as everybody is agreed, they will serve.[20] They are economical, because they collect an abundance of particulars into "short sounds," and they can never (except to enthusiasts!) become the instigators of perverse thoughts, because they are always definable. That is, they can always be resolved back into their components. Since they "depend on such collections of ideas as men have made, and not on the real nature of things," [21] there is no need to fight about them: if a dispute threatens, all we need do is to take apart the complex idea in question, see what differences appear in our respective inventories of impressions, and so come to an accommodation. "A definition is best made by enumerating those simple ideas that are combined in the signification of the term defined." [22]

That the terms of theology and ethics, the words over which Christendom had been rent, were "mixed modes," Locke was well aware; he thought he might do "some service to truth, peace, and learning, if, by any enlargement on this subject, I can make men reflect on their own use of language," because this would be to make them aware that both they and their opponents might have good words in their mouths "with very uncertain, little, or no signification." [23] They might even, he insinuated, begin to suspect that because the revealed will of God happens to be clothed in words, doubt and uncertainty unavoidably attend that sort of conveyance; whereas in nature, in the realm of the simple ideas, "the precepts of Natural Religion are plain, and very intelligible to all mankind, and seldom come to be controverted." [24] If the concept of predestination, for instance, is in fact nothing but a bundle of particulars, then unloosening the thongs and spreading out the collection of elements may make for pleasant discourse over the port—"for easier and readier improvement and communication of their knowledge" [25]—but surely not for the splitting of skulls.

Berkeley, as is well known, improved upon this logic by insisting that Locke did not go far enough. The premise being that language is separable from reality, a word would therefore have meaning only so long as it could be attached, either immediately or by stopping to think, to an idea framed in the mind of speaker and listener; consequently, the name of a complex idea would be viable only so long as both agreed that if they took the time to investigate it they would turn up the same array of simple ideas. Thereupon Berkeley pounced upon Locke's admission that in social intercourse, men do get along without the investigation, that for indefinite periods the word serves from man to man without anybody really entertaining the idea. If the idea can be dispensed with temporarily, need it ever be required? If it is unnecessary, does it exist? "It is one thing for to keep a name constantly to the same *definition*, and another to make it stand everywhere for the same *idea*: the one is necessary, the other useless and impracticable." [26] In other words, it is entirely logical, on the basis of the sensational psychology, to argue that the names of complex ideas, being only human constructions for social ends, for converse over the port, do not stand for any ideas at all and never have stood for any; that they are merely words and nothing but words. If a bundle has to be resolved back into its particulars in order to be defined, the particulars are the definition, and bundles are simply "fictions and contrivances of the mind." [27]

For certain words—Berkeley concentrated on "matter"—there obviously are no corresponding ideas; the whole business is a social makeshift, and Locke, for all his precaution, had failed to hound nature in her wanderings. Those indeed advise well, Berkeley continued, who tell us to attend our ideas and not the absurd opinions which grow out of words, but they have not heeded their own counsel "so long as they thought the only immediate use of words was to signify ideas, and that the immediate signification of every general name was a determinate abstract idea." [28] Locke and the Lockeans had, in short, fallen into the error of contending, in the face of their own logic, that whereas no word can engender a simple idea, a word standing for an intricate conception, if susceptible of definition, can communicate a nexus of ideas. The result was that they still tried to use such a word as "matter" as though it could summon up an idea, when to the simplest introspection it was evident that no such idea ever had existed or could exist. But Locke, we remember, had classified the concept of matter, along with all mixed modes and substances, under the head of complex ideas, which included also the propositions of Christian theology, such as resurrection, regeneration, and reprobation. Was Berkeley alone or peculiar in sensing a terrible deficiency in the very center of the rational optimism? Did he, in fact, realize how enormous the deficiency was? Was it the century's desire for stability and its want of logical acumen that induced so many businessmen and divines to accept Locke with a sigh of relief, in the confidence that life could now become genial, enthusiasm unfashionable, and Christianity reasonable, that language could at last be so brought under control that it would no longer "insinuate wrong ideas, move the passions, and thereby mislead the judgment"? [29]

Suppose there were a mind as acute as Berkeley's, no less prepared to seize upon the weakness of the sensational rhetoric and yet equally convinced that the terms of the analysis were correct; and suppose that this mind, not so much concerned with the purely metaphysical issue of materialism and appreciating that there never had been an age "wherein strength and penetration of reason, extent of learning, exactness of distinction, correctness of style, and clearness of expression, did so abound," was also convinced that never was there an age "wherein there has been so little sense of the evil of sin." If this mind, fully possessed of the doctrine of the sensational rhetoric, were also persuaded that "our people do not so much need to have their heads stored, as to have their hearts touched; and they stand in the greatest need of that sort of preaching, that has the greatest tendency to do this," [30] would he be content with refinements on the Lockean metaphysics, or would he see in the Lockean theory of language a help to that of which the people had greatest need? What would he therefore do with it? What could he do?

II

There is no evidence that Jonathan Edwards ever read Berkeley. He did read Locke, probably in 1717 when he was fourteen years of age—read him with more pleasure, he recollected, "than the most greedy miser finds, when gathering up handfuls of silver and gold, from some newly discovered treasure." [31] In 1727 he went up the river to become colleague pastor with his magnificent grandfather at Northampton, and two years later to assume the sole spiritual dictatorship of the most turbulent town in New England. He went there to preach, to touch the people's hearts and not to store their heads, but his own head was full of Newton and Locke; while Newton had impressed upon him the inviolable connection of cause and effect, Locke had taught him that in general the words used by parsons "signified nothing that really existed in nature." [32] The frontiersmen, farmers, aspiring merchants, and land speculators who made up pioneer Northampton existed in nature, and to them Edwards was to preach the New England theology, as complicated a collection of mixed modes as could be imagined, having read in Locke that the mixed modes which constitute the propositions of theology are "for the most part such whose component parts nowhere exist together." Hence his mission was defined for him: "It is the mind alone that collects them, and gives them the union of one idea: and it is only by words enumerating the several simple ideas which the mind has united, that we can make known to others what their names stand for." [33]

As a student and tutor at New Haven, Edwards had already jotted down his "Notes on the Mind," which to historians have seemed so to echo Berkeley that they have supposed an influence; but in fact the similarity stems from Edwards' having also, and precociously, grasped the implication of the Lockean postulate. For Berkeley it led inescapably to a stylistic injunction: "Whatever ideas I consider, I shall endeavour to take them bare and naked into my view"; [34] for the young Edwards, acceptance of the sensational psychology was a commitment, for a lifetime of effort, "to extricate all questions from the least confusion of ambiguity of words, so that the ideas shall be left naked." [35]

Within a few years at Northampton he was preaching naked ideas in this fashion:

How dismal will it be, when you are under these racking torments, to know assuredly that you never, never shall be delivered from them; to have no hope: when you shall wish that you might but be turned into nothing, but shall have no hope of it; when you shall wish that you might be turned into a toad or a serpent, but shall have no hope of it; when you would rejoice, if you might but have any relief, after you shall have endured these torments millions of ages, but shall have no hope of it; when after you shall have worn out the age of the sun, moon, and stars, in your dolorous groans and lamentations, without any rest day or night, or one minute's ease, yet you shall have no hope of ever being delivered; when after you shall have worn out a thousand more such ages, yet you shall have no hope, but shall know that you are not one whit nearer to the end of your torments; but that still there are the same groans, the same shrieks, the same doleful cries, incessantly to be made by you, and that the smoke of your torment shall still ascend up forever and ever; and that your souls, which have been agitated with the wrath of God all this while, yet will still exist to bear more wrath; your bodies, which shall have been burning and roasting all this while in these glowing flames, yet shall not have been consumed, but will remain to roast through an eternity yet, which will not have been at all shortened by what shall have been past.[36]

By such rhetoric he whipped up a revival in 1734, and a still greater one in 1740, which, with the help of Whitfield, spread over all New England, became a frenzy and a social upheaval, and then burned itself out in a sullen resentment against its begetter and resulted in Edwards' expulsion from Northampton. Students have worried over how Edwards ever got from his early devotion to Locke, with the denunciation of "magisterial, positive, and imperious" ways of "imposing our own sense and interpretation" [37] on the Bible, to his later and indubitably imperious utterance. They have assumed that he could not have read Locke carefully; actually, he read Locke so profoundly that the progress from Book III of the *Essay* to the apocalyptic terrors of his revival sermons seemed to him not only logical but irresistible.

Edwards became a revolutionary artist in the midst of the eighteenth century because he took with painful seriousness Locke's theory that words are separable from all reality, natural or spiritual, and in themselves are only noises. "Sounds and letters are external things, that are the objects of the external senses of seeing and hearing"; therefore, he told his people, "ideas of certain marks upon paper, such as any of the twenty-four letters, in whatever order, or any sounds of the voice, are as much external ideas, as of any other shapes or sounds whatsoever." [38] Hence, "words are of no use any otherwise than as they convey our own ideas to others." [39] Out of the Lockean psychology, for instance, he could readily explain the failure of the educational methods employed by his enemies in Stockbridge upon the Indian children, who were being taught, Edwards reported, to read words merely as sensations and not as signs of ideas, "without any kind of knowledge of the meaning of what they read." They were being permanently disabled from ever getting knowledge by their "habit of making such and such sounds, on the sight of such and such letters, with a perfect inattentiveness to meaning." The proper method, "a rational way of teaching" either in the schoolroom or in the pulpit, would be to attach every word to an idea, so that eventually the words would provoke the concept: "Being long habituated to make sounds without connecting any ideas with them, they so continue until they come to be capable of well understanding the words, and would perhaps have the ideas, properly signified by the words, naturally excited in their minds on hearing the words, were it not for an habitual hearing and speaking them without any ideas." Edwards was an unbreakable, and unbendable, man; he would never admit that the methods he used to instigate the Awakening were wrong, even after they betrayed him; in the midst of his bitter exile, he unrepentantly insisted, "The child should be taught to understand *things,* as well as *words.*" [40]

In his notebooks Edwards came back again and again to the troubling theme which was the crux, as he saw it, not only of his own problem but, in view of what the people most needed, of the age. The one incontrovertible and yet disastrous fact, "duly considering human nature," was simply that a great part of our discourse about things can be conducted without "the actual ideas" of the things in our mind, that "the mind makes use of signs instead of the ideas themselves." [41] This ability was obviously a consequence of the sensational psychology; it was immensely useful in practical affairs because it saved time; it enabled a man to run his eye down a page and take in a staggering array of abstract terms—"God, man, angel, people, misery, happiness, salvation, destruction, consideration, perplexity, sanctification"—without having to stop and frame a conception for every word. "If we must have the actual ideas of everything that comes in our way in the course of our thoughts, this would render our thoughts so slow as to render our power of thinking in great measure useless." [42] But granted these conveniences, nevertheless a terrible prospect followed: thinking can get along without being employed about things or ideas; it can operate entirely with those artificial signs which the mind habitually substitutes for reality. Profitable though the device may be for warfare, business, and speculation, what is it but the supreme manifestation of original sin? It is the negation of life, the acceptance of substitutes, of husks without the corn. Actually to know something, actually to live, is to deal with ideas themselves, for which words must remain forever the inadequate, because arbitrary, symbols:

To have an actual idea of a thought, is to have that thought we have an idea of then in our minds. To have an actual idea of any pleasure or delight, there must be excited a degree of that delight. So to have an actual idea of any trouble or kind of pain, there must be excited a degree of that pain or trouble. And to have an idea of any affection of the mind, there must be, then present, a degree of that affection.[43]

In one of the several astonishing passages of his notebooks, Edwards worked out in a significant image the immense distinction between knowledge of the word and knowledge of the actuality for which the word is a substitute:

> When we have the idea of another's love to a thing, if it be the love of a man to a woman [whom] we are unconcerned about, in such cases we have not generally any further idea at all of his love, we only have an idea of his actions that are the effects of love, as we have found by experience, and of those external things which belong to love and which appear in case of love; or if we have any idea of it, it is either by forming our ideas so of persons and things as we suppose they appear to them that we have a faint vanishing notion of their affections, or—if the thing be a thing that we so hate that this can't be—we have our love to something else faintly and least excited: and so in the mind, as it were, referred to this place, we think this is like that.[44]

To know the love of a woman only from the *signe* displayed by another man in love, and to deduce from this that what he feels must resemble some lesser feeling of one's own, bears the same relation to one's actually loving a woman that the word bears to the idea.

When we come to the words of theology, the problem of getting from the term to the idea becomes difficult in the extreme. Instead of striving with ourselves to excite in ourselves the constituent ideas of the complex conception, "and so having actually such an abstract idea as Mr. Locke speaks of," we content ourselves with "only an idea of something in our mind, either a name, or some external sensible idea, that we use as a sign to represent that idea." [45] But in the face of this dilemma, it never occurred to Edwards, as it had to Berkeley, to solve his problem by denying the reality of the abstract idea—which is presumptive proof that Edwards was unaffected by Berkeley. He remained, on this point, faithful to Locke: the way to comprehend an abstract idea was, for him, not to deny it, but to define it. "If we are at a loss concerning a connection or consequence, or have a new inference to draw, or would see the force of some new argument, then commonly we are put to the trouble of exciting the actual idea, and making it as lively and clear as we can; and in this consists very much of that which we call at-

tention of the mind in thinking." [46] But to excite the actual idea
of certain realities, of the love of woman or the fear of God, for
example, does indeed put us to "trouble." And it was precisely
here that Edwards went beyond Locke, far beyond him! He
reached into a wholly other segment of psychology, the realm
of the passions, and linked the word not only with the idea but
also with that from which Locke had striven to separate it, with
the emotions.

Edwards' great discovery, his dramatic refashioning of the
theory of sensational rhetoric, was his assertion that an idea in
the mind is not only a form of perception but is also a determination of love and hate. To apprehend things only by their signs
or by words is not to apprehend them at all; but to apprehend
them by their ideas is to comprehend them not only intellectually
but passionately. For Edwards, in short, an idea became not
merely a concept but an emotion. Thus he could achieve, to the
bewilderment of his opponents, his radical definition of grace as
"a new simple idea," and thereby elevate the central Christian
experience entirely above the ambiguities of the mixed modes.
He went so far as to distinguish the emotional from the intellectual apprehension by calling it the truly "sensible" method, and
to whisper to himself in the seclusion of his study, "Perhaps this
distribution of the kinds of our knowledge into Speculative and
Sensible, if duly weighed, will be found the most important of
all." [47] For Edwards it was the most important achievement of his
life and the key to his doctrine and practice.

Again he presents a strange parallel to Berkeley, though now
with an important difference. As soon as Berkeley had proved,
out of Locke's own principles, that words can function in communication without there being any idea involved or, as with
abstractions, even existing, he was ready to suggest that words,
simply as physiological stimuli, could operate not by actually
communicating anything but by "the raising of some passion,
the exciting to or deterring from an action, the putting the mind
in some particular disposition." He entreated his readers to
answer honestly if they had not, upon hearing certain discourses,
experienced passions of fear or love or admiration "without any
ideas coming between." Yet even with his logical destruction

of abstract ideas to support him, Berkeley knew that when he claimed for language the right of working as a mere provoker of emotion, without the intermediacy of concepts, he was challenging the reigning complacency of the age: it is "commonly supposed," he noted, that "the communicating of ideas marked by words is . . . the chief and only end of language." [48] The Lockeans were positive on this point: consigning emotion to the pathology of enthusiasm, Locke explicitly limited the function of language to making known one man's thoughts or ideas to another, to doing it easily, and to conveying the knowledge of things.[49] Once more Locke was resolutely consolidating the gains of the recent scientific offensive; Sprat, for example, had lamented that tropes and figures, which originally had been intended to "bring Knowledge back again to our very senses, from when it was at first deriv'd," were in this degenerate age being used, in defiance of reason, to correspond "with its Slaves, the Passions!" [50] Locke's triumph, by restricting the validity of words to their matching ideas, seemed to preclude their ever being used again by civilized men as the goads of passion; and yet by 1710 Berkeley was soberly maintaining that, since there are words which symbolize abstract ideas, when in reality no such ideas can be conceived, at least such words must be used in the ordinary affairs of life only to "excite in us proper sentiments or dispositions to act in such a manner as is necessary for our well-being, how false soever they may be if taken in a strict and speculative sense." [51]

Edwards, as we have seen, remained a true Lockean, in that he persisted in taking abstract ideas for realities; had he in other respects remained as literal a disciple of Locke he would have frowned, as did his opponents in Boston, Lockeans like Chauncy and Mayhew, upon any use of words to arouse affections. On the other hand, had he followed the line of Berkeley and denied the existence of complex abstractions, he might have given way entirely to employing words for their emotional excitement without bothering about ideas, and so have gone along with the enthusiasts who turned the Awakening into an orgy. His greatness is that he did neither. Instead, he redefined "idea." He so conceived it that it became a principle of organization and of

perception not only for the intellectual man, but for the passionate man, for the loving and desiring man, for the whole man.
He conceded readily that a word can act as an emotional stimu-
lus, not because like Berkeley he separated emotion from the
mind, but because, having consolidated the mind with the passions, he was ready to maintain that an emotional response is
also an intellectual, or that an intellectual, in the highest sense,
is also emotional. A passionate grasping of meaning from a thing
or a word is as much an idea—a more clear and distinct idea—as
a theoretical grasping. He argued that the purport of a symbol
can be appreciated not only by the human head, but more accurately by the human heart. An "ideal apprehension" is not only
a proposition, it is a "sense"—"whereby things are pleasing or
displeasing, including all agreeableness and disagreeableness, all
beauty and deformity, all pleasure and pain, and all those sensations, exercises and passions of the mind that arise from either
of those." [52]

In other words, Edwards did not deny what Berkeley maintained, that the noise of a word can produce a visceral response
which has nothing to do with any intelligibility. He was too
rigorous a sensationalist not to see that such a phenomenon was
altogether likely, and had he been doubtful, the extremists of the
Awakening gave him empirical verification. What Edwards saw
was that a purely physiological—or, as we might say, "aesthetic"
—reaction to a word is of no use to anybody; what he denied
was that the appeal to the emotions must always be made at the
cost of the idea; what he insisted upon was that by the word
(used in the place of a thing) an idea can be engendered in the
mind, and that when the word is apprehended emotionally as
well as intellectually, then the idea can be more readily and
more accurately conceived. When the word sets in train a sequence of passions, out of it—not invariably, but frequently—
there emerges, like Venus from the foam, a "sensible" concept.
This was possible, he argued, because an idea is a unit of experience, and experience is as much love and dread as it is logic.
To go from the word to a mechanical response, in preaching or
in literary criticism, is a direct, natural, scientifically explicable
process; but to get from the sensational impact of a word,

through the emotion, to the saving, comprehending idea, there must be an indirect, a supernatural, a mysterious leap. And yet, wonder of wonders, it happens! It happens because, while the saving and comprehending idea is not an effect of which the word is the cause, still, in the marvelous order of divine providence, the preliminary application of the word is, for the producing of that idea, absolutely indispensable.

Hence it seemed obvious to Jonathan Edwards that the sounding of the word, out of which the new simple idea would or might be born, had to be of a word that stood for reality; and reality, to any objective consideration, is grim as well as beautiful. "I am not afraid to tell sinners, that are most sensible of their misery, that there case is indeed as miserable as they think it to be, and a thousand times more so; for this is the truth." [53] Edwards was the heir of a tradition which often found its happiest formulations in the terms of formal logic, and he sometimes expounded the rationale of his apocalyptic preaching by drawing upon old distinctions: the nature of a cause, he pleaded, is not always to be deduced from the nature of an effect, nor that of an effect from the cause, "when the cause is only *causa sine qua non*, or an occasional cause: yea, that in such a case, oftentimes the nature of the effect is quite contrary to the nature of the cause." [54] But Edwards could not have explained by the logic of old Puritanism and by the scholastic psychology how his naked preaching of terror could become an "occasional cause"; the old Puritanism would have suspected, as Edwards' opponents in fact did during the 1740's, that the effect was merely the efficient work of the word and so was entirely "natural." Edwards decisively departed from the old Puritanism by his appropriation of the new psychology of sensation. By defining grace in this novel frame of reference as a new simple idea, and by keeping in the center of his thinking the principle that an undefinable simple idea can be learned only from experience, he committed himself as a preacher to a rhetoric in which words were obliged to stand in the place of engendering objects, in spite of the fact that there is never any inherent reason why any particular word should stand for any specific object. He was prepared to stake his life upon the assurance that words which were disciplined into becoming "naked" embodiments of ideas could thence become, at least for those capable of receiving the concept, the source or the occasion of an ideational discovery. But if his rhetoric was to achieve such an effect, it had to be not only naked, but so passionately presented that the passions of listeners would heed it. "I should think myself in the way of duty, to raise the affections of my hearers as high as I possibly can, provided that they are affected with nothing but truth, and with affections that are not disagreeable to the nature of what they are affected with." [55] Because the terror of damnation is a truth, and fear is an affection agreeable to it, Edwards preached terror and fear.

To step for a moment outside history, let us look a century ahead of Edwards to Kierkegaard's observation that the teacher can give the learner not truth but only the condition necessary for understanding truth. By conceiving of the word as the occasional rather than the efficient cause, Edwards was maintaining, in the idiom of colonial New England, essentially Kierkegaard's position; in their different phrases both claimed that there is a fundamental limitation upon all literature, namely, that after the artist has provided the verbal environment, at this point another power must intervene if the beholder is to collect out of it the true conception.

But one who gives the learner not only the Truth, but also the condition for understanding it, is more than teacher. All instruction depends upon the presence, in the last analysis, of the requisite condition; if this is lacking, no teacher can do anything. For otherwise he would find it necessary not only to transform the learner, but to re-create him before beginning to teach him. But this is something no human being can do; if it is done, it must be done by God himself.[56]

In Edwards' version, the statement runs that a person can indeed respond to words in terms of his knowledge of natural good or evil, but for him to react to the spiritual import of rhetoric—since spiritual good or evil will never consist in any consonancy whatsoever with human nature—"it must be wholly and entirely a work of the Spirit of God, not merely as assisting and coworking with natural principles, but as infusing something above nature." [57]

Yet this did not mean for Edwards—any more than for Kierkegaard—that the rhetorician simply builds up a wall of words around the listener, and then reclines, to let the Spirit of God work or not work. Had Edwards evaded the issue by taking so easy a way out, he too could be accused, as have most of the followers of Locke, for having surrendered to a "passive" notion of intelligence and to a naïve environmentalism. Edwards' point was that the sensory impression, and especially the sensible word, comes to the human spirit bearing significances of love or terror, and the leap to a saving understanding proceeds out of the natural. Though a sense of spiritual excellency is required for salvation, it is not the only kind of ideal apprehension that is concerned in conviction: "It also partly depends on a sensible knowledge of what is natural in religion." The mind, being convinced of the truth, "thence naturally and immediately infers from this fitness" what is originally beyond the contrivance of man.[58] So the word must be pressed, and rhetoric must strive for impression; it is a strength, not a weakness, of language that no matter how sensational it becomes, it has to depend upon something happening to the recipient outside and above its own mechanical impact. If this fact imposes a limitation upon the efficacy of art, it bestows at the same time an infallible criterion for its success: "There is a great difference between these two things, viz., lively imaginations arising from strong affections, and strong affections arising from lively imaginations." If Edwards' artistry was an accidental effect or a consequence of real passion, it would be genuine; but if it produced in the listener or reader an emotion that contained no more than what the rhetoric imparted, "then is the affection, however elevated, worthless and vain." [59] I think Edwards meant the affection of both speaker and listener, for he never spared himself. To this paradoxical and yet logical conclusion, this desperate and yet exhilarating insight, the sensational concept of language led in the reasoning of America's greatest sensationalist.

Notes

1. *Dialogues,* ed. Mary Whiton Colkins (New York, 1929), pp. 281–82.
2. *Ibid.,* p. 123.
3. *An Essay Concerning Human Understanding,* bk. III, chap. ix, par. 21.
4. *Ibid.,* chap. x, par. 2.
5. *Ibid.,* par. 22.
6. *Ibid.,* chap. ii, pars, 1, 8.
7. Bacon, *Works,* ed. Spedding, Ellis, and Heath (Boston, n.d.), VIII, 412.
8. Preface to Thomas Sprat, *The History of the Royal Society* (London, 1667).
9. *Ibid.,* p. 62.
10. *Essay,* bk. III, chap. ii, par. 7.
11. *An Essay on Criticism,* vv. 309–10.
12. Adam Smith, "Considerations on the First Formation of Languages," reprinted in *Essays Philosophical and Literary* (London, n.d.).
13. Hugh Blair, *Lectures on Rhetoric and Belles Lettres* (Dublin, 1783), I, 115.
14. Essay, bk. III, chap. iv. par. 11.
15. *Ibid.,* chap. ii, par. 1.
16. *Ibid.,* chap. i, par. 2.
17. *Ibid.,* chap. ii, par. 6; chap. iii, par. 7.
18. *Ibid.,* chap. iii, par. 16.
19. *Ibid.* chap. iii, pars. 4, 11.
20. *Ibid.,* chap. v, pars. 4, 7.
21. *Ibid.,* chap. vi, par. 1.
22. *Ibid.,* chap. iii, par. 10.
23. *Ibid.,* chap. v, par. 16.
24. *Ibid.,* chap. iv, par. 23.
25. *Ibid.,* chap. iii, par. 20.
26. Berkeley, *A Treatise Concerning the Principles of Human Knowledge* (London, 1710), Intro., par. 18.
27. *Ibid.,* par. 13.
28. *Ibid.,* par. 23.
29. *Essay,* bk. III, chap. x, par. 34.
30. Jonathan Edwards, *Works* (New York, 1844), III, 336.
31. Sereno E. Dwight, *The Life of President Edwards* (New York, 1830), p. 30.
32. *Essay,* bk. III, chap. x, par. 16.
33. *Ibid.,* chap. xi, par. 18.
34. *Treatise,* Intro., par. 21.
35. Dwight, *Life,* p. 702.
36. *Works,* IV, 278.
37. *Essay,* bk. III, chap. ix, par. 23.
38. *Works,* III, 80.
39. *Ibid.,* I, 532.
40. Dwight, *Life,* pp. 475–76.
41. Perry Miller, "Jonathan Edwards on the Sense of the Heart," *Harvard Theological Review,* XLI (April 1948), 129.
42. *Ibid.,* p. 133.
43. *Ibid.,* p. 131.
44. "Miscellanies, No. 288," Jonathan Edwards Manuscripts, Yale University Library (quoted by permission).
45. Miller, p. 131.
46. *Ibid.,* p. 134.
47. *Ibid.,* p. 138.
48. *Treatise,* Intro., par. 20.
49. *Essay,* bk. III, chap. x, par. 23.
50. Sprat, *History,* p. 112.
51. *Treatise,* pt. I, par. 52.
52. Miller, p. 136.
53. *Works,* III, 338.
54. *Ibid.,* p. 290.
55. *Ibid.,* p. 335.
56. Robert Bretall, *A Kierkegaard Anthology* (Princeton: Princeton University Press, 1946), p. 158.
57. Miller, p. 141.
58. *Ibid.,* pp. 143, 145.
59. *Works,* III, 124.

COLERIDGE ON
THE FUNCTION OF ART

Walter Jackson Bate

I

English romantic criticism, as it evolved in the later eighteenth century, is distinguished by a general moderation and compromising eclecticism. As such, it shares the historic ability of British thought as a whole, which has perennially adapted traditional concepts and values to changing aims and circumstances. The fragmentary critical writings of Coleridge illustrate one aspect of this talent for compromise. Broadly viewed, almost the entire body of his criticism, after his early infatuation with the Hartleian psychology, consists of a long series of spasmodic attempts to harmonize the traditional rationalistic precepts of classicism with the romantic vitalism that Whitehead has described as "a protest on behalf of the organic view of nature." [1] The direction of Coleridge's attempts to achieve this end may be best summarized by his statement that art, in its broadest function, "is the mediatress between, and reconciler of, nature and man." [2] His discussions of the relation of the universal and the particular, his conceptions of the nature of beauty and of the role of imitation in art, his isolated observations on such matters as imagery and meter, and his wholesale plundering, for the exposition of these and other subjects, of divergent philosophies and critical assumptions, all seem guided by a central desire to extend and convince himself and others of the truth of this essentially classical standpoint: that the aim of art is to make nature, or ultimate truth, comprehensible and realizable to human response. Moreover, it is only by noting the ways in which Coleridge tried to ramify this fundamental principle that one can rightly grasp his elaborate and rather confused theory of the imagination. For Coleridge's theory of the imagination, which has too often been approached directly as a separate unit or even as a fulcrum for his other critical ideas, was essentially no more than a roundabout psychological justification for his conception of the mediating function of art.

II

Coleridge tends to accept the familiar distinction between classicism and romanticism which the Schlegels in particular had popularized.[3] Classical art, that is, reveals the rational harmony inherent in ordered nature. It distinguishes carefully in the objects it presents: it is concerned with classes and types; and, in subduing its objects to a proper decorum, it tends to circumscribe them as "fixed" and "self-sufficient." The romantic spirit is more restless: its goal is less to depict the fixed and formal quality of the object than to suggest a dynamic fluctuation which lies beneath exterior distinctions. Neglecting clear-cut boundaries and "self-existent perfection," it penetrates at once, as A. W. von Schlegel said, to the fluid reality of nature, "is perpetually striving after new and marvellous births," and hence "approaches more to the secret of the universe."[4] It is only fair to state that Coleridge did not labor the distinction between classic and romantic as essentially a distinction between the "fixed" and "dynamic." He shared the belief of many other contemporary critics that art achieves a profounder and more essential truth if it presents life, not in its "simple, clear . . . and self-sufficient" aspects—which Schlegel considered the aim of classicism—but as a vital evolving of process. Coleridge's use of the antithesis between classic and romantic seems to have been merely a hasty device for illustrating this belief. An instance would be his statement that, whereas the classical dramatist portrays "fixed" types and decora, Shakespeare, as a "romantic" dramatist, presents "our *inward* nature, the working of the passions in their most retired recesses."[5] The statement is relevant to Coleridge's general conviction that "the artist must imitate that which is within the thing, that which is active through form and figure": it is thus that he catches "each thing that lives" in its "moment of self-exposition," and can "interpret and understand the symbol, that the wings of the air-sylph are forming within the skin of the caterpillar." [6]

The vitalism that Coleridge prized and tended at times to bracket as "romantic" may be generally described, therefore, as a successive unfolding of potentiality within concreteness. As such, it has certain romantic implications for his practical criticism of Shakespeare, as well as for his theoretical antithesis between classicism and romanticism. One may note this in the way it qualified and colored his theory of "organic unity." [7] It led him, for example, to depart somewhat from the Aristotelian precept that the event, the situation—and hence, in dramatic poetry, the plot or design—is of primary importance, and that the characters are to be shown as they reflect or participate in this ordered action. In Shakespeare, as Coleridge and other romantic critics regarded him, the essential thing is character; and events and circumstances are viewed as they reveal and evolve from the various facets, feelings, and reactions of the characters. Moreover, the characters of Shakespeare do not exemplify predominant types, attributes, or passions as such, but emerge in a vital verisimilitude with their various qualities as an inherent part or outgrowth of them. Even in those comic characters which come close to burlesque, their features are never more than an "exquisitely characteristic" part of them:

however awry, disproportionate, and laughable, yet like his Bardolph's nose [they are] still features. But Jonson's are either a man with a huge wen, having a circulation of its own, and which we might conceive amputated, and the patient thereby losing all his character; or they are mere wens instead of men—wens personified.[8]

Similarly, when Shakespeare lays bare the working of a given passion or reaction in one of his characters, we have not an abstraction, description, or even presentation of that passion as a passion, but rather the living fluctuation of feeling taking its natural outlets, so that we see not the passion but the man. An example would be the flow of Capulet's anger when Tybalt prepares to challenge Romeo for coming to the celebration at Capulet's house. After bidding him, without success, to drop the matter, Capulet's anger rises at the flouting of his authority in his own house; then, observing that the lights are burning dimly, he breaks off suddenly, and his anger is simply shifted, as it were, upon the servants. In this transition of his anger to another object,

we see that no one passion is so predominant, but that it includes all the parts of the character, and the reader never has a mere abstract of a passion, as of wrath or ambition, but the whole man is presented to him—the one predominant passion acting, if I may so say, as the leader of the band to the rest.[9]

Coleridge's stress on the concretely vital and organic thus displays a certain romantic naturalism like that of the Schlegels. On the other hand, in contrast with the Schlegels and others who were to accept their antithesis between classicism and romanticism, the critical writings of Coleridge reveal a repeated struggle to combine or reconcile this organic naturalism with the Platonic ideal of absolute universality. Accordingly, he seems to have conceived of "nature" as a kind of field on which opposites can converge, reconcile, and achieve significance. At its "apex," nature is essential spirit which is above strictly human terms and can be fully realized only by the help of analogy: "the fulness of nature is without character, as water is purest when without taste, smell, or color; but this is the highest, the apex only,—it is not the whole. The object of art is to give the whole *ad hominem*." [10] Art, as an "abridgment of nature," employs other aspects of nature—such as are suggested by the terms "color, form, motion, and sound"—that are also symbols by which man familiarly thinks. It uses them in such a way as to make the whole of nature, both its phenomenal reality and its "apex," realizable *ad hominem*. Hence Coleridge's further extension of his statement that art

is the mediatress between, and reconciler of, nature and man. It is, therefore, the power of humanizing nature, of infusing the thoughts and passions of man into every thing which is the object of his contemplation; color, form, motion, and sound, are the elements which it combines, and it stamps them into unity in the mould of a moral idea.[11]

The high calling that Coleridge is here giving to art is as much opposed to extreme romantic sensibility as it is to the most arid mechanism. To judge a drama purely by its capacity to stimulate sensibility is to place it, as he said, on a level with the onion, which also possesses the power to draw tears. When Coleridge emphasizes the importance, therefore, of "humanizing nature"— of making nature realizable to human feelings—he is not, as Irving Babbitt and others have charged, sanctioning the projection of one's personal sentiment upon nature, which one may then call reality and interpret as beautiful and benevolent or as empty and cruel, according to one's subjective mood.[12] Nor is this accusation strengthened by dwelling on the lyrical suggestiveness of Coleridge's own verse. "For my own part," as he frankly said, "I freely own that I have no title to the name of poet, according to my own definition of poetry." [13]

Indeed, by postulating an objective reality and the possibility of conceiving it, Coleridge's critical theory, in intention if not in achievement, also stands apart from more serious forms of contemporary subjectivism. What appears to have been his general conception of nature is only confused, for example, by stressing his verbal parallels with Schelling. Such parallels—or appropriations—are, of course, frequent in Coleridge. To apply them to his basic aesthetic tenets, however, can obscure the main outlines of his thought even further: it encourages the common mistake that Coleridge's idealism is a distorted echo of German subjective transcendentalism rather than a reassertion of the absolute ideas of the Platonic tradition. Whether Coleridge succeeded in reconciling his romantic naturalism with Platonic idealism, or whether even his attempt to do so reveals a lack of philosophical discrimination and is merely a result of a desire to have his cake and eat it too, are aside from the point. The fact remains that he did aspire to such a reconciliation. One example is simply his successive interest in various philosophers because of his hope that each might offer "the key-stone of the arch"—as he said on one occasion of Fichte—and then his subsequent abandonment of them when their ultimate implications appeared too materialistic or subjectivistic. His youthful interest in the Hartleian psychology, which he abruptly terminated, thus set a pattern that was to continue. If he rejected Hartley's associationism partly because it did not really "mark," as he had at first believed, "the *ideal* tribes/Up the fine fibres to the sentient brain," he also finally parted company with what he called the "dynamic philosophy" of Kant and his followers because of its incompatibility with "the objective reality of the Ideas," and its final "grounding all on an equivoque of the word I." [14] One may therefore agree with Mr. Raysor and Mr. Eliot, among others, that Coleridge lost rather than gained by his loose terminological borrowings from Kant, Fichte, and Schelling. Indeed, such borrowings, with their subjectivistic implications, only clouded his ultimate aim, as Coleridge himself seems finally to have felt.[15] One may best approach Coleridge, therefore, by disregarding, wherever possible, the superstructure which these borrowings form, and by viewing him in the line of British empirical intuitionalists who have occasionally sought to yoke their customary premises of thought with the Platonic tradition.[16]

III

Coleridge's occasional remarks on the role of the universal and the particular in art appear as one extension of his reconciliatory position. On the one hand, he adopts "with full faith the principle of Aristotle, that poetry . . . is essentially *ideal* . . . that its apparent individualities . . . must be *representative* of a class." [17] This much is to be taken for granted. Indeed, poetry, in its highest function, discloses the ultimate and permanent universals of nature itself. They are not to be confused with the mere generalizations which the mind constructs on the basis of experience, but are grasped by a higher faculty of mind than discursive generalization and abstraction. They are the formative aim and guide of a process which Coleridge elsewhere calls the "apex" of nature, the particular existing merely as the "organ" of the universal, "as the lungs in relation to the atmosphere, the eye to light, crystal to fluid, figure to space." [18] But if the particular is meaningless except as it is seen to reveal the universal— its self-sufficiency being only "a framework which the human imagination forms by its own limits, as the foot measures itself on the snow" [19]—the universal, on the other hand, is comprehensible only through the particular. It is, in ordinary human terms, "without character," in the sense that "water is purest when without taste"; and art, in order to make it realizable, must show it as "the substance capable of endless modifications,"[20] working in and through the particulars with which human reaction is familiar.

In doing so, art presents an "abridgment" of reality itself. For "universal" and "particular" are mutually dependent in nature. Reality, that is, consists in the manner in which value or form becomes definite and emergent in the particular: reality is the bridge between concreteness and value. Value becomes *real* at the same point where the concrete exemplifies the *ideal*. In this sense, therefore, the *ideal* and the *real* are one and the same, and "Idealism" is at the same time "the truest and most binding realism."[21] This conception is crucial for the whole of Coleridge's thought. If his critical writings generally have a rather puzzling, hieroglyphic quality, this fundamental standpoint, when completely understood, can be used as something of a Rosetta stone, by the aid of which other principles and assumptions are seen to fall into place. Yet it is also at this decisive point that one is tempted, even more than usually, to echo Dr. Johnson's sentiments about the shadowy member of his household menagerie, Poll Carmichael: "I had some hopes for her at first, but . . . she was wiggle-waggle, and I could never persuade her to be categorical." For in a broad sense, Coleridge's premise is simply a repetition of Aristotle's basic thesis that universal and particular, form and matter, exist only through each other.

Yet we find Coleridge, in his famous distinction between "Platonists" and "Aristotelians" using the terms as a division between the sheep and the goats; his point being that for Plato— and hence Coleridge, as one of the sheep—the universals are "constitutive," while for Aristotle they are only "regulative."[22] Perhaps the only point of difference is that, for Coleridge, Aristotle did not go far enough by regarding form and matter as simply two sides of reality, without separate existence except through artificial abstraction; whereas Coleridge himself wished to emphasize that such a union of form and matter presupposes a prior if "deficient" existence of form. His apparent inconsistency, therefore, rests largely on loose terminology. The universals exist independently, but they become "real"—that is, they attain fulfillment and thus a higher degree of being—only as they are emergent in the particular. It is as though one took Plotinus' conception of universality as being both transcendent and yet immanent within individuality, and then maintained that the universal achieves a "higher reality"—that is, a fuller manifestation—through being immanent. Indeed, it is here that the qualified Neoplatonism of Jakob Boehme could appeal so much to Coleridge and take its place on his eclectic shelf. Universality, to Boehme, presupposes immanence for its fulfillment: unity, for example, may exist as a universal, but it also achieves its complete realization only when there is "opposition" to be unified. In its full value, it exists as *process:* it should then be thought of as "unifying" rather than as "unity."

Similarly, for Coleridge, the realization of the universal might be better expressed by the active participle than by the noun; hence his general emphasis on thinking in terms of "an *act,* instead of a *thing* or a *substance*" [23]—a statement which is misinterpreted if it is connected solely with a vague organic vitalism. Indeed, Coleridge seems generally to use the word "universal" when he is speaking of a principle, existing separately (for example, "unity"), and to apply the term "idea" to the "act" (for example, "unifying") in which the universal becomes manifest. Accordingly, he refers to "ideas" as "real," "living," "seminal," and the like. The universal, then, as he uses the term, is not a "mere abstraction" of the mind; it has objective existence. But it becomes an "idea" only as it executes its function of a controlling and formative principle, and such a principle is not controlling unless there is something being controlled. It is therefore necessarily immanent in concrete individuality, the "controlling" and the "being controlled" substantiating and fulfilling each other in the same act. Hence Coleridge defines the "idea" as "the universal *in* the individual, *or the individuality itself,*—the glance and exponent of the indwelling power." [24] Similarly, in art, "the ideal consists in the happy balance of the generic with the individual," since "nothing *lives* or is *real,* but as definite and individual." [25]

The focal point for the artist, therefore, is neither the "universal" nor the "particular" as such, but a point of union which

sustains and fulfills both. It is the "germ" of universal potentiality in the particular itself which biases and directs the particular to its own "self-exposition," and thus creates individuality,
while at the same time it "elaborates essence into existence" by
exhibiting value at the point where it attains reality. It is this, as
the basic premise of Coleridge's thought, which underlies his
criticism of Shakespeare, whose dramas, like nature itself, have
"a vitality which grows and evolves from within." Indeed, it is
because he so habitually turns to Shakespeare as the grand exposition of his entire aesthetic theory, that we begin to feel, in reading Coleridge's criticism, that Shakespeare is almost the only poet,
and Coleridge is his prophet. For it was the prerogative of
Shakespeare

to have the *universal* which is potentially in each *particular*, opened
out to him . . . not as an abstraction of observation from a variety of
men, but as the substance capable of endless modifications, of which
his own personal existence was but one, and to use *this one* as the
eye that beheld the other, and as the tongue that could convey the
discovery.[26]

In this sense, Shakespeare himself may be viewed as a particular
"modification" through which the universal is declared. His dis-
closure of the active thread of connection which binds the specific
with the general is thus opposed, for example, to the pseudo-
universality of Beaumont and Fletcher, who portray only "what
could be put together and represented to the eye." Far from
grasping the living potentiality inherent in the particular, they
viewed the particular *ab extra,* and constructed a piecemeal
synthesis on the basis of their empirical observation. It is as
though one

might fit together a quarter of an orange, a quarter of an apple,
and the like of a lemon and a pomegranate, and make it look like one
round diverse colored fruit. But nature, who *works from within by
evolution and assimilation* according to a law, cannot do it. Nor could
Shakespeare, for he too worked in the spirit of nature, *by evolving the
germ within by the imaginative power according to an idea.*[27]

Art, as it achieves this aim, is accordingly viewed as analogous to
the fulfillment of religion itself. For religion acts "by a contraction of universal truths into individual duties, such contraction

being the only form in which those truths can attain life and reality": as the universal revealed concretely, religion

is the echo of the *voice of the Lord God walking in the garden.* Hence in all ages and countries of civilization religion has been the parent and fosterer of the fine arts . . . the common essence of which consists in a similar union of the universal and the individual.[28]

IV

If reality consists in the "evolution and assimilation" of particular and universal, beauty, in Coleridge's aesthetic theory, may be described as the means by which reality is best comprehended by the total mind. Beauty, that is, is not itself the character or meaning of nature; it is not truth. It is that quality which sustains the peculiarly human conception or awareness of that reality. Only to this extent is it subjectivistic. For far from being a mere pleasant feeling which arises when one's personal associations are agreeably stirred by whatever happens to appeal to one as an individual, beauty—which may even involve "the rupture of association"—is present only when that which is being conceived is the objective truth of the dynamic and vital taking universal form and value. "The BEAUTIFUL is thus at once distinguished both from the AGREEABLE, which is beneath it, and from the GOOD, which is above it." [29] Since it is a means rather than the ultimate object of the act, it is not the good; beauty is a process of approaching the good, and hence is subservient to it. Similarly, since beauty is ultimately directed to the good and the true, it is not merely the agreeable. Agreeableness, of course, accompanies the beautiful. But beauty is not beauty because it happens to please, as some of the "taste-meter" associationists have urged. Rather, it pleases because it is beautiful.[30]

Thus, just as art itself is the mediator between nature and man, "Beauty," says Coleridge, "is the shorthand hieroglyphic of Truth —the mediator between Truth and Feeling, the Head and the Heart." [31] Beauty, in other words, though it is not truth itself, is that which makes truth immediately realizable. As such, it imitates the reality of nature by presenting a "reduction of many to one" in symbols familiar and meaningful *ad hominem.*[32] "It is, in the abstract, the unity of the manifold, the coalescence of the diverse; in the concrete [that is, art], it is the union of the shapely (*formosum*) with the vital." Accordingly, Coleridge praises Raphael's Galatea as showing, he says, the balance and reconciliation "effected between these two conflicting principles of the FREE LIFE, and of the confining FORM! How entirely is the stiffness . . . of the latter, *fused* and . . . almost *volatilized* by the interpenetration and electrical flashes of the former." [33] Using an illustration common in later eighteenth-century aesthetics,[34] Coleridge cites how, among simple visual forms, "rectilineal" lines exemplify the rigidity of pure form as such, "determined *ab extra*"; while, in the curved line, the restraining form is met and modified by the inner movement of a "self-justifying" vitality:

The beautiful in the object may be referred to two elements . . . the first belonging to the shapely . . . and in this, to the law, and the reason, and the second, to the lively, the free, the spontaneous, and the self-justifying. As to lines, the rectilineal are in themselves the lifeless, the determined *ab extra* . . . The curve line is a modification of the force from without by the force from within, or the spontaneous. These are not arbitrary symbols, but the language of nature, universal and intuitive.[35]

In the balance and reconciliation of "these two conflicting principles," form and content embody each other, as a crystal contains and gives shape to light and yet is lost within it:

Something there must be to realize the form, something in and by which the *forma informans* reveals itself . . . An illustrative hint may be taken from a pure crystal, as compared with an opaque, semiopaque, or clouded mass, on the one hand, and with a perfectly transparent body, such as the air, on the other. The crystal is lost in the light, which yet it contains, embodies, and gives a shape to; but which passes shapeless through the air, and, in the ruder body, is either quenched or dissipated.[36]

Yet the simile is insufficient. For the balance desired is not static, but dynamic and emergent: reconciliation, by its very nature, implies process, a movement *into* unity. It is this active progression, then, and not the final unity itself, which constitutes beauty. Accordingly, art attempts not to suggest "the apex only," but to present, as he says, "a harmonized chaos." For "harmony"—

and Coleridge is here echoing the general premise of Jakob Boehme—becomes manifest only as it opposes and subdues "chaos": it presupposes, that is, something which is being harmonized.[37] Such a "fusion to force many into one" may characterize the unfolding of an entire drama. In the form of a "feeling . . . made to modify many others" it may also be shown in a particular character, as when the anguish of Lear "spreads the feeling of ingratitude and cruelty over the very elements of heaven." Or, in a single image, it may produce "out of many things, as they would have appeared in the description of an ordinary mind, described slowly and in unimpassioned succession, a oneness"; and Coleridge cites his favorite example of the flight of Adonis from Venus in the dusk of evening, where, as he says, the brightness of Adonis, the rapidity of his flight, the hopeless yearning of Venus, together with "a shadowy ideal character thrown over the whole," are all united:

> Look! how a bright star shooteth from the sky,
> So glides he in the night from Venus' eye.[38]

This principle of reduction into unity is so intrinsic and pervasive in beauty that it is also echoed in the emergence of likeness from difference—"the coalescence of the diverse"—when an original is imitated in a given medium of art. Like Kames, Adam Smith, and other writers of the century before, Coleridge points out, for example, the lack of aesthetic response when resemblance between original and imitation is too obvious and close. For in this case the sense of unity and likeness does not emerge through and replace that of difference. Rather, it comes first, with patent flatness, and is followed by the disappointing and anticlimactic notation of differences: the progression, that is to say, is not from difference to likeness but from likeness to difference. Thus, in seeing wax figures, we may at first almost mistake them for men and women; and then,

not finding the motion and the life which we expected, we are shocked as by a falsehood, every circumstance of detail, which before induced us to be interested, making the distance from truth more palpable. You set out with a supposed reality and are disappointed and disgusted with the deception; whilst, in respect to a work of genuine imitation, you begin with an acknowledged total difference, and then every touch of nature gives you the pleasure of an approximation to truth.[39]

Art, then, imitates what is essential in nature—the reconciliation of universal and particular—by presenting, within its own given medium, a similarly active progression of "multeity into unity," and of difference into likeness. The symbols which it employs, therefore, are themselves an active repetition of "the germinal causes in Nature" and may be distinguished from mere "copying," which produces "masks only, not forms breathing life."[40] It is thus that one should interpret the statement that the "symbol," as distinct from "allegory," "always partakes of the reality that it renders intelligible."[41] Moreover, Coleridge's distinction between "organic" and "mechanical" form falls into place as a further ramification of this standpoint; nor can it be understood otherwise. Form is mechanical when it is superimposed instead of "arising out of the properties of the material": when, that is to say, a work of art—the unfolding of a plot, the revelation of a character, an image, a symbol—does not offer, within its own medium, an organic progression in which unity issues through and by means of a given multeity. But "organic" form proceeds directly and intrinsically from such a multeity. It will be remembered that the "idea," in Coleridge's metaphysics, is "the universal in the individual"; it is the universal become active and formative. It therefore evolves the particular, while, as a controlling principle, it necessarily fulfills itself through the very act of controlling. Similarly, "organic" form in art "shapes [its material at the same time] as it develops itself from within." It thus symbolically duplicates nature, "the prime genial artist," in which form is also "the physiognomy of the being within, the true image reflected and thrown out of the concave mirror."[42]

As distinct from truth or the good, therefore, beauty is a means rather than an end. It offers in symbols which are apprehensible and persuasive to man a faithful "abridgement of nature," a "shorthand hieroglyphic of truth," and thus, in its function of mediating between nature and man, is at once a transcriber and a conveyor or admitter. "As light to the eye, even

such is beauty to the mind . . . Hence the Greeks called a beautiful object . . . [a] *calling on* the soul." [43]

v

It is probable that no other interest engrossed Coleridge so
much as the nature and working of the human mind. Yet his
psychology, in which his theory of the imagination occupies a
unique place, cannot be considered apart from his conceptions
of nature itself, of beauty, and of the mediating function of art.
Indeed, no broad outline or direction can be descried in his
aesthetic psychology unless it is viewed as an unfinished extension of these conceptions. It is, so to speak, the roof rather than
the foundation of his aesthetic. Moreover, his fragmentary remarks on the mind, however suggestive, possess an elusiveness
and contradictory electicism—unusually marked even for Coleridge—which make it doubly futile to approach them independently. Such an approach forces one to grasp at straws which are
of little help. A particular instance would be the attempt to as-
certain and then reconcile the implications of Coleridge's borrowings as they are found in their original sources: the assumption
being that if, on the basis of these borrowings, we dexterously
combine elements from Hartley, Kant, and Schelling, not to mention others, we may reconstruct Coleridge's theory of the mind.
But the terms, phrases, and definitions which he took over from
various philosophers—at least those he adopted from his contemporaries or near-contemporaries—are not fixed stones in a systematic structure: they were appropriated because they seemed
at the moment to express or coincide with his own intuitions.
Used as a starting point, they have not only proved of little value,
but have actually complicated and obscured the question need-
lessly; whatever value they may have as borrowings is illustrative rather than fundamental and directing.

Viewed in the light of his general conception of nature, the
cornerstone of Coleridge's psychology, aesthetic or otherwise, is
to be found in his distinction between "reason" and "understanding," both the importance and character of which may be easily
misinterpreted. Its importance for Coleridge is almost unique:

he clung to it during the last twenty-five years of his life with a tenacity which was rare in one so prone to passing terminological enthusiasms. To establish it, he said, was "one main object" of his periodical, *The Friend* (1809); he emphasized it with unusual frequency thereafter; and four years before his death he spoke of it as the "Gradus ad Philosophiam." [44] Though the implications of his distinction changed a bit over a period of years, it may be generally described as an attempt on Coleridge's part to explain the means by which the mind conceives both the concrete particular and at the same time the ultimate universals which comprise the "apex" of nature. The "understanding" is "discursive" rather than immediate, and is directed to the world of material phenomena; "reason," on the other hand, is "the immediate and inward beholding of the spiritual as sense is of the material." The understanding classifies, reflects, and generalizes upon the content of empirical experience. Its exclusive concern is with

the quantities, qualities, and relations of particulars in time and space. The understanding, therefore, is the science of *phaenomena,* and of their subsumption under distinct kinds and sorts (*genera* and *species*). Its functions supply the rules and constitute the possibility of experience . . . The reason, on the other hand, is the science of the universal.[45]

The aim of this distinction is illustrated by comparing it with Kant's discrimination between *Verstand* and *Vernunft,* of which it has often been regarded as an echo. The Kantian faculty of understanding (*Verstand*) is directed to the impressions which sense receives from the phenomenal world; it projects upon them the categories inherent in its own subjective working, classifies and interprets them by means of these categories, and elaborates them into concepts and judgments. Reason (*Vernunft*), however, attains a higher synthesis: it arranges and interprets the judgments of understanding in the light of certain universally valid "ideas." But these ultimate "ideas," for Kant, are not objects of knowledge; they are merely necessary hypotheses or points of view rather than realities existing outside the mind. In Coleridge's distinction, however, the word "reason" is in marked contrast with the implications of Kant's term, *Vernunft:* man is not shut off from knowledge of ultimate reality. The universals have objective existence, and reason is the means by which they are known.[46]

At least one half of Coleridge's distinction, therefore, swings back from Kant's subjective idealism to the objective and rationalistic idealism of the Platonic tradition; and "reason," as he conceived it, has the full connotation of Plato's *nous*. Indeed, upon this point he tended to divide all philosophies, including Kant's and his own:

> Whether ideas are regulative only, according to Aristotle and Kant; or likewise constitutive, according to Plato, and Plotinus . . . is the highest problem of philosophy, and not part of its nomenclature.[47]

Hence the famous statement—which Irving Babbitt considered an "extravagant compliment" to humanity—that "every man is born an Aristotelian or a Platonist." On another occasion, Coleridge qualified himself, stating that Fichte had distorted Kant's position into a "crude egoismus," and that Kant really must have meant more by the "THING IN ITSELF, than his mere words express." [48] As the years passed, Coleridge placed him back again on the side of the "Aristotelians," but compromised a bit by permitting him to lean on the fence:

> There are two essentially different schools of philosophy, the Platonic and the Aristotelian. To the latter but with a somewhat nearer approach to the Platonic, Emmanuel Kant belonged; to the former . . . I profess myself adherent . . . He for whom Ideas are constitutive, will in effect be a Platonist—and in those, for whom they are regulative only, Platonism is but a hollow affectation.[49]

It is on this "highest problem of philosophy," then, that Coleridge, being "born a Platonist," ultimately parted from Kant. Indeed, his distinction between "reason" and "understanding" from the beginning bore less resemblance to that of Kant, despite its initial impetus and certain similarities in the conception of "understanding," than it did to the traditional division, which is as old as Plato and is found in medieval and especially Renaissance writers, between discursive and intuitive reason. Coleridge himself increasingly intimated this.[50]

Southey, writing of Coleridge's state of mind in his early thirties, had said that "Hartley was ousted by Berkeley, Berkeley

by Spinoza, and Spinoza by Plato; when last I saw him [1804]
Jacob Behmen had some chance of coming in." [51] The remark was
prophetic. For all philosophies, in the development of Coleridge's
thought, were ultimately ousted by Plato (substantiated and
ramified by elements from Plotinus and Boehme). Perhaps
"ousted" is too strong a term. It is rather a case in which "the
One remains, the many change and pass." For in Coleridge's life-
long attempt to formulate a system which reconciles the universal
and the particular, the One and the Many, his interest in various
philosophers and his use of them become themselves a characteristic symbol of his aim: Plato representing the "One," to which
he clung as a pivotal center, while the others, including Kant, are
the "many," and may be regarded as successive means by which
Coleridge sought to declare and ramify the Platonic position.
Coleridge would not have been displeased at the inference. He
would possibly have felt that the process fulfilled his requirements
for a good symbol by presenting unity emerging through and by
means of multeity.

VI

Coleridge's conception of the imagination can be approached
only as a necessary concluding hypothesis in his theory of the
mind; by means of it, he attempted to synthesize his psychological justification of the mediating function of art. If his psychology starts as a house divided against itself, the imagination
is the final crossbeam; as such, it cannot be considered apart from
what it is intended to unite. In order to maintain the ability of
the mind to realize both the universal and the particular, Coleridge had asserted the existence of two faculties, "reason" and
"understanding." But this very distinction into separate faculties
was, by itself, inconsistent with his own organic conception of
nature. For reality, as he had emphasized, is to be found in neither
the universal nor the particular as such, but in the process of fulfillment where each declares the other; and value and concreteness, the "ideal" and the "real," become one in mutual substantia-
tion. If the human mind is to grasp this reality, therefore, it could
be only through some capacity which brings together and coa-

lesces what man's respective faculties have to offer. To this capacity, which he postulated as necessary, Coleridge gave the word "imagination."

Such a process of awareness would duplicate the creative impulse of nature itself. It could in this sense be described as "a repetition in the finite mind of the eternal act of creation," and would serve as "the living Power and prime agent of all human Perception."[52] For if the concrete world has, in the human mind, a counterpart in the form of the senses and the understanding, and if the universal possesses its counterpart in man's reason, in a similar way the energizing creativity of nature, which unites the universal and the particular, is matched by the imaginative capacity, which welds the insights of reason with the impressions and conceptions drawn from the concrete. Thus, as reality itself is the bridge, the point of meeting and emergence, between concreteness and value, the imagination is a similar bridge between the various faculties of the mind: it is "the spirit of unity, that blends, and (as it were) *fuses,* each into each," revealing itself in the balance "of sameness, with difference; of the general, with the concrete; the idea, with the image; the individual, with the representative."[53] Accordingly, in what is perhaps his most specific single definition, Coleridge describes the imagination as

that reconciling and mediatory power, which incorporating the reason in images of the sense, and organizing (as it were) the flux of the senses by the permanent and self-circulating energies of the reason, gives birth to a system of symbols, harmonious in themselves, and consubstantial with the truths of which they are the conductors.[54]

In postulating this "completing power," as he called it on one occasion, Coleridge reflects an influence from Kant and especially Schelling which may be noted but should not be overstressed. In the Kantian psychology, the imagination is the means by which sense and the understanding can come together: it is the conveyor-belt, as it were, by which the data of the "sense manifold" is able to reach and fill the forms and categories of the understanding.[55] Coleridge, for his own purposes, could find little in this conception of the imagination beyond a general emphasis upon its unifying position among the faculties. Just as the other

functions of the mind are limited, for Kant, to the phenomenal
world, the imagination, as he regarded it, had no contact with
objective reality: it was far from being "a repetition in the finite
mind of the eternal act of creation." But in Schelling, Coleridge
could and did find an emphasis on the imagination as a means
of ultimate insight and as an analogue of "the eternal act of
creation." Indeed, and it is here that Coleridge also parted company with him, the imagination, for Schelling, is not merely an
analogue of the creative process of nature: it is identical with
it. The imagination and nature, the ego and the non-ego, are
aspects of the same substance, which is ultimately no more than
a neutral principle, a point of "indifference" where contraries
become "reconciled." Coleridge was, of course, right in finally
concluding that Schelling's philosophy was essentially a form of
monistic pantheism. The widespread emphasis on the organic
and vital unity of nature had led many contemporary writers,
especially in Germany, to a peculiarly romantic interpretation
and adoption of Spinoza's pantheism—an interpretation, needless
to say, which Spinoza himself would hardly have sanctioned.
Coleridge himself, under the influence of Spinoza, had for a short
while followed suit. But, as in so many other respects, his attempt
to reconcile organic vitalism with the Platonic tradition again
places him apart from his contemporaries. He increasingly fought
shy of pantheism and came to bracket it on the side of the enemy,
in the company of materialism and frank idealistic subjectivism,
with both of which he had also dallied. It was, in fact, the most
tempting result of any reasoning "in which the intellect refuses
to acknowledge a higher or deeper ground than it can itself
supply." [56] The diverging of his theory of the imagination from
that of Schelling thus follows the characteristic direction of
Coleridge's thought as a whole.

The imagination, then, is less a "faculty" than it is a *process*
of realization by which the products and insights of two distinct
aspects of mind become transmuted and funneled into a single
stream of awareness. On the one hand, it is turned to the images
and objects of the concrete world, which, since they are rendered
by the senses and the understanding, appear "fixed and dead."
But by sensing the dynamic potentiality inherent in these par-

ticulars and behind the static "masks" they seem to have, it volatil-
izes the impressions of them and the conceptions to which they
give rise; it charges and lifts them, as it were, to a state of fusible
intensity. At the same time it draws down the forms, the universals, which reason has descried, converting them into a similarly vital response. Indeed, it is only at this point of active fulfillment that universal conceptions become "ideas"; and it is in this
sense that Coleridge defines an "idea" as an "educt of the imagination actuated by the pure reason." [57] In the reconciling centrality of the imagination, therefore, both the form and the concrete
potentiality become *processed* into each other, as they are in
nature, the imagination thus serving as "the laboratory in which
thought elaborates essence into existence." [58] Art, in its highest
function, is the repetition and expression of such a process as it is
translated into the terms of a given medium: hence the statement
that Shakespeare evolved "the germ within by the imaginative
power according to an idea." [59] Similarly, in the response to art,
"taste," as one mode of the imagination, "connects the active with
the passive powers of our nature, the intellect with the senses,"
and involves the ability "to elevate the *images* of the latter, while
it realizes the *ideas* of the former." [60]

At least the broad outlines of Coleridge's conception of the
imagination may thus be ascertained if it is viewed, in his own
phrase, as a "completing power," which he assumed as a concluding synthesis to more basic principles and assumptions. Indeed, it is doubtful whether one can approach it profitably in
any other way. His specific remarks on the imagination itself are
surprisingly few. Least of all should one take as a starting point
the rather overstressed definition of the imagination that concludes chapter thirteen of the *Biographia Literaria*. As a matter
of fact, if it had not been so often cited in the belief that it was
in some way profound—Hazlitt would have cited it for a very
different reason—the passage could just as well be neglected.
Coleridge had contemplated for this place, he tells us, an analysis
of the subject which would not "amount to so little as an hundred
pages"; and the chapter bears the promising title, "On the Imagination, or esemplastic power." But, as Basil Willey says, "face to
face at last with his central problem, and alarmed by his own

chapter-heading," Coleridge slips "lizard-like from sight . . . leaving in our hands his tail only—a letter from himself to himself about his forthcoming masterpiece." [61] The letter is a blatant example of Coleridge's obliging habit of placing ammunition in the hands of his critics. It states that, "to *unprepared* minds," his "speculations on the esemplastic power would be utterly unintelligible"; and he therefore prints only the final statement:

> The primary IMAGINATION I hold to be the living Power and prime Agent of all human Perception, and as a repetition in the finite mind of the eternal act of creation in the infinite I AM. The secondary Imagination I consider as an echo of the former, co-existing with the conscious will, yet still as identical with the primary in the *kind* of its agency, and differing only in *degree*, and in the *mode* of its operation. It dissolves, diffuses, dissipates, in order to recreate; or where this process is rendered impossible, yet still at all events it struggles to idealize and to unify. It is essentially *vital*, even as all objects (*as objects*) are essentially fixed and dead.[62]

This rather artificial distinction between "primary" and "secondary" imagination is not among Coleridge's more lucid contributions to aesthetics. Shawcross, whose interpretation has been generally followed during the last generation, assumed that it was a paraphrase of Schelling's distinction between the unconscious imaginative molding of perception, common to all mankind, and the more conscious and restricted use of the imagination in the creation of art. This is perhaps supported by Coleridge's statements that the "primary" imagination is the "prime Agent of all human *Perception*," and that the "secondary" is "an *echo* of the former, co-existing with the conscious will." It is equally possible to interpret the distinction in a very different way. For one thing, the entire direction of Coleridge's criticism is opposed to the belief that he regarded the poetic imagination as merely an "echo" of a capacity common to all. It is rather the highest exertion of the imagination that the "finite mind" has to offer; and its scope, as we have seen, necessarily includes universals which lie beyond the restricted field of the "secondary" imagination. For the appointed task of the "secondary" imagination is to "idealize and unify" its objects; and it can hardly "unify" the universals. Indeed, its field is explicitly stated to consist of "objects" which "(*as objects*) are essentially fixed and dead."

On the other hand, the "primary" imagination, as it is defined in this passage, seems directed in every way to the universals: it is stated to be a repetition, in the human mind, of those same ultimate principles which, "in the infinite I AM," formatively control and evoke the creative unfolding of nature. It is in this sense that it functions as "the living Power and prime Agent of all human Perception." Nor need the word "Perception" prove a stumbling block. It is not consistently used by Coleridge; in its loose context, and in its capitalized form, it may be applied to the direct awareness of reason. In this case, the "primary" imagination may simply refer to that aspect of the creative capacity which draws down the rational insight of the universal into an individualized form of response, thus repeating "the eternal act of creation" whereby value becomes fulfilled in concrete particularity. Similarly, the "secondary" imagination would apply to the same creative and energizing power as it is directed to the world of material phenomena—of "objects," which, as they appear to sense and the understanding, are "essentially fixed and dead"; and these objects it "struggles to idealize and unify." In its twofold aspect, the imagination would thus draw upon nature in its totality and present an analogous synthesis.

The passage may therefore be regarded as simply a cryptic phrasing of what one may discover in other ways to be Coleridge's general theory of the imagination. But this interpretation of the distinction need not be labored. Whatever its meaning, Coleridge does not dwell upon it elsewhere. As it now stands, in its fragmentary form, it is neither clear nor particularly helpful; indeed, isolated concentration on it has perhaps distracted attention from other remarks which are potentially more fruitful. Coleridge himself, for that matter, probably regarded the distinction as a straw across the path; for, as Shawcross notes, he considered removing it.[63] Perhaps the main value of the passage is in introducing the clearest single statement of another and slightly more important distinction, in which the imagination as a whole is contrasted with "fancy":

FANCY, on the contrary, has no other counters to play with, but fixities and definites. The Fancy is indeed no other than a mode of

Memory emancipated from the order of time and space . . . But equally with the ordinary memory the Fancy must receive all its materials ready made from the law of association.[64]

Coleridge's famous distinction between "fancy" and "imagination" may be viewed simply as a means of emphasizing the unique function that he assigned to the imagination. He wished to divorce the term from any lingering traditional connotations of an "image-making" faculty which reproduces, separates, or joins together images derived from sensation. The mind possesses such a faculty, of course. There is an obvious form or mode of memory, that is, which can retain or repeat sensations without being limited by their original contexts, and which is to this extent "emancipated from the order of time and space"; it can transpose, divide, and combine impressions of "fixities and definites" according to the various laws of association. To this ability, Coleridge gave the name "fancy" in order to distinguish it from both the power of organic fusion and the total exertion of mind, including reason, which enter into the creation of art. Nor was he, in doing so, making any such radical breach with English critical terminology as has usually been thought.[65] William Duff in 1767, for example, had defined "fancy" in much the same way, and applied "imagination" to a "plastic" power which discloses "truths that were formerly unknown," and which "generates and produces a form of its own"; while Dugald Stewart in 1792 viewed the imagination as a creative synthesis of several facets of the mind, and assigned the word "fancy" to a restricted "habit of association" directed wholly to "the appearances with which our senses are conversant."

Coleridge's distinction has had an impressive list of detractors and admirers. It is possible that both have overstressed or misinterpreted its importance for him. It is not, as has occasionally been charged, an arbitrary division of the creative process into chemical "fusion" and mere "aggregation," nor, least of all, between two levels of imaginative "intensity." On the other hand, one can hardly agree with Mr. Willey that it is anything so important as the distinction between reason and understanding "transposed into another key."[66] For "fancy" does not even extend to the conceptions of the understanding, while the entire provinces

of both understanding and reason are exploited by the imagination as the creative unifier of the faculties. Coleridge's own remarks on the subject, and his fondness for recurring to it, seem
to illustrate what he himself admitted to be his peculiar "grievous
fault": that he used "five hundred more ideas, images, reasons,
etc., than there is any need of . . . My illustrations swallow up
my thesis . . . Bring me two things that seem the very same, and
then I am quick enough [not only] to show the difference, even
to hair-splitting, but to go on from circle to circle." [67] The distinction between "fancy" and "imagination" may be regarded as
one of these "illustrations" which one should not permit to "swallow up" his thesis: it is a means of stating what the imagination
is not.

VII

As an energizing capacity, immanent throughout all the faculties of the mind, the imagination not only unites reason with
sense and understanding. Its reach also extends to the most basic
emotional impulses of human nature, through appealing to which
it achieves a heightened awareness and a more formative realization. For it is in this substratum of response that human motiva-
tion is actualized and secured, and not in the mechanical jostling
of what the associationists call "ideas" or impressions. Indeed,
association itself

depends in much greater degree on the recurrence of resembling states
of feeling than on trains of ideas . . . a metaphysical solution, that
does not instantly *tell* you something in the heart is grievously to be
suspected as apocryphal. I almost think that ideas *never* recall ideas, as
far as they are ideas, any more than leaves in a forest create each
other's motion. The breeze it is that runs through them . . . the
state of feeling.[68]

The imagination is thus not only the synthesizing and creative
insight into truth; but, as a corollary to this function, it also
transmutes that insight into beauty, "the mediator between Truth
and Feeling." The corollary process ideally follows as the inevitable accompaniment of the former. Hence the remark that,
in Shakespeare's nondramatic poems, the "intellectual energy,"

which conceives the original conception, and the "creative power," which renders this conception into symbols *ad hominem,* "wrestle as in a war embrace. Each in its excess of strength seems to threaten the existence of the other. At length in the DRAMA they were reconciled, and fought each with its shield before the breast of the other." [69]

In such a process, therefore, the transmutation of the conception into the "mediating" form of beauty is not accompanied by loss or intrinsic change. The original insight, being the unique achievement of the imagination itself, remains present, with formative and ready effect, in the continuing imaginative process which, as a natural and automatic supplement, translates its conception into terms or symbols persuasive to human feelings. The symbol or resultant product thus evolves with inevitable and organic derivation, remaining "consubstantial" with the original conception. This is the significance of the statement that, in organizing "the flux of the senses by the permanent and self-circling energies of the reason," the imagination

gives birth to a system of symbols, harmonious in themselves and consubstantial with the truths of which they are the conductors. These are the *wheels* which Ezekiel beheld, when the hand of the Lord was upon him . . . *Whithersoever the Spirit was to go,* the wheels *went, and thither was their spirit to go:—for the spirit of the living creature was in the* wheels *also.*[70]

It is this standpoint and not romantic subjectivism, then, which underlies the occasionally misinterpreted statement that the artist "must out of his own mind create forms according to the severe laws of the intellect, in order to generate in himself that coordination of freedom and law . . . which assimilates him to nature, and enables him to understand her." [71] By evolving derivatively from an objective conception, the symbol, as its "conductor," thus retains an appeal to the total mind. Coleridge's distinction between "allegory" and "symbol" is primarily a means of emphasizing just this point. The appeal of allegory is restricted to sense and to a given mode of the "understanding": it is merely a "translation of abstract notions into a picture language, which is itself nothing but an abstraction from objects of the senses." The symbol, however, as the "wheel" conveying truth to feeling, renders what is meaningful, on the one hand, to sense and understanding, portraying what is specifically individual in the particular and also what, to the understanding, is "general" in that specific individuality; at the same time, it reveals what, to the reason, is truly "universal" in the generality which the understanding forms or descries. This seems to be the point of the rather involved statement that the symbol should be

characterized by a translucence of the special in the individual, or of the general in the special, or of the universal in the general; above all by the translucence of the eternal through and in the temporal.[72]

By insisting on the objective appeal of the symbol, therefore, Coleridge does not fundamentally depart from the spirit of Aristotle's belief that poetry should offer an imitation of an original rather than symbolic representations. For Aristotle's attitude seems to be explained by the view that symbols rely upon what we now call "convention";[73] and conventions, of course, change. But symbolism, to be sure, does not imply complete relativism, either local or personal, unless one adopts subjectivistic premises which would equally restrict any other theory of communication. Eighteenth-century associationism, which virtually created the theoretical interest in symbols, had nonetheless emphasized their value in proportion as they in some way rise above the "local and temporary" and appeal to the universal principles of human nature. Coleridge's standpoint involves this much and more: he is not speaking of symbols which rest upon conventions alone, or, least of all, private association and subjective emotion, but of "imitation" in the broadest sense of the word. He is speaking, that is, of objective conception transmitted into terms of feeling—the "union and reconciliation of that which is nature with that which is exclusively human."[74]

Coleridge's emphasis on feeling as a necessary accompaniment to genuine insight is thus characteristic of moderate English romanticism in general. It is not a primitivistic trust in the beauty of sheer, unschooled instinct or impulse: "On such meagre diet as feelings, evaporated embryos in their progress to *birth,* no moral being ever becomes healthy."[75] Almost as much as his later critic, Irving Babbitt, he distrusted what he called "the temperamental pro-virtues." [76] Nor does art, any more than morality, consist of a drawing out and expression of subjective feelings in their "original" and primitive state. It is characteristic, for example, that "those only who feel no originality . . . are anxious to be thought original"; nor is it a matter for congratulation that "modern poetry is characterized by the poet's *anxiety* to be always striking." [77] Indeed, like that of Hazlitt, Coleridge's standpoint is by no means unclassical. Feeling, by itself, is blind and helpless. It may offer the distinctively human content to complete realization; but prior to the imaginative inducement of that realization, the significance of feeling is only potential, like clay waiting to be molded. What Coleridge says of the mind in general is especially applicable to feeling: "Events and images . . . are like light, and air, and moisture," without which it "would else rot and perish," and it must "assimilate and digest the food which it thus receives from without." [78]

Far from being an organ of insight, therefore, feeling is merely a process of response, neutral in aim, which is peculiar and inevitable to our physical being: it is passive in being dependent for direction on what is outside it, and active in responding to what it has received. In this sense, "Our notions resemble the index and hand of the dial; our feelings are the hidden springs which impel the machine, with this difference, that notions and feelings react on each other reciprocally." [79] Art, as the rendering of truth *ad hominem*, exploits and develops this interaction. In one of its functions, therefore, it incites an expectant tension; but it does so only for the purpose of increased receptivity. The use of meter in poetry would be one example. Meter "tends to increase the vivacity and susceptibility both of the general feelings and of the attention," but only as a means. Its effects, however pervasive, should not themselves be "objects of distinct consciousness," but should act "as a medicated atmosphere, or as wine during animated conversation":

Where, therefore, correspondent food and appropriate matter are not provided for the attention and feelings thus roused, there must needs be a disappointment felt; like that of leaping in the dark from the last step of a stair-case, when we had prepared our muscles for a leap of three or four.[80]

Similarly, in the creation of art, "sensibility" is a necessary accompaniment of genius:

> But it is not less an essential mark of true genius, that its sensibility is excited by any other cause more powerfully than by its own personal interests; for this plain reason, that the man of genius lives most in the ideal world . . . and because his feelings have been habitually associated with thoughts and images, to the number, clearness, and vivacity of which the sensation of *self* is always in inverse proportion.[81]

Consequently, "A poet's heart and intellect should be *combined*, intimately combined and unified with the great appearances of nature." [82] Sensibility finds its fulfillment, that is, in sympathy. A widespread and pervasive emphasis on the importance of sympathetic identification is one of the most marked characteristics of English romanticism; [83] Coleridge's statements on the subject may be viewed as one extension of this characteristic, though he takes it for granted that sympathy is not an inherent guide but a product or result formed and developed through the imagination. Still, the potential aspiration of feeling, dependent as it is on what it "receives from without," is toward sympathy, as though the "body" itself were "but a striving to become mind." [84] It is for this reason that what is originally "the same feeling" becomes modified and altered in the conception of different forms. For example: "The Heaven lifts up my soul, the sight of the ocean seems to widen it." The difference of feeling, in each case, is that which

> we should feel in actual travelling horizontally or in direct ascent . . . For what are our feelings of this kind but a motion imagined, [together] with the feelings that would accompany that motion, [but] less distinguished, more blended, more rapid, more confused, and, thereby, coadunated? Just as white is the emblem of one in being the confusion of all.[85]

Feeling, then, achieves value and becomes the handmaiden to realization to the degree that it is developed outward, through the imagination, into sympathy, and is modified by what it absorbs. It is through this means that, "in energetic minds, truth soon changes by domestication into power." [86] Such a developed sensibility is one of the distinctive qualities of Shakespeare, who, far from being a mere "automaton" of original genius, "studied patiently, meditated deeply, understood minutely, till knowledge, become habitual and intuitive, *wedded itself to his habitual feelings.*" [87] Accordingly, he possessed the "chief requisite" of the poet: the ability to "project his mind out of his own particular being," and to arouse in others "that sublime faculty by which a great mind becomes that on which it meditates." [88] This capacity should be distinguished from and is indeed directly opposite to what Coleridge called "ventriloquism," in which the poet "distributes his own insipidity" by projecting himself upon a phenomenon rather than into it.[89] Sympathetic identification achieves its highest pertinence, of course, in the dramatic portrayal of character. In this sense, particularly, Shakespeare is without rival. Like Hazlitt, Coleridge was fond of comparing him to Proteus, in classic mythology, who could transform himself into diverse shapes, of whatever sort: [90] "to *think* ourselves into the thoughts and feelings" of others, whatever their circumstances, "*hic labor, hoc opus;* and who has achieved it? Perhaps only Shakespeare." [91] Milton, by contrast, "attracts all forms and things to himself, into the unity of his own IDEAL," [92] while Wordsworth and Goethe, in another way, are "spectators *ab extra*,—feeling for, but never with, their characters." [93]

Such poets, however, appear external to their subject only when compared with the unique achievement of Shakespeare; and sympathetic absorption, as a fundamental requisite for poetry, has more general implications than the specific needs of the drama. Whether his aim is dramatic or not, the imagination of any poet must have as its complement "the threefold form of sympathy with the interesting in morals, the impressive in form, and the harmonious in sound." [94] For poetry secures its peculiarly human appeal through the active harmonizing fusion of the imagination working in conjunction with the natural imitative and sympathetic capacity of feeling, and transmuting objective conception into emotional participation. It is by combining "a more than ordinary sympathy with the objects, on a more than common sensibility, with a more than ordinary activity of . . . the imagination," that poetry succeeds in its aim of producing "a more vivid reflection of the truths of nature and of the human heart, united with a constant activity modifying and correcting these truths." [95]

The imagination, then, duplicates nature, where universal and particular develop themselves, by presenting a conception in which the insights of reason have been united with the impressions and judgments of sense and understanding. But it also reiterates this process by reconciling its conception "with that which is exclusively human." In this latter function, feeling may itself be viewed as potentiality to be fulfilled through form by the imaginative process. Art implies and rests upon both functions of the imagination. From the former, it secures its objective fidelity to truth. Through the latter, it transmutes truth into actualized response. "The *heart* should have *fed* upon the *truth*," Coleridge wrote to Southey, "as insects on a leaf, till it be tinged with the colour, and show its food in every . . . minutest fibre." [96] Art is thus not only the "mediatress between, and reconciler of, nature and man," in the sense that it makes truth realizable to him. But in its capacity of "reconciler," it is also formative; it "assimilates him to Nature," and directs the process of human fulfillment whereby "to know is to resemble." By ramifying and supporting the implications of this standpoint as he did, Coleridge occupies a unique position not only in English but in European romantic criticism as a whole: he represents, that is, a suggestive and in some respects challenging attempt to unite the traditional rationalistic values of classicism with the organic vitalism to which the romantic movement aspired, and to substantiate and rest this union upon an ultimate metaphysical basis. One may grant that it was only an attempt, and both the fragmentary results and the aim itself may be variously viewed. But it must not be forgotten that, from his hope of achieving such a synthesis, Coleridge's critical writings possess their only unity.

Notes

1. *Science and the Modern World* (New York, 1925), p. 138.
2. "On Poesy or Art," appended to *Biographia Literaria,* ed. J. Shawcross (Oxford, 1907), II, 253.
3. Cf., for example, *Coleridge's Shakespearean Criticism,* ed. T. M. Raysor (Cambridge, Mass., 1930), I, 196–198, 222, 241, 243, and *Coleridge's Miscellaneous Criticism,* ed. Raysor (Cambridge, Mass., 1936), pp. 7, 11, 12, 190, and 412.
4. *Lectures on Dramatic Art and Literature,* tr. John Black (London, 1815), II, 98–99 (lecture 12).

5. *Shakespearean Criticism,* I, 198.

6. "On Poesy or Art," p. 259, and *Biographia Literaria,* I, 167.

7. For general discussion of this theory, see Gordon McKenzie, "Organic Unity in Coleridge," *University of California Publications in English,* vol. VII (1939), no. 1.

8. *Miscellaneous Criticism,* pp. 56–57.

9. *Shakespearean Criticism,* II, 131.

10. "On Poesy or Art," p. 262.

11. *Ibid.,* p. 253.

12. See the comprehensive and effective disposal of this charge in Clarence D. Thorpe, "Coleridge as Aesthetician and Critic," *Journal of the History of Ideas,* V (1944), 387–414.

13. *Shakespearean Criticism,* I, 45.

14. *Biographia Literaria,* I, 100–102, 246–248. Coleridge's departure from contemporary German thought is best exemplified in his distinction between "reason" and "understanding." See below, sect. IV.

15. This assumption is further substantiated by René Wellek's careful proof of how little Coleridge has in common with contemporary German thought. See *Immanuel Kant in England* (London, 1931), chap. iii.

16. This point of view, I believe, is supported by Mr. Thorpe in his statement (p. 390, n. 12, in his article cited above) that Coleridge's "idealism . . . was a blend of idealisms, and it was, moreover, modified by a strain of English empirical sensationalism." Cf. chap. xii of *Biographia Literaria.*

17. *Biographia Literaria,* II, 33; cf. *Miscellaneous Criticism,* p. 300.

18. *Statesman's Manual,* App. B, *Works,* ed. H. N. Coleridge (London, 1839), I, 268n.

19. *The Friend* (sect. 2, essay 11), *Works,* IV, 211.

20. "On Poesy or Art," p. 262, and *Miscellaneous Criticism,* p. 44. Cf. "Treatise on Logic" (Brit. Mus. MS. Eg. 2825–2826), II, 466.

21. *Biographia Literaria,* I, 178. Cf. John Heraud, *Oration on the Death of S. T. Coleridge* (London, 1834): "Of Kant's system, he remarked to me, that it was a scientific fiction . . . [Coleridge] brought philosophy back again to the recognition of the Oldest Realism . . . that all the phenomena we perceive, together with the matter in which they inhere, substantially exist . . . But not only did Coleridge restore Reality to the material World, but, in an especial manner, was it his delight, to find the Real in the Ideal" (pp. 9–11).

22. See above, sect. IV.

23. *Biographia Literaria,* I, 101.

24. "On Poesy or Art," p. 259 (my italics); cf. above, sect. V.

25. *Biographia Literaria,* II, 187.

26. *Miscellaneous Criticism,* p. 44. I cannot understand Mr. Raysor's belief (note to p. 44) that this passage illustrates the "characteristic and all-important theme of Coleridge's aesthetics—the priority of subjective to objective elements in art." It does not seem to me that such a dichotomy is relevant to the passage; granting it, however, I should say that the opposite interpretation is indicated both in this passage and in Coleridge's aesthetics as a whole.

27. *Ibid.,* pp. 42–43 (my italics).

28. *Statesman's Manual,* pp. 260–61.

29. "On the Principles of Genial Criticism," appended to *Biographia Literaria*, II, 239; cf. "On Poesy or Art," p. 257.

30. "On the Principles of Genial Criticism," pp. 223–227, 236–37. Coleridge, of course, somewhat exaggerates the relativism of the associationist position (cf. my study, *From Classic to Romantic* [Cambridge: Harvard University Press, 1946], pp. 97–128).

31. MS. *Semina Rerum* (cited in J. H. Muirhead, *Coleridge as Philosopher* [London, 1930], p. 195).

32. "On the Principles of Genial Criticism," pp. 238–39. "This unity in multeity," which is "the principle of beauty . . . is equally the source of pleasure in variety, and in fact a higher term including both" ("On Poesy or Art," p. 262).

33. "On the Principles of Genial Criticism," pp. 235, 237.

34. Somewhat stimulated by the vogue of Hogarth's winding "line of beauty," the associationist critics frequently discussed the aesthetic symbolism of simple geometrical figures and of straight and curved lines (see Bate, *From Classic to Romantic*, pp. 106–7, 146–47, 151–52). The intention was usually to urge "uniformity in variety" as the fundamental basis of beauty, or, at times, to suggest something approaching to empathy. Though the illustration is the same, Coleridge's meaning, of course, has further implications.

35. Egyptian art would be an instance of the imposition of form, *ab extra*, without the corresponding "freedom" ("Fragment of an Essay on Beauty," appended to *Biographia Literaria*, II, 251). Cf. "On Poesy or Art," p. 257, and similar statements in *Anima Poetae*, ed. E. H. Coleridge (Oxford, 1895), pp. 82–83, 86.

36. "On the Principles of Genial Criticism," p. 238.

37. "On Poesy or Art," pp. 262–63; "virtue consists not simply in the absence of vices, but in the overcoming of them. So it is in beauty. The sight of what is subordinated and conquered . . . should be exhibited by the artist either inclusively in his figure, or . . . beside it to act by way of supplement and contrast."

38. *Shakespearean Criticism*, I, 212–13; cf. II, 93.

39. "On Poesy or Art," p. 256; cf. *Shakespearean Criticism*, I, 128, and *Anima Poetae*, p. 76.

40. For relevant distinctions between "imitation" and "copy," see especially *Shakespearean Criticism*, I, 128, 200, 204, and II, 80–81, 117–18n.

41. *Statesman's Manual*, pp. 230–31.

42. *Shakespearean Criticism*, I, 224. Cf. "On Poesy or Art," p. 262: "Remember that there is a difference between form as proceeding, and shape as superinduced;—the latter is either the death or the imprisonment of the thing;—the former is its self-witnessing and self-effected sphere of agency."

43. "On the Principles of Genial Criticism," p. 243. Whether or not his ingenious etymology is legitimate (see Shawcross' note, p. 314), the intention is plain.

44. *Biographia Literaria*, I, 110, and *Table Talk*, May 30, 1830. Coleridge's main discussions of the distinction are to be found in *The Friend*, vol. I, essay 5; *Statesman's Manual*, App. B; and *passim* throughout "Aphorisms on Spiritual Religion," in *Aids to Reflection* (1825), especially pp. 207–228.

45. *Statesman's Manual*, p. 259.

46. Coleridge thus differs also from his noted contemporary, Friedrich

Jacobi, to whom, at first glance, he appears similar. Jacobi, in a manner which permanently shook the Kantian metaphysic, attempted to prove the objective existence of the ideas; yet he assumes that they transcend reason and can exist only as objects of faith. One may agree with Mr. Thorpe ("Coleridge as Aesthetician and Critic," p. 408) that there has hardly been "any critic since the world began who has had more to say for the value of intellect and reason than Coleridge."

47. *Statesman's Manual*, App. E, p. 302.

48. *Biographia Literaria*, I, 100–01.

49. Letter to Gooden, January 14, 1820, *Unpublished Letters*, ed. E. L. Griggs (London, 1932), pp. 264–266.

50. He even felt (*Biographia Literaria*, I, 109) that his use of the actual terms was "confirmed by the authority of our genuine divines and philosophers before the revolution"; and he cited *Paradise Lost*, V, 485–488: ". . . both life and sense, Fancy and *understanding*, whence the Soul *Reason* receives, and reason is her being, Discursive, or Intuitive." But Coleridge, of course, had no genuine and clear-cut precedent in his terminology, despite the commonness of the idea behind it; and he elsewhere admitted as much, attributing its absence "in Hooker, and the great divines of his age" to "an occasional carelessness in the use of the terms" (*Note on English Divines*, ed. Derwent Coleridge [Oxford, 1853], I, 18). Mr. Claud Howard (*Coleridge's Idealism* [Boston, 1924]) is certainly right in stressing the background of Renaissance Platonism in Coleridge; but his discussion is vitiated by the extraordinary belief that not only Coleridge's "idealism" as a whole but "practically all the essential principles" of Kant's metaphysics as well were "anticipated" by the Cambridge Platonists.

51. Letter to William Taylor, July 11, 1808, *Memoir of the Life and Writing of William Taylor*, ed. J. W. Robberds (London, 1843), II, 216. We may remember that Schelling himself was at the same time moving mildly away from subjective idealism, passing successively from the influence of Fichte through that of Spinoza to Jakob Boehme and other Neoplatonists. The parallel indicates nothing more, however, than a vague similarity of temperament; what influence Schelling had on Coleridge came largely from his earlier writings.

52. *Biographia Literaria*, I, 202.

53. *Biographia Literaria*, II, 12. The position of the imagination is thus far more comprehensive and intricate than the function attributed to it, in Coleridge's thought, by Shawcross (I, lxxiv): "It is not the power of intellectual intuition . . . but the faculty of the true apprehension of things sensible as the data and material of philosophical reflection."

54. *Statesman's Manual*, pp. 228–29.

55. For Coleridge, the imagination, as the general reconciler for the faculties, naturally includes this as one of its functions. Thus, in a rather Kantian passage (*Statesman's Manual*, App. B, p. 266), he states that the forms of the understanding, considered apart from the content of sense, are analogous to "clearness without depth" and comprise "a knowledge of superficies without substance . . . The completing power which unites clearness with depth, the plenitude of the sense with the comprehensibility of the understanding, is the imagination, impregnated with which the understanding itself becomes intuitive, and a living power."

56. *The Friend* (sect. 2, essay 11), *Works*, IV, 214.

57. *Statesman's Manual,* Appendix E, p. 302. See above, sect. II. Cf. the definition of "ideas" as truths, "the knowledge and acknowledgment of which require the whole man" (*Coleridge on Logic and Learning,* ed. A. D. Snyder [New Haven, 1929], p. 100).

58. *Anima Poetae,* p. 158.

59. *Miscellaneous Criticism,* p. 43.

60. "On the Principles of Genial Criticism," p. 227.

61. *Coleridge on Imagination and Fancy* (British Academy, Wharton Lecture on English Poetry, 1946 [London: Geoffrey Cumberlege, 1947]), p. 3. One is reminded of Hazlitt's statement, in his review of the *Biographia Literaria,* that Coleridge, "in a state of suspended animation, 'twixt dreaming and awake," devotes his pages to *"promising* us an account of the Intellectual System of the Universe, and putting us off with a reference to a *promised* dissertation on the Logos, introductory to an *intended* commentary on the entire Gospel of St. John" (*Works,* ed. A. R. Waller and Arnold Glover [London, 1902–1906], X, 138).

62. *Biographia Literaria,* I, 202.

63. *Ibid.,* I, 272. Sara Coleridge stated (*Biographia Literaria* [1847], I, 297) that, in his copy of the book, he "stroked out" the sentence distinguishing the "primary" imagination, but that she decided to leave it in, "especially as it has been quoted." She would have grounds for self-congratulation at the number of times it has been quoted since.

64. *Ibid.,* I, 202. Presumably the omitted discussion of "the esemplastic power" was also to include observations on "fancy." Cf. the prefatory remarks in chap. iv of the *Biographia Literaria,* which Hazlitt, in his review, called a "barren ridge of clouds" from which Coleridge "deludes us with a view of the Promised Land that divides the regions of Fancy from those of Imagination." For other statements of the distinction, see especially *Shakespearean Criticism,* II, 124; *Miscellaneous Criticism,* pp. 387–88, 435–36; and *Anima Poetae,* p. 199.

65. There had been a growing tendency in eighteenth-century criticism and philosophy to differentiate the terms; Coleridge simply followed suit, and, in at least four instances, very closely. (See J. M. Bullitt and W. J. Bate, "Distinctions between Fancy and Imagination in Eighteenth-Century Criticism," *Modern Language Notes,* LX [1945], 8–15).

66. *Coleridge on Imagination and Fancy,* p. 10.

67. *Anima Poetae,* pp. 87–88.

68. To Southey, August 7, 1803, *Letters,* ed. E. H. Coleridge (London, 1895), I, 427–28. Coleridge is, of course, using the word "ideas" in the associationist sense.

69. *Biographia Literaria,* II, 11. If one wishes to adopt, in a general way, Shawcross' belief that the distinction between "primary" and "secondary" imagination is a distinction between a faculty common to the "Perception of all and the poetic use of the imagination, one can then develop and clarify it only along these lines. The "primary" imagination, in this case, would achieve a synthesized insight by uniting all the faculties, including reason (which is still a very different thing from the "ordinary perception" that Shawcross' followers have considered to be the field of the "primary" imagination); while the "secondary" imagination would connote the supplementary creative process by which the insight is transformed into symbols or art. Yet some of the objections cited before would still apply.

70. *Statesman's Manual,* p. 229.

71. "On Poesy or Art, p. 248.

72. *Statesman's Manual*, p. 230.

73. Cf. Samuel H. Butcher, *Aristotle's Theory of Poetry and Fine Art* (London, 1895), pp. 118–19.

74. "On Poesy or Art," p. 254.

75. *Anima Poetae*, p. 143.

76. Cf. the statement (*Aids to Reflection*, p. 53): Where virtue is already present, sensibility emerges as its "Attire," and "On certain occasions it may almost be said to *become* Virtue. But Sensibility and all the amiable Qualities may likewise become . . . the pandars of Vice and the instruments of Seduction."

77. *Anima Poetae*, pp. 135, 139.

78. *Preliminary Treatise on Method*, ed. A. D. Snyder (London, 1934), p. 7.

79. *Shakespearean Criticism*, II, 12.

80. *Biographia Literaria*, II, 51. "A whole Essay might be written on the Danger of thinking without Images" (*Unpublished Letters*, I, 163). Cf.: "by excitement of the associative power passion itself imitates order and the order resulting produces a pleasurable *passion* (whence metre)"; poetry thus impregnates objects with an interest "by means of the passions, and yet tempers the passions by the calming power which all distinct images exert on the human soul" (*Miscellaneous Criticism*, pp. 205–06).

81. *Biographia Literaria*, I, 30.

82. *Letters*, I, 403–04.

83. Cf. W. J. Bate, "The Sympathetic Imagination in Eighteenth-Century English Criticism," *Journal of English Literary History*, XII (1945), 144–164.

84. "On Poesy or Art," p. 258.

85. *Anima Poetae*, p. 86. Cf. the extension of this standpoint in the characteristic remark: "What is the body, but the fixture of the mind—the steretotype impression? . . . Is terror in my soul?—my heart beats against my side. Is grief?—*tears* pour in my eyes. In her homely way, the body tries to interpret all the movements of the soul" (*Lectures and Notes on Shakespeare*, ed. T. Ashe [London, 1883], p. 114).

86. *Biographia Literaria*, I, 62. Cf. "I regard that alone as genuine *Knowledge*, which sooner or later will re-appear as *Power*" ("Outline of . . . the formation of the Mind and Character," *Literary, Philosophical and Miscellaneous Remains* [Brit. Mus., MS. Eg. 2800–2801], II, 198).

87. *Biographia Literaria*, II, 19 (my italics).

88. *Lectures and Notes on Shakespeare*, p. 218; see also p. 68, and *Miscellaneous Criticism*, p. 433.

89. *Shakespearean Criticism*, I, 82, and II, 162, 145; *Biographia Literaria*, II, 109; and *Miscellaneous Criticism*, pp. 54, 90, 411.

90. *Lectures and Notes on Shakespeare*, pp. 56, 379; *Biographia Literaria*, II, 20; *Anima Poetae*, p. 74.

91. *Letters*, I, 372.

92. *Biographia Literaria*, II, 20; *Lectures and Notes*, p. 532.

93. *Miscellaneous Criticism*, p. 415; cf. *Biographia Literaria*, II, 122–23.

94. *Shakespearean Criticism*, I, 230.

95. *Shakespearean Criticism*, I, 164.

96. *Letters*, I, 91.

NEWMAN'S ESSAY ON POETRY
AN EXPOSITION AND COMMENT

Geoffrey Tillotson

I

The intellectual range and powers of Newman as a young don are nowhere concentrated more splendidly than in his essay on poetry.[1] "Poetry with Reference to Aristotle's Poetics" was furnished in response to a request of Blanco White,[2] who had been asked to edit a new magazine, and who looked to his friend Newman for a secular contribution to it: "Give me an article on any subject you like," he pleaded, "Divinity excepted for the present, for of that I expect a flood."[3] Blanco White had known the young Newman for the few years during which his "reputation as a thinker pure and simple—though confined to a comparatively small circle—was [perhaps] at its highest, [the days] when the bent of his mind was towards liberalism,"[4] and he knew him well enough to know "how difficult it is to persuade a mind like [his] to write without preparation."[5] Fearing a refusal because of short notice, he offered anxious advice: "I should strongly advise you to venture upon the strength of your *household stuff*— on the reading and reflection of many years. Write without much concern";[6] advice not unmixed with flattery: "You are sure to write well . . . imagine yourself in our Common-Room [at Oriel], myself in the corner, Dornford passing the wine, &c., and tell us your mind on paper."[7]

Newman responded with enthusiasm: he promised the essay requested and another besides. The first, on poetry, is that now under discussion; but the one on music never reached manuscript, or if manuscript, not print, the reason being, presumably, that the *London Review* ceased publication with its second number.[8] (So that Newman on music has to be pieced together from scattered sources, of which there happen to be two minor ones in the course of the essay on poetry.)

Newman took about two months to write his 11,000 words: Blanco White's letter asking for the essay bears the date September 11, 1828, and his letter rejoicing over its receipt the date November 8. But though Newman could on occasion produce literature at as fast a rate as anybody—witness the race won against the clock in the composition of the *Apologia* and of some of the *Tracts for the Times*—it is unlikely that he found much leisure during those two autumn months. His essay is unusually packed with matter, and packed with matter which is drawn from a wide and seemingly fresh reading in Greek drama and English poems and novels. And in 1828 Newman was unused to writing for print: the only things he had published so far (apart from the undergraduate poem, "St. Bartholomew's Eve," of which he was part author only, and the few pages he had contributed to the *Logic* of his "gentle and encouraging instructor," [9] Whately) were three articles in the *Encyclopaedia Metropolitana* on Cicero, Apollonius Tyanaeus, and the miracles of Scripture. Moreover, the public that would read a new London magazine was a more numerous and worldly public than that which read anonymous minor poetry and books on logic, or encyclopedia articles, or even than that which he was already drawing round his pulpit in St. Mary's: the public proposed was the whole "liberal" reading public of England. And, again, though he took Blanco White's tip and drew on household stuff, that household stuff was difficult in two ways: insofar as his theme was Aristotle, Greek drama, and poetry in general, it was a theme for a scholar-critic and a philosopher; and insofar as it was certain contemporary British novels and popular contemporary British poems, it was one in which every "liberal" person held expert opinions.

In its original form, the essay started off with a review of a contemporary work on Greek drama ("Take up any work of the day," [10] Blanco White had cajoled, advised, commanded), and, after criticizing Aristotle's remarks on the same subject, proceeded to its main business, a discussion of poetry in general in the threefold form of stating Aristotle's theory, explaining it, and modifying it,[11] with the help of "illustrations." [12]

The essay appeared in the first number of the *London Review* in January 1829.[13] When Newman reprinted it among the *Essays* in 1871, he cut out the review section,[14] replaced it by one sentence as introduction, and, according to his Note, had the rest set up from his original manuscript, Blanco White having altered "several sentences" by virtue of what his victim generously conceded as "an editor's just prerogative." [15]

II

Newman's essay dives into its subject, and its subject, to begin with, is not so much Aristotle's *Poetics* as Newman's personal preference for a great number of other Greek tragedies over the tragedy which Aristotle "is constantly thinking of . . . as he writes his Poetic," [16] the *Oedipus Tyrannus* of Sophocles, an author whom the young Newman had described as "dry, stiff, formal, affected, cold, prolix, dignified." [17] What it comes to is that Newman cannot accept the high valuation which Aristotle accords the element of plot in drama. Aristotle's scheme he summarizes as follows:

> Aristotle considers the excellence of a tragedy to depend upon its plot—and, since a tragedy, as such, is obviously the exhibition of an action, no one can deny his statement to be abstractedly true. Accordingly, he directs his principal attention to the economy of the fable; determines its range of subjects, delineates its proportions, traces its progress from a complication of incidents to their just and satisfactory settlement, investigates the means of making a train of events striking or affecting, and shows how the exhibition of character may be made subservient to the purpose of the action.

Aristotle derives great satisfaction from the elaborate, dovetailed plot of the *Oedipus Tyrannus,* but Newman sees the plot of that play as something too obviously produced by an ingenious application of "workmanship." The word "workmanship" is crucial: Newman dislikes any evidence of skill.[18] And, leaving Aristotle to his preference, he turns to the many plays of Aeschylus, Sophocles, and Euripides that are "beautiful," "exquisite," endowed with "grace and interest," and all this when at the same time they are plainly defective by the standards which center in the *Tyrannus:* one play is found to provide little "interest," one to be "stationary," one "irregular," one "inartificial" (that is, constructed without art), one to exist merely as a pretext for "the introduction of matter more important than itself," and "sometimes [a plot] either wants or outlives the catastrophe." Newman takes pleasure in listing these defects because he believes all such defects to be nugatory. "Gods, heroes, kings, and dames, enter and retire: they may have a good reason for appearing,—they may have a very poor one; whatever it is, still we have no right to ask for it. The question is impertinent." What he wants from a tragedy is not so much its tragic course as its moments of poetic greatness. And he departs from Aristotle because he sees that "the inferior poem may, on his principle, be the better tragedy." His point is clinched, to his own liking, by reference to the "sudden inspiration . . . of the blind Oedipus, in the second play bearing his name, by which he is enabled, 'without a guide,' to lead the way to his place of death," an incident which in Newman's judgment "produces more poetical effect than all the skilful intricacy of the plot of the Tyrannus. The latter excites an interest which scarcely lasts beyond the first reading—the former 'decies repetita placebit.' " [19]

Newman unfortunately simplifies Aristotle's conception of plot, crediting a critic he otherwise finds almost entirely sound and subtle with the belief that plot is an external contrivance. Newman's simplification is almost that of Miss Dorothy Sayers, who has amusingly adopted Aristotle as the patron saint of detective novelists. And though Newman missed seeing his low estimate of the *Tyrannus* reduced to the absurd by the thousand masterpieces of twentieth-century detective fiction, he had a ready means of restraining himself from error in his own experience of the play of Sophocles, an experience which, on his own showing, was complete enough to have saved him: these are his words introducing a comparison of the play with the *Agamemnon* of Aeschylus and the *Bacchae* of Euripides:

> The action of the Oedipus Tyrannus is frequently instanced by [Aristotle] as a specimen of judgment and skill in the selection and combination of the incidents; and in this point of view it is truly a masterly composition. The clearness, precision, certainty, and vigour with which the line of the action moves on to its termination is admirable. The character of Oedipus, too, is finely drawn, and identified with the development of the action.

And later we get this testimonial, a surprising one in view of the rest of the essay: "The sweet composure, the melodious fulness, the majesty and grace of Sophocles." Now if these are qualities of the *Tyrannus*, what becomes of the remark that the play "excites an interest which scarcely lasts beyond the first reading"?

Is it true that a play which is well constructed and nothing more can only "interest" us once? Even if the *Tyrannus* offered nothing worth our attention but its plot (which, as plot, Newman admits to be very good), we should still be able to read and see it a second time, if only because we do not trouble to remember the particular moves by which the parts of the action slide into place, and are quite happy to sit back and watch them happen afresh: after an interval, people can even reread a detective novel. But Newman would not have allowed any play that showed "sweet composure . . . melodious fulness . . . majesty and grace" to herd with the detective novels. And yet the greatness of the *Tyrannus*, and its characteristic greatness as a play, brings it nearer to the detective novel than to the lyric poem: for the first reason that it is a great play is because it is a detective novel and something more. It is a question of the end for which the materials are used. No one goes to a thriller to read of the nature of man and the universe. Novels in that form exist, it is true, in a relationship with those august matters, but the relationship is a perfunctory one. These base themselves on the law that requires a sin against society to be punished by society; but all their effort goes in constructing something with that law as foundation accepted and then forgotten. They exist to build a superstructure and to stock it with architectural surprises.

The *Tyrannus*, however, works to a different end. It gives us the free run of the elaborate building in order to make us remember the foundation. Oedipus has killed his father and married his mother in ignorance of their identity, and the play consists of the series of jolts by which his guilt is uncovered as piece by piece his ignorance is removed. The word "guilt," if not "ignorance," serves to show the distance separating the *Tyrannus* from the detective novel with its plot-for-plot's-sake. The plot of the *Tyrannus* is a vehicle, the vehicle of a criticism of the nature of man and the universe. The plot is the criticism. And not only

that: the criticism consists in the very elaboration of the plot.
The play exists to protest against a "scheme of things," and the
protest would have been strong even if the plot had been simpler,
even if knowledge of the horrid facts had come on Oedipus like
a bolt from the blue. But the strong protest made by a plot that
was simple would merely have repeated the strong protest made
by the prime facts of the tale themselves, the initial killing and
marriage, facts which, already known to the audience, had already pointed the audience to the conclusion that fate was cruel.
Sophocles writes his play because he can take his audience
farther than they have gone of themselves. And his means of
taking them farther is the construction of the plot, his making
Oedipus learn the facts of his history one by one.

It is this process that embodies the dramatist's addition to the
criticism already made by the audience: a fate already known
as cruel is seen as more cruel still because it craftily arranges that
Oedipus' enlightenment shall be a crescendo of torture.

> I play the torturer, by small and small
> To lengthen out the worst that must be spoken.[20]

Moreover, this course of torture is the more painful for Oedipus
and for the audience because it is his own goodness as a man
and a king that has put him in its way—he has decreed that the
offense which has brought the plague on his city shall be punished, not knowing that he himself is its perpetrator. The elaboration of the plot is therefore an elaboration of the suffering of a
man who is doing his duty. Newman allows that "the character
of Oedipus . . . is finely drawn, and identified with the development of the action," but he does not see how this identification
excites more emotion and thought in the audience because the
action develops ingeniously.

III

The critic who discusses Newman's conception of the role of
the plot goes to great lengths to put him right, only to find his
criticism virtually acknowledged in certain judgments scattered
over the essay. What can we make of the following sentences but

a confession that elements which Newman professes to admire most can defeat the ends of elements he confesses, on this occasion, to admire even more, elements that are in the keeping of the plot? Caught off his guard, he well sees the dilemma to which the lauded "carelessness" of Euripides may lead:

Moral excellence in some characters may become even a fault. The Clytemnestra of Euripides is so interesting, that the divine vengeance, which is the main subject of the drama, seems almost unjust.

And why, if Newman believes that "poetry" is more necessary than plot, should he look to plot, if not to save poetry, at least to improve it:

The original conception of a weak or guilty mind may have its intrinsic beauty; and much more so, when it is connected with a tale which finally adjusts whatever is reprehensible in the personages themselves. Richard [III] and Iago are subservient to the plot.

And finally, why this on Byron?

[The] bearing of character and plot on each other is not often found in Byron's poems. The Corsair is intended for a remarkable personage. We pass by the inconsistencies of his character, considered by itself. The grand fault is, that whether it be natural or not, we are obliged to accept the author's word for the fidelity of his portrait. We are told, not shown, what the hero was. There is nothing in the plot which results from his peculiar formation of mind. An every-day bravo might equally well have satisfied the requirements of the action.

And so on to some remarkable sentences about *Childe Harold,* which I shall quote in another connection.

If Newman is talking sense in these passages, his objections to the *Tyrannus* are nonsense. And nonsense, whether or not he might have invoked in defense the distinction between plots simple and plots complex. The plots of *Richard III* and *The Corsair* are less complicated than those of *Othello* and the *Tyrannus,* but the degree of complication, while it may make the identifying of plot and character a harder task for the dramatist, does not affect the status accorded that identity. In any play or poem concerning human beings, that status is primary. And though the capacity to identify plot and character may not be a poetical capacity, it is a crucial one for any poet setting up to write narrative, whether in play or poem. If, writing in those forms, he fails to achieve that identification, any poetry he supplies in his capacity as lyric poet is a mockery, flowers without roots. For it is the plot and the characters who embody the plot, creating it and being created by it, that convey the very meaning of the work. How can we attend to what goes on, if we think the pains and pleasures of the action fall on dummies, even if on dummies endowed with poetry—with a poetry which, being beside the point, can never be more than pretty? Many poets, in every age from the Elizabethan to our own, have neglected this consideration, and in consequence a thousand poetic dramas are, if they are anything at all, poems to feed the anthologist rather than plays to be played.

IV

But even if Newman had gained a surer grasp of the *Poetics* in the way Butcher [21] did, it is still unlikely that he would have accepted its doctrines about "action": Newman's simplification merely makes him fly further away from a critic he was bound to detach himself from in any event. When all is allowed for, there exists the estranging incompatibility of temperament implied in Newman's remark that "we may be allowed to suspect [Aristotle] of entertaining too cold and formal conceptions of the nature of poetical composition, as if its beauties were less subtle and delicate than they really are." Moreover, different as were their temperaments, Newman and Aristotle also differed in their assumptions as psychologists dealing with the mind of poets. Neither saw that mind as abnormal: Aristotle treated it as he treated the mind of any man; and Newman found so much poetry abroad in the world that not all its possessors could be madmen. Newman believed that Aristotle expected work from a poet's mind which no poet's mind can do. The difference appears at its widest when it is a question of composition, of composition in general, not only of the composition of anything with a plot. For Aristotle the datum is that the poetry exists written down (or uttered by actors): the poet for him is by definition a maker, and his poem a thing made. But for Newman in the nineteenth century there is "an ambiguity in the [very] word 'poetry,' which is taken to signify both the gift itself, and the written composition which is the result of it." For Newman poetry exists apart from pen and paper, and, moreover, only exists at its most characteristic and pure when so existing, since "the poet's habit of mind lead[s] to contemplation rather than to communication with others."

Newman almost begrudges the putting of the poem on paper, as if "the spirit of poetry" suffers when an attempt is made to fit it with a body. He sees composition as the mere consequence of the poet's decision to communicate his poetry, and he sees that decision almost as dependent on accident. A poem is an "accessory," "no essential part of poetry, though [obviously] indispensable to its exhibition," "the artificial part," "dexterity," "accomplishment"; [22] and the "talent for composition" is compared to those of dancing, of elocution, and even of typesetting.

> Poetical composition requires that command of language which is the mere effect of practice. The poet is a compositor; words are his types; he must have them within reach, and in unlimited abundance.

Newman considers that Aristotle's insistence on a "laboured and complicated plot" deflects the poet's mind away from his proper function when composing, "tend[ing] to withdraw [it] from the spontaneous exhibition of pathos or imagination to a minute diligence in the formation of a plot"; and whereas Aristotle sees a play as "an exhibition of ingenious workmanship," Newman sees it, if it is poetical, as "a free and unfettered effusion of genius." He leaves us in no doubt on the point, even going so far as to see plot itself as a by-product, as happening of itself, as something "breathed" out of the mind, "effused" along with the characters and their voices of joy and sorrow: Aristotle's sort of counsel, it is held, "leads to negative, more than to positive excellence; [plot, 'the artificial part'] should rather be the natural and, so to say, unintentional result of the poet's feeling and imagination, than be separated from them as the direct object of his care."

If the poet does write a poem, then it is bound to be obscure for one reason or another, and to one degree or another. The degree will depend on the several counts, for example, on the kind of poem he is writing (he will be "less [obscure] in epic, or narrative and dramatic representation,—more so in odes and choruses"), and on the "depth of his feelings" and their "acuteness," both these poetical qualities causing him to shrink "from any formal accuracy in [their] expression."

Newman, who himself strove so hard to write simply, always disliked what, in the sermon on "The Danger of Accomplishments," he called "unreal words"; [23] and in the essay on poetry we find him deprecating a technical care lavished in excess of what the initial inspiration warrants. He scorns

the power of throwing off harmonious verses, which, while they have a respectable portion of meaning, yet are especially intended to charm the ear. In popular poems, common ideas are unfolded with copiousness, and set off in polished verse—and this is called poetry.

Newman's view may be put in something like this way. The poet is inspired like an Old Testament prophet and may write the inspired poem down. He is inspired with his poem complete, and, as far as the poem is concerned, inspired once for all. There is no opportunity, therefore, for further inspiration while composition is proceeding. (Newman would have countered Dryden's remark that the act of rhyming often helped him to a thought with "So much less poetical the thought.") The poet ought to write his poem down (if write he must) simply; he should not require the given inspiration to sponsor more than its own direct expression; this held for small things, as it clearly held for great:

When a deed or incident is striking in itself, a judicious writer is led to describe it in the most simple and colourless terms, his own being unnecessary; for instance, if the greatness of the action itself excites the imagination, or the depth of the suffering interests the feelings. In the usual phrase, the circumstances are left to "speak for themselves."

Newman considers Pope an offender under this head: he sees him as elaborating his couplets too independently of the poetry that originally prompted their existence. They are beautiful as couplets, but beautiful only as Chippendale's furniture is beautiful: Chippendale made his furniture by reference to a pattern laid up in his head, which was how Pope made his couplets. If

you must have elaborate art, then let your poems be like those
of Virgil and Milton:

> Though Virgil is celebrated as a master of composition, yet his
> style is so identified with his conceptions, as their outward develop-
> ment, as to preclude the possibility of our viewing the one apart from
> the other. In Milton, again, the harmony of the verse is but the echo
> of the inward music which the thoughts of the poet breathe.

v

Newman's theory, then, may be called Protestant, or better,
Evangelical. Like Protestants, the poet is justified rather by faith
than by works; like Evangelicals, rather by "spiritual-minded-
ness" [24] than by faith. Newman is unconsciously applying to
poetry his religious discoveries up to date. In 1828 he was still
much of an Evangelical. Until 1825 he had "[taken] for granted,
if not intelligibly held, the opinions called Evangical," [25] and nine
years later he could still "go on . . . a great way with [them]." [26]
When he left them behind in the *Lectures on Justification* of
1838, he did so mainly because, like the poets he thought most
poetical, they were people exclusively concerned with their "spir-
itual-mindedness," their "experiences," their "sensation." [27] Much
later, in the *Idea of a University*, he was to describe their religion in words all of which he might, and some of which he did,
apply to poetry; describing it as consisting "in the affections,
in the imagination, in inward persuasions and consolations, in
pleasurable sensations, sudden changes, and sublime fancies." [28]
When Newman threw off his Evangelical views, he only threw
off what he came to see as wrong in them. After all, spiritual-
mindedness was not wrong in itself, but only being stuck fast
in it: the better Christian was spiritual-minded and something
more. Newman went so far as to exclaim that it was to an
Evangelical, to Thomas Scott, that "(humanly speaking) I almost
owe my soul," [29] and no development in doctrine could call on
him to discard that. But Newman as literary critic is too much
for keeping the poet where the Evangelicals kept the Christian.
In 1832 he had shown Luther as a reformer who "found Chris-
tians in bondage to their works and observances," and had gone

on to show the Evangelicals as having landed Protestants in another bondage, that to "their feelings." [30] His many attacks on the Evangelical system are an attempt to rescue Evangelicals from a bondage he was willing to keep poets in.

VI

In the same way that Newman's evaluation of the *Oedipus Tyrannus* looks different after the advent of the detective story, his view that plot grows (so to speak) independently of the poet looks different after Max Beerbohm's "Savonarola Brown":

> "I've hit on an original idea," [Brown] said, "and that's enough to start with. I gave up my notion of inventing a plot in advance. I thought it would be a mistake. I don't want puppets on wires. I want Savonarola to work out his destiny in his own way." [31]

The production of literature is surely more of a dialectic than Newman allows, and of a compromise which takes account of elements Newman will not frankly acknowledge. We have only to think of the many different requirements which Shakespeare, for instance, had to satisfy, when, as most often, he was writing a play, requirements imposed from several quarters including the groundlings and his own need to create something solidly and intricately balanced out of chaotic materials. Newman's views apply best to certain kinds of short lyric poems, the kind which Wordsworth called "effusions," and of which his voluminous poetical works contain only ten instances; [32] and after all, if an extempore lyric comes right first time, it comes right because the hand, like Giotto's hand making the circle, is a practiced one. The upshot is that Newman's eloquent statement of a romantic and unworldly position is useful mainly as a corrective against an explanation that makes the writing of poetry too much a mechanical thing. But one would have thought his own experience of composition would have led Newman to a more balanced view: we know how thoroughly his prose drafts were disciplined into sense and grace, and may suspect that the drafts of his poems had a similar evolution—a similar evolution up to a point: they seldom achieve the grace of the prose works.

That more balanced view had to wait till those excellent pages of his *Lectures . . . on University Subjects* which are devoted to the great writer who subjects his work to severe correction.[33] But even here Newman assigns the need for such correcting to initial clumsiness and inadequacy: the battle of pen strokes is seen as nothing more than improving attempts to say what from the start had been seen. He does not make enough allowance for the poet whose "wheels," to use Coleridge's words, "take fire" while driving. When he praises Virgil and Milton, he forgets that he never saw their eyes glittering with inspiration, but can only infer their glitter from the printed page, and therefore cannot be sure at what point the inspiration, which it is agreed the verses embody, became available. On the evidence of Milton's manuscripts, some of it happened very charily and had only finished happening with the last of the many corrections: it seems that there were some things which Milton won his way through to seeing for the first time in the process of winning his way through to saying what he may have thought he had seen clearly from the start.

VII

Something of the nature of poetry as Newman sees it may be gathered from his word *breathe,* a word used several times in the course of the essay. When he used it in the sentence on Milton (quoted above), he was adapting Gray's line which attributed to Dryden

Thoughts that breathe, and words that burn.[34]

At an even earlier date, however, than "The Progress of Poesy," *breathe* had begun its long history of metaphor. It seems to have been the young Shakespeare who inaugurated that history in England, speaking of "breathing war" (an expression taken over by Gray).[35] In "Hero and Leander," Marlowe compared "every street" to "a firmament," and said that it "glistered with breathing stars," that is, with women. Milton followed, calling nymphs "the breathing roses of the wood." [36] (The rosy nymphs are breathing because they are alive, and their breath is like the smell of roses because it is sweet.) When Pope borrowed Milton's phrase, he stripped it of half its metaphor:

> Here western winds on breathing roses blow,[37]

but restored the other half in his epistle "To Mr. Jervas":

> Yet still her [the Muse's] charms in breathing paint engage,[38]

which, since Jervas was a painter of portraits, was an adaptation of the "spirantia . . . aera" of Virgil,[39] and of the "breathing statues" which, until a late edition, stood in his own "Temple of Fame." [40] Joseph Warton took over this use,[41] but he, too, drew on the other half of Milton's metaphor in his "breathing Mead," and in his "ambrosial Hair, /Breathing rich Odours" (cf. *Paradise Lost*, II, 244–45: "his altar breathes /Ambrosial odours").[42] This last phrase of Warton's becomes the "breathing tresses" which Collins bestowed on evening, a gift that was bold, but not too bold: if roses and meadows can breathe, then Collins can count on "breathing tresses" to mean hair emitting a scent. That was in 1747, and from then onward the word figured so often in poetical writing that it aroused the protest of that excellent small critic, Sir Henry Taylor, the author of *Philip van Artevelde*. Taylor saw Byron as the chief offender, and we know how much Newman read Byron's poems, and, with reservations, how much he admired them. In a passage from his essay on Wordsworth, which cogently criticized the romantic poetry of the time, Taylor wrote:

> "The mind, the music *breathing* from her face," [43] is suggestive of as much false metaphor as could well be concentrated in a single line; but it conveyed some vague impressions of beauty and fervour, and was associated with the feelings with which Lord Byron's writings were usually read; and "to breathe" became thenceforth, amongst the followers of Lord Byron, a verb poetical which meant anything but respiration. Indeed the abuse seems to have spread to a circle which might be supposed to be remote from Lord Byron's influence; for a book was published two or three years ago with the title of "*Holy Breathings*." [44]

Newman, however, had an unusual right to make use of this fashionable verb since, like Keble, he placed most value on those

manifestations of life which are gentlest, most intimate and commonplace: the Abbé Brémond has drawn attention to the quiet
stroke "blushing for joy" in *Callista*.[45] We can allow a critic to
use *breathe* when his essay on poetry exists to effect a dematerialization of poetry—breath is an appropriate symbol: like breath,
poetry exists whether or not it voices words. Newman found
poetry in the pages of, say, Shakespeare, and equally in the wordless minds of children ("Alas! what are we doing all through life,
both as a necessity and as a duty, but unlearning the world's
poetry, and attaining to its prose!"),[46] and in the often wordless
minds of young people, especially in the season of spring (see
chapter iii of *Loss and Gain*), and in the ritual of the church.[47]
When Newman visited the Keble household, he thought "Keble's
verses are written (as it were) on all their faces,"[48] the only difference being that John had the capacity and took the trouble to
seize the beautiful poetry that fell to his share, and extended its
manifestation to paper. The world has its poets, as it has its saints,
without knowing it has them. But it is only in the estimation of
men that the mute Miltons are inglorious Miltons: in the estimation of God, who looketh on the heart, the mute Miltons are as
glorious as the Milton who, instead of being mute, wrote *Paradise
Lost*. For Newman the thing is to be a poet: the rest is a question of showing or not showing, a question which is ultimately
beside the point for one who, like Newman, "rest[ed] in the
thought of two and two only supreme and luminously self-evident
beings, myself and my Creator";[49] for one who, like Newman,
saw the Christian as "the greater part of his time by himself, and
when he is in solitude, that is his real state";[50] and for one who,
like Newman, saw the poet as a person whose "habits of mind
lead to contemplation rather than to communication with
others."

VIII

So far I have drawn mainly on the opening and closing sections of Newman's essay, and in these sections one of the virtues
of his argument is, despite lapses, its clarity. It does not take
account of enough material; it says nothing about Aristotle's doc-

trine of catharsis;[51] nor has it any sense of the historical—after
all, certain allowances are due imperatively to literature surviving out of the past, especially the distant past. Newman tells us
in the *Apologia* that Whately was very "dissatisfied" with the
essay.[52] But the clarity of the essay so far is delightful. When
we proceed to investigate the remaining middle sections, however, we meet a fullness which is embarrassing because obscure.
It could scarcely be other than obscure being so full: how much
surer is the argument of the lecture on literature,[53] its sureness
being the result of the same maturity which prompted Newman
to confine himself to a more compassable subject. Part of the
trouble with the essay on poetry is that it attempts to cover too
much ground—in his dedication of the collected *Essays* to William
Froude, Newman confessed that "portions of their contents
[were] not always in agreement with each other." In the middle
sections of the present essay, he has no line of argument, but
instead a great tidied-up heap of odds and ends of thought. Some
of the odds and ends are tidied up with a brilliant show of
pattern-making: the spiritedness of the whole procedure is delightful to watch; in these middle sections Newman is indeed the
talker in the Oriel common room, "Dornford passing the wine."
And so it is one of those essays that can only receive adequate
treatment by critics willing to pay it the disproportionate honor
of a thorough analysis and a thorough reconstruction: and critics
equal to this task prefer to construct their systems *ab initio*.
I propose to make only a few comments on these teasing middle
sections.

The concern in these middle sections is to state, to illustrate
and to modify Aristotle's "general doctrine of the nature of
poetry," a doctrine which Newman holds to be "most true and
philosophical." Here are the most ambitious of the paragraphs:

Poetry, according to Aristotle, is a representation of the ideal.
Biography and history represent individual characters and actual
facts; poetry, on the contrary, generalizing from the phenomenon
of nature and life, supplies us with pictures drawn, not after an
existing pattern, but after a creation of the mind. Fidelity is the
primary merit of biography and history; the essence of poetry is
fiction. "Poesis nihil aliud est," says Bacon, "quam historiae imitatio
ad placitum." It delineates that perfection which the imagination

suggests, and to which as a limit the present system of Divine Providence actually tends. Moreover, by confining the attention to one series of events and scene of action, it bounds and finishes off the confused luxuriance of real nature; while, by a skilful adjustment of circumstances, it brings into sight the connexion of cause and effect, completes the dependence of the parts one on another, and harmonizes the proportions of the whole. It is then but the type and model of history or biography, if we may be allowed the comparison, bearing some resemblance to the abstract mathematical formulae of physics, before they are modified by the contingencies of atmosphere and friction. Hence, while it recreates the imagination by the superhuman loveliness of its views, it provides a solace for the mind broken by the disappointments and sufferings of actual life; and becomes, moreover, the utterance of the inward emotions of a right moral feeling, seeking a purity and a truth which this world will not give.

It follows that the poetical mind is one full of the eternal forms of beauty and perfection; these are its material of thought, its instrument and medium of observation,—these colour each object to which it directs its view. It is called imaginative or creative, from the originality and independence of its modes of thinking, compared with the commonplace and matter-of-fact conceptions of ordinary minds, which are fettered down to the particular and individual. At the same time it feels a natural sympathy with everything great and splendid in the physical and moral world; and selecting such from the mass of common phenomena, incorporates them, as it were, into the substance of its own creations. From living thus in a world of its own, it speaks the language of dignity, emotion, and refinement.

In all this Newman is certainly taking full advantage of his program of modified Aristotle. For him the poet was a man gifted to discover, and gifted to write down for the good of others, an aspect of the actual otherwise overlooked, the general in the particular. That was all the base in the *Poetics* for Newman's dazzling superstructure, though he was also indebted to another view drawn from Aristotle indirectly, the view that "in general art partly completes what Nature is unable to elaborate, and partly imitates her." [54] What else exists in Newman's paragraphs belongs to Plato and to what intervening critics have dreamed over their Aristotle and Plato.

There is only the narrowest basis in Aristotle for what Newman managed to work into his essay about revealed religion. Blanco White had expressly forbidden theology, but could not object when theology was softened into religion, and religion, however strongly emphasized, emphasized in the midst of the secular. Newman writes:

> According to the above theory, Revealed Religion should be especially poetical [55]—and it is so in fact. While its disclosures have an originality in them to engage the intellect, they have a beauty to satisfy the moral nature. It presents us with those ideal forms of excellence in which a poetical mind delights, and with which all grace and harmony are associated. It brings us into a new world—a world of overpowering interest, of the sublimest views, and the tenderest and purest feelings. The peculiar graces of mind of the New Testament writers is as striking as the actual effect produced upon the hearts of those who have imbibed their spirit. At present we are not concerned with the practical, but the poetical nature of revealed truth. With Christians, a poetical view of things is a duty,—we are bid to colour all things with hues of faith,[56] to see a Divine meaning in every event, and a superhuman tendency. Even our friends around are invested with unearthly brightness—no longer imperfect men, but beings taken into Divine favour, stamped with His seal, and in training for future happiness. It may be added, that the virtues peculiarly Christian are especially poetical—meekness, gentleness, compassion, contentment, modesty, not to mention the devotional virtues; whereas the ruder and more ordinary feelings are the instruments of rhetoric more justly than of poetry—anger, indignation, emulation, martial spirit, and love of independence.

In this passage the link with Aristotle is discernible, but only just. According to Aristotle, the poet sees something in the world which men who are not poets cannot see: the Christian, says Newman, sees a brightness in his friends invisible to non-Christians. But he calls the brightness "unearthly," whereas for Aristotle the general which poets see in the particular is a part of the actual. And for Newman not only is the brightness "unearthly," but it is partly bestowed by the Christian as well as discerned: "we are bid to colour all things with hues of faith." Newman is modifying Aristotle to some purpose.

Newman ascribes to revealed religion the quality of being "poetical." The poet accordingly is free to write about it. But if revealed religion is a suitable subject for a poet, then the poet surrenders some of the qualities which, following Aristotle, Newman had fixed on him. How can revealed religion be a proper object of poetry if the poet's business is to "generalize," to imitate for the sake of pleasure (*ad placitum*), to bound and finish off, to improve? The best comment on this absurdity is Dr. Johnson's: in his "Life of Waller" he takes occasion to argue his dislike of pious poetry, his argument providing this weighty logic:

> Poetry pleases by exhibiting an idea more grateful to the mind than things themselves afford . . . but Religion must be shown as it is; suppression and addition equally corrupt it, and such as it is, it is known already.

Or we can confute early Newman by later Newman:

> [In theology] the simple question is, what is revealed? . . . If we are able to enlarge our views and multiply our propositions, it must be merely by the comparison and adjustment of the original truths; if we would solve new questions, it must be by consulting old answers. The notion of doctrinal knowledge absolutely novel, and of simple addition from without, is intolerable to Catholic ears . . . Revelation is all in all in doctrine; the Apostles its sole depository, the inferential method its sole instrument, and ecclesiastical authority its sole sanction. The Divine Voice has spoken once for all, and the only question is about its meaning.[57]

IX

Newman's essay culminates in his paragraph on revealed religion, but despite this he is still "liberal" enough in 1828 to ascribe not only virtue but religion and holiness to authors of poetry which he thinks good poetry, and even to speak of religion without insisting on the distinction between religion and Christianity. He gladly joins all those Renaissance critics who see the good poet as a good man. He is indeed quite unembarrassed by the ease with which the formula applies itself. Here are his sentences on Burns:

> Burns was a man of inconsistent life; still, it is known, of much really sound principle at bottom. Thus his acknowledged poetical talent is in no wise inconsistent with the truth of our doctrine, which will refer the beauty which exists in his compositions to the remains of a virtuous and diviner nature within him.

And then more generally:

> Nay, further than this, our theory holds good, even though it be shown that a depraved man may write a poem. As motives short of

the purest lead to actions intrinsically good, so frames of mind short
of virtuous will produce a partial and limited poetry. But even where
this is instanced, the poetry of a vicious mind will be inconsistent and
debased; that is, so far only poetry as the traces and shadows of holy
truth still remain upon it.   On the other hand, a right moral feeling
places the mind in the very centre of that circle from which all the rays
have their origin and range; whereas minds otherwise placed command
but a portion of the whole circuit of poetry.   Allowing for human in-
firmity and the varieties of opinion, Milton, Spenser, Cowper, Wordsworth, and Southey, may be considered, as far as their writings go, to
approximate to this moral centre. The following are added as further
illustrations of our meaning. Walter Scott's centre is chivalrous honour;
Shakspeare exhibits the characteristics of an unlearned and undisci-
plined piety; Homer the religion of nature and conscience, at times
debased by polytheism. All these poets are religious. The occasional
irreligion of Virgil's poetry is painful to the admirers of his general
taste and delicacy. Dryden's Alexander's Feast is a magnificent composition, and has high poetical beauties; but to a refined judgment
there is something intrinsically unpoetical in the end to which it is
devoted, the praises of revel and sensuality. It corresponds to a process
of clever reasoning erected on an untrue foundation—the one is a
fallacy, the other is out of taste. Lord Byron's Manfred is in parts
intensely poetical; yet the delicate mind naturally shrinks from the
spirit which here and there reveals itself, and the basis on which the
drama is built. From a perusal of it we should infer, according to the
above theory, that there was right and fine feeling in the poet's mind,
but that the central and consistent character was wanting. From the
history of his life we know this to be the fact.[58] The connexion between
want of the religious principle and want of poetical feeling, is seen
in the instances of Hume and Gibbon, who had radically unpoetical
minds. Rousseau, it may be supposed, is an exception to our doctrine.
Lucretius, too, had great poetical genius; but his work evinces that
his miserable philosophy was rather the result of a bewildered judgment than a corrupt heart.

In later years Newman was to apply to poets, and to authors
generally, a more crucial religious test. As, for instance, in the
sermon "Nature and Grace," preached soon after he became a
Catholic:

Many are the tales and poems written now-a-days, expressing high
and beautiful sentiments; I dare say some of you, my brethren, have
fallen in with them, and perhaps you have thought to yourselves, that
he must be a man of deep religious feeling and high religious profes-
sion who could write so well.   Is it so in fact, my brethren? it is not
so; why? because after all it is *but* poetry, not religion.[59]

And so to a definition of poetry drawn up by Newman the theologian:

[Poetry] is human nature exerting the powers of imagination and reason, which it has, till it seems also to have powers which it has not. There are, you know, in the animal world various creatures, which are able to imitate the voice of man; nature in like manner is often a mockery of grace.

And in conclusion:

The truth is, the natural man sees this or that principle to be good or true from the light of conscience; and then, since he has the power of reasoning, he knows that, if this be true, many other things are true likewise; and then having the power of imagination, he pictures to himself those other things as true, though he does not really understand them. And then he brings to his aid what he has read and gained from others who *have* had grace, and thus he completes his sketch; and then he throws his feelings and his heart into it, and meditates on it, and kindles in himself a sort of enthusiasm, and thus he is able to write beautifully and touchingly about what to others indeed may be a reality, but to him is nothing more than a fiction.

The most telling statements of this later position are those made in *The Idea of a University* [60] and in the lecture on English Catholic literature. Here is the latter of them. Newman has been speaking of the indecency of French and Italian literature, and concludes:

These are but specimens of the general character of secular literature, whatever be the people to whom it belongs. One literature may be better than another, but bad will be the best, when weighed in the balance of truth and morality. It cannot be otherwise; human nature is in all ages and in all countries the same; and its literature, therefore, will ever and everywhere be one and the same also. Man's work will savour of man; in his elements and powers excellent and admirable, but prone to disorder and excess, to error and to sin. Such too will be his literature; it will have the beauty and the fierceness, the sweetness and the rankness, of the natural man, and, with all its richness and greatness, will necessarily offend the senses of those who, in the Apostle's words, are really "exercised to discern between good and evil."

It is a pity that Newman did not stop at this point. Instead he proceeds with:

"It is said of the holy Sturme," says an Oxford writer, "that, in passing a horde of unconverted Germans, as they were bathing and gambolling in the stream, he was so overpowered by the intolerable scent which arose from them that he nearly fainted away." National literature is, in a parallel way, the untutored movements of the reason, the plungings and the snortings, the sportings and the buffoonings, the clumsy play and the aimless toil, of the noble, lawless savage of God's intellectual creation.[61]

On Newman's own showing, these savages are no fit symbol for the natural man. They are merely disgusting, only more faintly so than Swift's Yahoos, and they have no right to the epithet "noble" which Newman perfunctorily attaches to them. They have nothing but fierceness and rankness, whereas the natural man and his product, literature, have beauty as well as fierceness, sweetness as well as rankness.

Another modification of Aristotle is worth noting. In the passage on revealed religion, Newman uses the words "especially poetical." Those words leave Aristotle for philosophers such as Plotinus who see poetry as choosing its material, or as preferring to choose it, from what is already beautiful. There are a score of straws, and bigger things, in the essay to show which way the gentle wind is blowing: such a phrase as "the loveliness of its views" could only be used of poetry by one for whom the poet's mind was a pristine garden of Eden. Further, Newman speaks of the imagination, "refined and delicate" in its "enjoyment," as preferring to "have the elements of beauty abstracted out of the confused multitude of ordinary actions and habits," and as neglecting not only their "improbabilities [and] wanderings," but their "coarsenesses." And in the discussion on originality, Newman marks off the originality of the poet from originality in general by discriminating the field of their operation. He had already said,

The poetical mind . . . is called imaginative or creative, from the originality and independence of its modes of thinking, compared with the commonplace and matter-of-fact conceptions of ordinary minds, which are fettered down to the particular and individual,

and he returns to discriminate the term originality, beginning with a question, "How does originality differ from the poetical talent?" and proceeding,

Without affecting the accuracy of a definition, we may call [poetical talent] the originality of right moral feeling.

Originality may perhaps be defined [as] the power of abstracting for one's self, and is in thought what strength of mind is in action. Our opinions are commonly derived from education and society. Common minds transmit as they receive, good and bad, true and false; minds of original talent feel a continual propensity to investigate subjects, and strike out views for themselves;—so that even old and established truths do not escape modification and accidental change when subjected to this process of mental digestion. Even the style of original writers is stamped with the peculiarities of their minds. When originality is found apart from good sense, which more or less is frequently the case, it shows itself in paradox and rashness of sentiment, and eccentricity of outward conduct. Poetry, on the other hand, cannot be separated from its good sense, or taste, as it is called; which is one of its elements. It is originality energizing in the world of beauty; the originality of grace, purity, refinement, and good feeling.

Poetry, that is, concerns itself not with the world in general (the world in general is the concern of originality in general), but with that part of the world which is capable of matching the "eternal forms of beauty and perfection" that exist in the poetic mind, and which is therefore capable of responding to grace, purity, refinement, and good feeling.

Newman here shows too much favoritism. He divides matter into poetical and unpoetical, and the poetical itself into poetical and "especially poetical." And his favoritism spreads more widely still: the unpoetical is made to include whatever does not square with Newman's scheme of morality. "Sometimes," he writes, "sometimes, and not infrequently in Shakespeare, the introduction of unpoetical matter may be necessary for the sake of relief, or as a vivid expression of recondite conceptions, and, as it were, to make friends with the reader's imagination." Matter that Newman considers unpoetical in this way is matter offending his sense of poetic justice: "Romeo and Juliet are too good for the termination to which the plot leads; so are Ophelia and the Bride of Lammermoor. In these cases there is something inconsistent with correct beauty, and therefore unpoetical." We can assign this delicate favoritism to Newman's native fastidiousness of mind, and also to his habit, at this time, of dividing sheep from goats. For all his liberalism, the essay on poetry is part of that movement which later became the Tractarian. It was noticeable that when he spoke of the Christian's vision of an "unearthly brightness," he made it invest not men in general, as for Wordsworth brightness invested children in general, but only "our friends." Newman was not yet equal to the humane sentence, which I shall quote later, about the people of Birmingham. Already the Tractarians are taking on each other's feelings: Hurrell Froude refused to Wordsworth the title of true poet on the score of his unchristian egotism.[62] For Aristotle there were none of these subdivisions of poetry: matter, of whatever sort, was fit for poetry if seen by a poet.

It is already clear that no one but Newman could have written this essay on poetry. Not even Keble, whose exquisite critical essays and lectures lack Newman's range of ancient and modern example (if the London Review failed because its writers were too "bookish and academical," not enough "attractive" and versed in "current literature," [63] Newman was not among those responsible). And if we weigh some of the subsidiary argument, Newman stands out as himself more clearly still.

Take, to begin with, his reference to Thomson as an instance of a modern writer who puts into verse material which, because it has not been seen with poetical originality, belongs rightfully to prose:

Empedocles wrote his physics in verse, and Oppian his history of animals. Neither were poets—the one was an historian of nature, the other a sort of biographer of brutes. Yet a poet may make natural history or philosophy the material of his composition. But under his hands they are no longer a bare collection of facts or principles, but are painted with a meaning, beauty, and harmonious order not their own. Thomson has sometimes been commended for the novelty and minuteness of his remarks upon nature. This is not the praise of a poet; whose office rather is to represent known phenomena in a new connection or medium. In L'Allegro and Il Penseroso the poetical magician invests the commonest scenes of a country life with the hues, first of a cheerful, then of a pensive imagination.

Perhaps the reference to Thomson ought not to be taken too seriously: Newman may be concerned only with what was sometimes said about The Seasons, not with the justice of what was said. But, even so, he does not remove the implication that Thomson is justly represented by the critics he is attacking. Whereas, of course, part of Thomson's praise as a poet—as the author, for example, of lines like

> The yellow wall-flower, stained with iron brown
> . . . auriculas, enriched
> With shining meal o'er all their velvet leaves—[64]

is precisely that he did paint facts with a meaning, beauty, and harmonious order not their own, and that he did represent known phenomena in a new connection or medium (by "medium" Newman means the intervening substance through which an object is seen).[65] The facts and phenomena drawn on by Thomson were known merely in the sense that they were perfunctorily and, so to speak, theoretically agreed to exist; and as it happens both Dr. Johnson and Hazlitt expressly state that Thomson added to them a meaning, beauty, and order of his own.[66] The poet whom Newman does take as his instance of a descriptive poet to be commended is the author of "L'Allegro" and "Il Penseroso." But since *The Seasons* would have served his purpose equally well, Newman's instance and his implication are at variance. And the explanation of this discrepancy is, I think, that Newman has little interest in descriptive poetry. If he likes "L'Allegro" and "Il Penseroso," that is because they are short, and because Milton, in the person of his cheerful or pensive deputy, is solidly present throughout either poem. Newman does not care for *The Seasons* because, in the main, they concern external nature rather than man. If his essay tells us anything at all about himself, it is that, much as he prized solitude, he did not go to poetry to escape from man into fantasy or into scenery either earthly or heavenly. There is corroboration of this inference in what follows. Newman quickly leaves the poet who deals in "natural history or philosophy" (material for poetry to which Newman only pays lip service) for the poet who uses description as an element in a poem otherwise realistically about man: "Ordinary writers . . . compare aged men to trees in autumn—a gifted poet will in the fading trees discern the fading men"; and the quatrain from *The Christian Year* follows in a footnote. Later, there is this remark on Byron:

Childe Harold . . . if he is anything, is a being professedly isolated from the world, and uninfluenced by it. One might as well draw
Tityrus's stags grazing in the air,[67] as a character of this kind; which
yet, with more or less alteration, passes through successive editions
in his other poems. Byron . . . did not know how to make poetry out
of existing materials. He declaims in his own way, and has the upper-
hand as long as he is allowed to go on; but, if interrogated on principles of nature and good sense, he is at once put out and brought to
a stand.

Byron offers an escape from the humdrum human lot, an invi-
tation which Newman will not accept.

Then again, in Newman's paragraph on lyric poetry, none of
the poems instanced there consist mainly of description. In other
words, Newman preferred lyrics of a very different content from
that, say, of Collins's "Ode to Evening" or of Keats's "To Autumn" (which he may not have read): the poets represented in
those odes would have seemed to Newman like the poet of
Childe Harold "a being professedly isolated from the world, and
uninfluenced by it." The paragraph he devotes to the lyric deals
with lyric poets very different from Collins and Keats:

Opinions, feelings, manners, and customs, are made poetical by
the delicacy or splendour with which they are expressed. This is
seen in the *ode, elegy, sonnet,* and *ballad;* in which a single idea, perhaps, or familiar occurrence, is invested by the poet with pathos or
dignity. The ballad of Old Robin Gray will serve for an instance, out
of a multitude; again, Lord Byron's Hebrew Melody, beginning,
"Were my bosom as false," etc.; or Cowper's Lines on his Mother's
Picture; or Milman's Funeral Hymn in the Martyr of Antioch; or
Milton's Sonnet on his Blindness; or Bernard Barton's Dream. As
picturesque specimens, we may name Campbell's Battle of the Baltic;
or Joanna Baillie's Chough and Crow; and for the more exalted and
splendid style, Gray's Bard; or Milton's Hymn on the Nativity; in
which facts, with which every one is familiar, are made new by the
colouring of a poetical imagination.

The list contains two instances of the picturesque and two of
the splendid, but as many as six of the kind we can call quietly
personal, religious, popular, homely. It is a list compiled by the
same persons who preferred the less exciting dramas of the Greeks
to the *Oedipus Tyrannus,* who exhorted us to go to those plays,
whether well- or ill-constructed, in order to "listen to [the] har-

monious and majestic language [of the characters], to the voices of sorrow, joy, compassion, or religious emotion,—to the animated odes of the chorus"; to listen and to find that "a word [68] has power to convey a world of information to the imagination, and to act as a spell upon the feelings; there is no need of sustained fiction,—often no room for it"; by the same person who looked to pastorals to provide more shepherd-like personages than those of Virgil's and Pope's; by the same person who here speaks of "the conciseness and simplicity of the poet" and who in his lecture on literature went so far as to speak of "that simplicity which is the attribute of genius." [69] Newman preferred the lyrical in plays, and, among lyrics, homely lyrics.

It was this quiet kind of poetry which Keble had written his essay on sacred poetry to commend. I have mentioned that Newman quotes a quatrain from *The Christian Year,* the only verses, except for a passage of three lines translated from a play of Euripides, included in the 1871 text:

> How quiet shows the woodland scene!
> Each flower and tree, its duty done,
> Reposing in decay serene,
> Like weary men when age is won.[70]

Newman honors Keble. He does not honor Blanco White, who in the previous year had published a sonnet which Coleridge was to hail as "the finest and most grandly conceived . . . in our language." [71] That sonnet, entitled "Night and Death," reads as follows:

> Mysterious Night! when our first parent knew
> Thee from report divine, and heard thy name,
> Did he not tremble for this lovely frame,
> This glorious canopy of light and blue?
> Yet 'neath a curtain of translucent dew,
> Bathed in the rays of the great setting flame,
> Hesperus with the host of heaven came,
> And lo! Creation widened in man's view.
> Who could have thought such darkness lay concealed
> Within thy beams, O sun! or who could find,
> Whilst fly, and leaf, and insect stood revealed,
> That to such countless orbs thou mad'st us blind!
> Why do we then shun death with anxious strife?
> If Light can thus deceive, wherefore not Life?

Though Newman's essay belongs to the period of his academic brilliance, his quoting Keble and not Blanco White (who, though editor of the magazine, could have been quoted, as Keble was quoted, anonymously) is a further indication that his essay belongs as securely to the Oxford Movement as do his parochial sermons and tracts, and as Keble's essay on sacred poetry. On the other hand, Blanco White's sonnet belongs to the grand deistic utterances of the eighteenth century: its aim was to enlarge and ennoble the human mind and to calm it, to calm it into a marmoreal repose. The human mind, as Newman and Keble saw it, needed rather to be humbled and refined.

To his list of lyrics Newman appends this caveat:

> It must all along be observed, that we are not adducing instances for their own sake; but in order to illustrate our general doctrine, and to show its applicability to those compositions which are, by universal consent, acknowledged to be poetical.

By "universal consent" Newman means nothing more august than "the consent of everybody in 1828 who reads English poems." It was Shelley, not Newman, who had the right to invoke a universal consent. In comparison with the grand and momentous instances of the *Defence of Poetry*, Newman's list of the poetical that is universally allowed is a very highways-and-byways affair. And this is a constant characteristic of his essay, which draws on the great, of course, for some of its instances— the Greek dramatists, Virgil, Spenser, Shakespeare, Pope, Scott, Byron—but also draws on Maria Edgeworth,[72] Southey, *Brambletye House*,[73] and contemporary writers of tracts ("which we must not be thought to approve, because we use them for our purpose"). We feel, accordingly, that we are in the presence of the essential Newman, of the Newman whose famous reply to the offer of an educated congregation in Rome has for its cornerstone "Birmingham people have souls." [74]

A final point. Newman's essay is not written as an indirect puff of the virtues of its author. This is clear from the basic assumption that "genius" is always of the romantic kind. Euripides is "careless"; we hear of the "wantonness of exuberant genius" and of the poet's "indolence of inward enjoyment." Newman himself is also a genius (to retain his term). And yet what could be more different from Newman's conception of genius than the form that genius took in himself? As a writer and thinker, his genius is summed up in his sentence: "Every thought I think is thought, and every word I write is writing." [75] Nothing could be further from careless wantonness, exuberance, indolence: instead, Newman is vigilant, exact, thorough; he is free from all idleness, and he has what he saw to be lacking in Blanco White, "power of working."

APPENDIX

In the Note appended to the essay in the collected edition of 1871, Newman recalls that "Blanco White goodhumouredly only called [the essay] 'Platonic'; [76] and, indeed, it certainly omits one of the essential conditions of the idea of poetry: its relation to the affections—and that, in consequence, as it would seem, of confusing the function and aim of poetry with its formal object ["object" in the sense of what it operates around, what it concerns itself with: see *NED*, sense 4]. As the aim of civil government is the well-being of the governed, and its object is expediency; as the aim of oratory is to persuade, and its object is the probable; as the function of philosophy is to view all things in their mutual relations, and its object is truth; and as virtue consists in the observance of the moral law, and its object is the right; so poetry may be considered to be the gift of moving the affections through the imagination, and its object to be the beautiful." The omission may be at its worst in the opening sections on the drama: for example, Newman makes the ridiculous statement that the Greek dramatists reveled "without object or meaning beyond [the] exhibition [of the imagination]." Newman, however, need not have accepted Blanco White's criticism completely. His essay does establish a connection between poetry and the "affections"; it discriminates some of the effects poetry produces on human minds and lives. If he did not say in so many words how poetry affected the reader practically, his telling him to be himself a poet was practical enough, since what affects being also affects doing. The practical effect which finds a place in Newman's essay is not so much the effect of somebody else's poetry as the effect of your own. In his essay on Keble, Newman made ample amends for any omission on this score:

[Keble] did that for the Church of England which none but a poet could do: he made it poetical. It is sometimes asked whether poets are not more commonly found external to the Church than among her children; and it would not surprise us to find the question answered in the affirmative. Poetry is the refuge of those who have not the Catholic Church to flee to and repose upon, for the Church herself is the most sacred and august of poets. Poetry, as Mr. Keble lays it down in his University Lectures on the subject, is a method of relieving the overburdened mind; it is a channel through which emotion finds expression, and that a safe, regulated expression. Now what is the Catholic church, viewed in her human aspect, but a discipline of the affections and passions? What are her ordinances and practices but the regulated expression of keen, or deep, or turbid feeling, and thus a "cleansing," as Aristotle would word it, of the sick soul? She is the poet of her children; full of music to soothe the sad and control the wayward,—wonderful in story for the imagination of the romantic; rich in symbol and imagery, so that gentle and delicate feelings, which will not bear words, may in silence intimate their presence or commune with themselves. Her very being is poetry; every psalm, every petition, every collect, every versicle, the cross, the mitre, the thurible, is a fulfilment of some dream of childhood, or aspiration of youth.[77]

But, if Blanco White's criticism is to be accepted because Newman in fact accepts it, then the omission he is charged with is an omission on the grand scale, Aristotle's doctrine of purgation being one of the main matters of the *Poetics*. And the leaving of so large a loophole for criticism is another indication that Newman was attempting too much in this essay in too short a time and at too immature an age. Butcher was forty-five when, shortly after Newman's death, he published his masterly *Aristotle's Theory of Poetry and the Fine Arts,* a work that makes only one reference to Newman's essay, and that merely to one of his "illustrations." Newman is not numbered among the few friends of the *Poetics* who were intent on trying to discover what Aristotle had originally meant. The value of Newman's essay lies in other departments.

Notes

1. *Essays Critical and Historical* (London, 1919), I, 1–26, to which is appended a Note, pp. 27–29. References to Newman's works are to those works as they appear in the collected edition.

2. See Wilfrid Ward, *Life of John Henry Newman* (London, 1912), I, 38. The *Concise DNB* gives the following summary of his various career: "White, Joseph Blanco (1775–1841), theological writer; born at Seville; studied for ministry; entered Seville University, 1790, and was ordained . . . priest, 1800; chaplain in Chapel Royal of St. Ferdinand, Seville, 1802; 'religious instructor' at Pestalozzian school at Madrid; gave up belief in Christianity, abandoned priesthood, and came to England, 1810 . . . again embraced Christianity, 1812, and qualified as English clergyman, 1814; studied at Oxford . . . published 'Evidences against Catholicism,' 1825; received degree of M.A. Oxford in recognition of his services to the church, and settled at Oriel College, 1826; became close friend of Whately, and when Whately was appointed archbishop of Dublin, 1831, accompanied him as tutor to his son . . . adopted unitarian views and resided at Liverpool, 1835 till death . . . He wrote the sonnet on 'Night and Death' (published in the 'Bijou,' 1828), which Coleridge declared to be 'the finest and most grandly conceived sonnet in our language.' "

3. *Letters and Correspondence of John Henry Newman,* ed. Anne Mozley (London, 1891), I, 193.

4. Ward's *Life,* I, 38.

5. *Letters and Correspondence,* I, 194.

6. *Ibid.*

7. *Ibid.*

8. Newman's reasons for the failure of the magazine, in so far as it was due to editor and contributors, are given in the note he appended to the reprint of his essay in 1871, and could scarcely be more telling: "The new publication required an editor of more vigorous health and enterprising mind, of more cheerful spirits, and greater power of working, and with larger knowledge of the English public, than Mr. White possessed; and writers, less bookish and academical than those, able as they were, on whom its fate depended . . . As a whole, the Review was dull" (*Essays Critical and Historical,* I, 27f).

9. *Apologia pro vita sua,* ed. Wilfrid Ward (London, 1913), p. 114.

10. *Letters and Correspondence,* I, 194.

11. These are Newman's own terms (*Essays Critical and Historical,* I, 20).

12. Unless otherwise stated, words and passages which are quoted derive from the essay under discussion. If any reader wishes to trace these quotations to their immediate context, he has only twenty-six pages to search: meanwhile other readers are spared the tedium of finding a flock of numerals related only to further numerals.

13. See *Essays Critical and Historical,* I, 26, and 27f.

14. In doing so, he sacrificed a Johnsonian paragraph of which the following is the latter half: .
"It is an officious aid which renders the acquisition of a language mechanical. Commentators are of service to stimulate the mind, and suggest

thought; and though, when we view the wide field of criticism, it is impossible they should do more, yet, when that field is narrowed to the limit of academical success, there is a danger of their indulging indolence, or confirming the contracted views of dullness. These remarks are not so much directed against a valuable work like the [book under review], the very perusal of which may be made an exercise for the mind, as against an especial fault of the age."

15. It was an excellent idea of Mr. Edmund D. Jones to include the essay in *Nineteenth-Century Critical Essays*, that admirable volume of the World's Classics series; but it is a pity that the text chosen for reproduction appears to be that of the *London Review*, a text which embodies Blanco White's tinkerings.

16. J. T. Sheppard, *The Oedipus Tyrannus of Sophocles, translated and explained* (Cambridge, 1920), p. xii. Since I do not read Greek, I can only know the works of Aristotle and the Greek dramatists in translation, and my criticism of Newman's views on the literature translated is prompted mainly by S. H. Butcher's *Aristotle's Theory of Poetry and the Fine Arts* (London, 1895).

17. Henry Tristram, "The Classics," *A Tribute to Newman*, ed. Tierney (Dublin, 1945), p. 256.

18. Cf. "Literature" (*The Idea of a University* [1889], p. 279): "'Poeta nascitur, non fit,'" says the proverb; and this is in numerous instances true of his poems, as well as of himself. They are born, not framed; and their perfection is the monument, not so much of his skill as of his power."

19. Matthew Arnold took up the cause of plot in the preface to his *Poems* (1853), but the position he adopts does not wholly contradict Newman's. Both see the importance of the "primary human" emotions and differ only in the way that they want them presented.

20. Shakespeare, *Richard II*, III, ii, 198–99.

21. See Appendix, pp. 189–190, above.

22. I have not attempted to relate Newman's essay to the criticism of the time. The influence of Wordsworth on it would be worth tracing and is particularly noticeable at this point. In the *Excursion* (I, 77ff.), Wordsworth had written:

> Oh! many are the Poets that are sown
> By Nature; men endowed with highest gifts,
> The vision and the faculty divine;
> Yet wanting the accomplishment of verse . . .

(with which, of course, compare the "mute inglorious Miltons" of Gray's *Elegy*). The American scholar, A. S. Cook, editing Newman's essay for a school edition (1891), gave many cross references to Shelley's *Defence of Poetry*. Similarities, however, between the views of Shelley and Newman cannot be due to borrowing, since Shelley's *Defence*, though written in 1821, was not published until 1840. Keble's essay, "Sacred Poetry," had appeared in 1825 and had related "inspiration" and composition in the way Newman does. Keble's essay, like Newman's, is a "liberal" attempt to enfold poetry in religion.

23. Sentences of this sermon might have found a place in the essay: "[Dangerous] too is the abuse of poetical talent, that sacred gift. Nothing is more common than to fall into the practice of uttering fine sentiments,

particularly in letter writing, as a matter of course, or a kind of elegant display" (*Parochial and Plain Sermons* [London, 1920], II, 376).

24. *Lectures on Justification* (London, 1874), p. 324.
25. *Letters and Correspondence*, I, 119.
26. *Ibid.*, II, 66.
27. *Ibid.*, II, 324–330.
28. *Ibid.*, II, 28.
29. *Apologia*, p. 108.
30. *Lectures on Justification*, p. 340.
31. *Seven Men* (London, 1920), p. 180.
32. See J. C. Smith, *A Study of Wordsworth* (Edinburgh, 1944), p. 16. Mr. Smith adds pointedly: "I doubt if even these were all what he calls one of them, 'extempore to the letter.'"
33. *Idea of a University*, pp. 282ff.
34. "Progress of Poesy," iii, 3 (v. 4). Newman, too, thought highly of Dryden. See, in particular, *The Idea of a University*, p. 279, where Dryden is set beside Homer, Pindar, Shakespeare, and Scott.
35. "The Alliance of Education and Government," v. 47.
36. "Arcades," v. 32.
37. "Spring," v. 32.
38. *Ibid.*, v. 55.
39. *Aeneid*, vi, 847.
40. See *Twickenham Edition of the Poems of Alexander Pope*, ed. John Butt, *et al.* (London, 1939–   ), II, 249.
41. "The Enthusiast" has "breathing Forms/By Fair *Italia's* skilful Hand" (vv. 131–32).
42. Both from "The Enthusiast" (vv. 56, 231–32).
43. Byron, *The Bride of Abydos*, I, 179. The expression was attacked before Taylor attacked it, and Byron defended it in a note (see the sixth edition and perhaps earlier ones).
44. Henry Taylor, *Notes from Books* (London, 1849), pp. 5–6. It is amusing to find Taylor himself writing: "one [sonnet] entitled 'Sorrow,' breathing a very full and noble strain of moral exhortation" (p. 214). I have been unable to trace the author of *Holy Breathings*. Later in the century appeared *Heart Breathings* by Agnes M'Neile Malden. Newman himself serves to bridge the use of the word by Byron and its use by devotional writers. The word is discredited by the time that a New York publisher, W. B. Ketcham, published two dictionaries in 1895–96. He called one a *Dictionary of Burning Words*, but avoided "breathing" by calling the other a *Dictionary of Living Thoughts*.
45. *The Mystery of Newman*, tr. H. C. Corrance (London, 1907), p. 247. See *Callista*, p. 221.
46. *Idea of a University*, pp. 331–32. Newman here is consciously indebted to Wordsworth, who "has asserted that a child is the only true poet, and has pictured in one of his poems . . . a child with all the poetry of childhood thrown around him, yet gradually losing these associations as he grew older, until when he arrived at manhood, he became a mere ordinary mortal" ("On the Characteristics of True Poetry," a reported lecture by Newman, *The Tablet*, July 21, 1849, reprinted by F. Tardivel, *La Personnalité littéraire de Newman* [Paris, 1937], pp. 388–89; cf. *The Sayings of Cardinal Newman* [London, 1890], p. 2).

47. For an early reference to this idea, see *Letters and Correspondence,*
p. 2, I, 338.

48. *Letters and Correspondence,* I, 190.

49. *Apologia,* p. 108.

50. *Parochial and Plain Sermons,* V, 69.

51. See Appendix, pp. 189–190.

52. *Apologia,* p. 114.

53. *Idea of a University,* pp. 268ff.

54. *Physics,* bk. II (B), chap. 8.

55. The word "poetical" is loosely used here: Newman means that it has
the qualities that he has remarked in the poet.

56. See p. 177 above: the poet's "mind is . . . full of the eternal forms
of beauty and perfection," and "they colour each object to which it directs
its view."

57. *Idea of a University,* p. 223.

58. By 1833, when Newman wrote the essay, the "Conversion of Augustine," he was more severe on Byron:

"We have seen in our own day, in the case of a popular poet, an
impressive instance of a great genius throwing off the fear of God, seeking
for happiness in the creature, roaming unsatisfied from one object to another, breaking his soul upon itself, and bitterly confessing and impart-
ing his wretchedness to all around him. I have no wish at all to compare
him to St. Augustine; indeed, if we may say it without presumption, the
very different termination of their trial seems to indicate some great difference in their respective modes of encountering it. The one dies of pre-
mature decay, to all appearance, a hardened infidel; and if he is still to
have a name, will live in the mouths of men by writings at once blas-
phemous and immoral: the other is a saint and a Doctor of the Church.
Each makes confessions, the one to the saints, the other to the powers of
evil. And does not the difference between the two discover itself in some
measure, even to our eyes, in the very history of their wanderings and
pinings? At least, there is no appearance in St. Augustine's case of that
dreadful haughtiness, sullenness, love of singularity, vanity, irritability, and
misanthropy, which were too certainly the characteristics of our own coun-
tryman. Augustine was, as his early history shows, a man of affectionate
and tender feelings, and open and amiable temper; and, above all, he
sought for some excellence external to his own mind, instead of concen-
trating all his contemplations on himself" (*Historical Sketches* [London,
1917], II, 144–45).

59. *Discourses Addressed to Mixed Congregations* (London, 1921), p.
156. I am indebted for this reference to Mr. Alvan S. Ryan's thoughtful
essay, "Newman's Conception of Literature," *University of Iowa Humanistic Studies,* VI (1942), 119ff.

60. *Idea of a University,* pp. 227ff.

61. *Ibid.,* pp. 316–17.

62. William Knight, *Principal Shairp and His Friends* (London and
Edinburgh, 1888), pp. 370–71.

63. See the Note appended by Newman in the edition of 1871.

64. *Spring,* vv. 533ff.

65. Hazlitt's "vapour of his brain" in the quotation in note 66 below.

66. G. Birkbeck Hill (Johnson's *Lives of the Poets* [Oxford, 1905], III, 289), has this note: "Johnson. Thomson, I think, had as much of the poet about him as most writers. Everything appeared to him through the medium of his favourite pursuit. He could not have viewed those candles burning but with a poetical eye [Boswell's *Johnson*, edited by G. B. Hill, 1887, I, 453]."

Hazlitt, in a criticism of Crabbe, says, "Even Thomson describes not so much the naked object as what he sees in his mind's eye, surrounded and glowing with the mild, bland, genial vapour of his brain" (*The Spirit of the Age* [London, 1825], p. 199).

67. The reference is to Virgil, *Eclogues*, I, 60.

68. Ryan, *op. cit.*, pp. 129–30, notes this interest in the single word as "a characteristic note of romantic criticism." Hurd had said that "a lucky word in a verse which sounds well and everybody gets by heart, goes farther than a volume of just criticism" (his instance is *clinquant*, applied by Boileau to Tasso, and which destroyed his fame. Hurd, *Letters on Chivalry and Romance*, ed. Edith Morley [London, 1911], p. 133).

69. *Idea of a University*, p. 283.

70. *The Christian Year*, XCIV: "All Saints' Day," vs. 9ff.

71. See note 2 above.

72. For Whately on Maria Edgeworth, see *Thoughts and Apothegms* (Philadelphia, 1856), pp. 190–91.

73. *Brambletye House, or Cavaliers and Roundheads*, by Horatio (or Horace) Smith (who collaborated with his brother in *Rejected Addresses*), was a best seller. Published in 1826, it had run through three editions in that year (see *Cambridge Bibliography of English Literature*, III, 417).

74. Ward, *Life*, II, 539.

75. *Letters and Correspondence*, I, 254.

76. *Apologia*, p. 114.

77. *Essays Critical and Historical*, II, 442–43.

MATTHEW ARNOLD
AND THE CELTIC REVIVAL

John V. Kelleher

I

When Matthew Arnold set out to describe the characteristics of Celtic literature and to analyze its effects, he paid the Celtic world the first valuable compliment it had received from an English source in several hundred years. However, the compliment, though enthusiastic, was guarded. Arnold noted this literature as the source of much of the lightness and brightness that rescued English literature from the heavy dullness of its Teutonic origin. He did not suggest that it rivaled English or classical literature in stature, or that any attempt should be made to revive it as a living mode. He took care, too, to be modest in his praise of its excellencies, to claim no more for it than could easily be justified—and this perhaps was his greatest service to the Celtic cause; for if he had shown too much enthusiasm, the audience he addressed would likely have dismissed his entire essay as another example of crackpot philo-Celticism. So carefully did he seem to measure and balance his thesis that the lectures became a contemporary classic of criticism, and in another generation had become the accepted doctrine, not only on Celtic literature, but on the literature of the Celtic Revival which Arnold had not contemplated. For all practical purposes it is the doctrine commonly accepted today.

The influence of Arnold's praise can be judged from the ease with which the Celtic Revival won popular critical support. As a literary movement the Revival began to be prominent in the early nineties. At about the turn of the century it became a large movement with a great many writers working within its boundaries; and nearly all, late or early, who were identified with it had a remarkably easy time getting themselves accepted. Even at the beginning, when its language and themes were awkward or unfamiliar, its authors obscure young people, it got unusually good notices and sympathetic handling in the English press. This cordiality lasted the life of the Revival—that is to say, for the quarter century between 1890 and the outbreak of the Irish Revolution—and it was expressed in almost exactly the same terms at the end as at the beginning. In other words, the critics had come by what they considered a satisfactory estimate of the movement as soon as it appeared, and later saw no reason to alter their decision substantially. As might be suspected from so general an agreement, no one of the contemporary critics had laid down the terms of the appraisal himself. Rather they were accepting in this, as in so much else, a commentary of Arnold's. And let it be noted, Arnold's commentary has gone virtually uncontradicted since it was made, in 1866.

This long immunity from criticism is one of the strangest things about the essay. From the start it must have been plain to Celtic scholars that Arnold, though a sympathetic partisan of their work, was not very well qualified to discuss it, at least in such sweepingly general terms. Then, too, not content with discussing literature, he had gone on to describe and pass judgment on the Celtic character in terms more kindly than complimentary. Though he assessed his own qualifications very modestly indeed, his modesty was not reflected in the way he cut up or retouched the passages he quoted to prove his points. And there was much that must have been plain irritating at any time about his calm assumption that the Anglo-Saxon, for all his faults, was head and shoulders above the Celt in any trait or talent that really counted in this world. Since most of the Celtic scholars were Celts themselves—or Germans, and in this essay Arnold seemed insultingly patronizing to the German character, or lack of it—it is really surprising that the publication of the essay, in 1867, was not followed at once by a series of competent rebuttals. As it was, no one did fire the shot at him. Apart from a polite footnote of Whitley Stokes's modifying one of Arnold's statements and Alfred Nutt's mild strictures in his critical edition of the essay, published in 1910, no one seems to have called Arnold to question for anything he said on the subject. Indeed, till this day, though it probably would be hard to find anyone to support Arnold's thesis, the only plain opposition to it is contained in *John Bull's Other Island,* where Shaw proves that every characteristic Arnold thought of as typically Celtic is typically English, and, of course, vice versa. And Shaw does not mention Arnold either in the introduction or the play.

There are plenty of reasons for this hands-off attitude, any of which might be sufficient to account for it. The most obvious is that those competent to criticize the essay at the time it appeared were not impressed by it or thought it too wide of the mark to discuss. Afterwards, it would be thought of as out of date and forgotten. There is, too, the fact that Arnold was sympathetic, which for the time made him unique of his kind and generation and one to be treated gently. But I think the most likely explanation is that the Celts and their few friends saw him only as one more of those perennial British reformers, kindly, innocent, and slightly foolish, who have always been ready to take a shot at solving the Anglo-Celtic question or some aspect of it without hurting anybody. Such Englishmen are always given free run in the Celtic provinces. It is well known that they don't bite.

Arnold was particularly that sort of Englishman. Besides *On the Study of Celtic Literature* (1867) he published, in the early eighties, two essays on Irish problems, one dealing with Gladstone's Land Act of 1881, the other with a subject he knew a good deal more about: the educational system in Ireland. He was always cautious—one never knew in those years when the latest round of concession and coercion would be punctuated with a blast of Fenian dynamite—but it is plain that he felt the basic question could be solved by sound British sense, a little fair give-and-take, and hands clasped all round. Maybe he was right. Those ideas were never fully tried. But the trouble with all those who thought like Arnold, and it is to England's credit that they were very many, is that they seem never to have considered seriously the third alternative to the kiss or the kick, that of letting the Irish have the limited independence and national recognition they were fighting for. Arnold really meant what he said about the Celts; and as we shall see, that meant no separation from

England, no throwback from the millennial advance of British progress. Present circumstances aside, it was for the Celts' own good that they should be absorbed by the Anglo-Saxon society that ruled them. Arnold could be sympathetic, particularly to that which touched his poetic sensibilities; but as a trueborn Englishman he would stand for no damned foolishness.

To the Irish, who were less inclined to ignore the present circumstances, Arnold's political and racial ideas could only seem a weary staleness. Well-intentioned Englishmen had been saying the same things about reason and light for a long time now, but they did not seem to affect the government of Ireland. Every concession the Irish won had to be fought for, no matter who agreed that it was obviously justified. The number of necessary concessions yet to be won was immense. And who in Ireland could take seriously the man who, in 1866, had come up with this whopper:

> The sensuousness of the Greek made Sybaris and Corinth, the sensuousness of the Latin made Rome and Baiae, the sensuousness of the Latinised Frenchman makes Paris; the sensuousness of the Celt proper has made Ireland.[1]

The Irishman proper of 1866, sensuously tightening his belt after a meal of sour milk and potatoes, could only reply that he hadn't quite made this Ireland all by himself, and turn his thoughts back to landlordism, rents, potatoes, rents, and landlords.

The chances are that, until 1892 or after, nobody in Ireland paid any serious attention to what Arnold had to say on any Celtic or Irish subject. After 1892 a great many young men did; but then the circumstances of Irish life were much changed; and Arnold was dead and not likely to contradict the young men's interpretation of his ideas. That the Celtic Revival and Arnold's plain influence on it came then shows, if you like, that in 1866 Arnold had been far in advance of his time. More likely it shows that he had been talking without any realistic observation in mind. Certainly he had neither predicted nor advocated a Celtic Revival: quite the contrary. Certainly it is plain that he had no notion of the circumstances under which literature of the type he described could prosper and become influential in the modern world. Very likely he would have been annoyed by the whole thing, at least until it had proved its merits, when his fair mind would have brought him to praise it as he praised all fine things. But he died in 1888.

II

The Celtic Revival expressed the mood of its time, and in Ireland that mood was established by the Parnellite disaster and by the double failure of the Fenian movement, first in its attempt at open rebellion, culminating in 1867, then in the involvement of the Fenian rank and file in the collapse of Parnell's party in 1891. The Fenian failure meant the end for a long time of effective revolutionary action. Parnell's fall, after he had brought the country so near to Home Rule, took away all real hope that the constitutional movement would get to its goal of a separate legislature for Ireland at any time in the near future. At least as important was the fact that the political split, coupled with the very substantial and continuing land reforms won in the eighties, had changed the spirit of the peasantry from the most radical in Europe to the caution of newly established or anticipant petty proprietors. There would be no further serious action in Ireland until these new gains had been consolidated, and until a new generation, brought up to a large share of political freedom, would declare for more. That it would so declare was by no means certain.

The advance of Irish prosperity from the 1880's onward was real and tangible. Rackrenting, pauperism, recurrent famine had at last come to an end. For the first time in centuries the Irish peasant and small farmer could look beyond this year's crop and plan for security. The economic basis of freedom was being established, which meant that if another bout of rebellion came Ireland would have some staying power, would not have to depend solely on the hope that a sudden fierce blow might catch England involved in greater difficulties and compel her to let Ireland go by default.

For all that, the mood of the strictly orthodox Nationalists was low. The older Fenians, those who like John O'Leary had refused to go along with Davitt and Parnell in combining land agitation with the political movement, had always insisted that to solve the land question before achieving the political solution would be to destroy the fighting spirit of the peasantry. Now it seemed as if they had been right. There was plenty of passion in Ireland in the years immediately following the Parnellite disaster, but it was no longer pure—it had been infected by materialistic motives. Truly the golden age of '98 and '48 and the silver age of '67 had passed, and the iron age had come. While Redmond and Dillon and Healy and O'Brien squabbled and fought for the leadership none could fill, the romance of Irish patriotism seemed to dim and wink out. Year followed dull prosperous year, each adding new thousands to the lists of small holders, and with every year the response to the old slogans became feebler and more prosaic, till at last Yeats would write,

> Romantic Ireland's dead and gone,
> It's with O'Leary in the grave,

mourning at once the greatest Fenian spirit and the apparent loss of all that that spirit had coveted.

What no one seemed to reflect upon was the plain truth that Irish romanticism had always been a middle-class notion, and that this iron age was establishing a middle-class Ireland. With the rise of prosperity from the eighties on, and the spread of education, the audience receptive to romantic nationalism was greatly increased. This was apparent enough in 1916 when a few hundred men could rise "in the name of God and of the dead generations," taking on the armed might of England in what they knew was a blood sacrifice; and when, in the same year, after the leaders had been executed, most of the country took up the challenge and accepted the consequences of revolution. Among the leaders of that rising were schoolteachers, minor poets, Gaelic enthusiasts, their heads full of Yeats's poetry and all the heroic antiquity his school had evoked. Yet Yeats himself was the last to recover from the shock of the Rising. He wrote the O'Leary poem in 1913.

The question of his responsibility for Easter Week, 1916,

dogged him to the end of his life, cropping up more and more insistently in his verse till the *Last Poems* are full of it.

> Did that play of mine send out
> Certain men the English shot?

It had; and not only the play *Cathleen ni Houlihan,* but his poetry, and all that he had preached in his earlier years. That he conceived of the poet's role as that of patriot and creative nationalist was clear enough, in 1892, when he had written:

> May not we men of the pen hope to move some Irish hearts and make them beat true to manhood and to Ireland? Will not the day come when we shall have again in Ireland . . . men like the men of '48, who lived by the light of noble books and the great traditions of the past? Amidst the clash of party against party we have tried to put forward a nationality that is above party.[2]

For many reasons—among them its date—that is a most important statement in regard to the Celtic Revival. It shows how soon Yeats had recognized what the character of Irish literature must be after Parnell. The poet's nationalism is henceforth "above party." He is to be like the men of '48, like Thomas Davis who had founded the Young Ireland school that still dominated Irish writing, and like them he is to appeal to Irish hearts through the "great traditions of the past."

Yet the poet would no longer be bound by Young Ireland's forms, however much he hoped to stand within their tradition. In the same year Yeats got the provisional committee of the Irish Literary Society to issue an appeal that amounted to a declaration of independence from Young Ireland:

> In recent years we have heard much of the material needs of Ireland, and little or nothing of her intellectual and literary . . . Without an intellectual life of some kind we cannot long preserve our nationality. Every Irish national movement of recent years has drawn a great portion of its power from the literary movement started by Davis, but that movement is over, and it is not possible to live forever upon the past. A living Ireland must have a living literature.[3]

That once firmly stated—though the older writers shortly afterwards tried to retract it—the new movement was begun. All that remained was to determine the style of the new literature and what it should be about.

That had practically determined itself. After the double defeat of the constitutional and revolutionary movements, to go on writing the sort of balladry in which Young Ireland had specialized for fifty years was so impossible that it could be taken for granted the new poetry would be almost diametrically opposite in tone, if not in purpose. If Irish nationalism was not to lose heart, too many failures had to be explained and justified for poetry to go on appealing to long past victories that had never seemed to win anything, anyway, no matter how enthusiastically one remembered them now. Irish self-confidence had received a terrible jolt. It could not restore itself with stale assurances—assurances that amounted to hearty repetition of the belief that one good Irishman could lick any ten Englishmen, providing only that he were fighting in the good cause and was not hamstrung by treachery. A more subtle rationale than this was needed to hearten a nation that was now used to defeating itself. Poetry in Ireland would have to accept the atmosphere of defeat as its first ingredient; and out of defeat and melancholy it must somehow make the ultimate victory not only credible but expected.

III

With that we return to Arnold and his description of the Celts, their literature, and their character. Twenty-six years had passed since he had lectured at Oxford on the study of Celtic literature; twenty-five, since he had published the lectures. They were now well known to everyone interested in the subject, and certainly no Irish writer would be ignorant of them. At the same time, it is useless to look for significant statistics on Arnold's influence in Ireland. It would be too painful for an evangelizing Celt to admit, even to himself, that he had got any substantial share of his gospel from an Englishman—even a good Englishman, now dead. Yeats in his essay, "The Celtic Element in Literature," first published in 1897, does "not think any of us who write about Ireland have built any argument upon [Arnold's ideas]." [4] We may still have our suspicions about it. Of course, it may have been entirely accidental that the Celtic Revival reproduced, element for element, Arnold's picture of Celtic literature, with the difference that every weakness Arnold deplored in the Celt and his works has now become a strange characteristic strength. Or it may be that the Revival did revive the true qualities of Celtic literature, and that Arnold had been uncannily right in his estimate of those qualities. Neither is very likely. That the resemblance between Arnold's idea and the ideas of the Revival was accidental might possibly be true. The second possibility is certainly wrong. Celtic Revival literature does not resemble Celtic literature very much at all; and Arnold's knowledge of the subject was neither wide nor trustworthy. For that matter, with the exception of Douglas Hyde—and his work was only adjunct to the Revival—Yeats and his followers did not know much about Celtic literature, either. And there is the real connection.

There would likely be little to choose between Arnold's Celtic knowledge in 1866 and Yeats's knowledge in the 1890's. Yeats had collected folk stories in the Irish-speaking west; he had spent much of his youth in Sligo; he had read most Anglo-Irish literature and knew the principal heroic tales in one English redaction or another. And he was an Irishman. Arnold had none of these advantages, but he had read many of the best books and apparently all the worst books on Celtic literature and history, and he had a pretty fair nose for what was ridiculous or unsound. He appreciated good scholarship. He could recognize from a distance the worth of a great scholar like Eugene O'Curry. Better still, though he felt that the era of genuine Celtic studies had just dawned, he could give intelligent praise, across sixty or a hundred and sixty years, to great collectors like Owen Jones and Edward Lhuyd. In the *Study* the range of his learning is unobtrusively apparent: he quoted from or referred to some thirty books, covering nearly every branch of the subject then studied and including the works of French and German Celticists. (His firsthand knowledge of several of these books is not certain, since his quotations from them can also be found in others on the list.) Few English or American critics who have dealt with a Celtic topic have been so well prepared to speak—which is still not much of a compliment.

Examination of his sources gives us another significant fact. With very few exceptions the books are all *about* Celtic literature or culture. As nearly as one can make out from his references and remarks, he seems to have read—in translation, of course, for he knew no Celtic language—very little of the literature itself. Of Welsh he had read Lady Guest's *Mabinogion* and possibly Williams ap Ithel's translation of *Brut y Tywysogion,* though he only quotes from the preface to that; for Breton he had Ville-marqué's French translations and Tom Taylor's English translation from Villemarqué. The rest of his quotations are from selections given in critical or descriptive works, that chiefly used being D. W. Nash's *Taliesin; or, The Bards and Druids of Britain* (1858), and as a distant second and the source of nearly every Irish passage, O'Curry's *Lectures on the Manuscript Materials of Ancient Irish History* (1861). In all, a singularly small foundation for comment on the native literatures of three countries and several provinces.

Next most remarkable is his free handling of what he had read. Take, for instance, that string of passages from the *Mabinogion,* through which, in the fifth lecture, he leads up to his illustration of Celtic "magic." The last two passages and Arnold's comment may be given here. I indicate in parentheses Lady Guest's words where Arnold has changed them; his wordings are italicized.

"And early in the day *Geraint and Enid* (they) left the wood, and they came to an open country, with meadows on one hand and mowers mowing the meadows. And there was a river before them, and the horses bent down and drank the water. And they went up out of the river by a *steep bank* (lofty steep), and there they met a slender stripling with a satchel about his neck, (but they knew not what it was); and he had a small blue pitcher in his hand, and a bowl on the mouth of the pitcher."

And here the landscape, up to this point so Greek in its clear beauty, is suddenly magicalised by the romance touch:—

"And *they* (he) saw a tall tree by the side of the river, one half of which was in flames from the root to the top, and the other half was green and in full leaf." [5]

The fault with Arnold's comment and the point he is making here is that the landscape is not thus "magicalised" for Enid and Geraint. The first passage is from the story of "Geraint the Son of Erbin," and the second is from the preceding story in the collection, "Peredur the Son of Evrawc." There are many pages in between the passages.[6] It is also interesting that Yeats, in the "Celtic Element in Literature," quoted twice from the same string of passages, emphasizing the one about the burning tree, and in both instances with Arnold's wording. To be sure, he acknowledged his source, but may we guess that, in 1897, he knew no more about Welsh literature than Arnold had known, or knew it chiefly from Arnold?

This is by no means a unique example of how Arnold stacked his cards. When he was convinced that a "Celt-lover" had written nonsense, he was not above embellishing the nonsense on his own, to make the poor man more ridiculous than he was. He certainly did it to Algernon Herbert, to whom he credits a worse translation than Herbert had actually used; [7] and there is in the first lecture a passage ascribed to Sharon Turner which conflicts with what Turner had to say and which I have not been able to find in Turner's book, *A Vindication of the Genuineness of the Ancient British Poems* (1803).[8] Indeed, after an examination of the *Study,* it seems fairly reasonable to conclude that Arnold had made up his mind about Celtic literature before he consulted most of his material on it. How else can one explain his bland insistence that Macpherson's *Ossian,* for all that it was a fraud, still had "a residue with the very soul of Celtic genius in it"? [9] Alfred Nutt pointed out that if Arnold had known any of the genuine Gaelic poems attributed to Oisin he would have noticed—and presumably have admitted—the utter difference in tone. Oisin, as Nutt truly said, does not weep about going forth interminably to battle and as consistently falling; rather, he does the knocking down and he enjoys it very much. Nutt, however, underestimated Arnold's resistance to what conflicted with the criteria he had himself established. At the end of the third lecture, quoting from Henry Morley's *English Writers,* where Morley spoke of "Oisin's dialogues with St. Patrick," Arnold changed the spelling to "Ossian." [10]

His reasons for preferring Macpherson are, I think, easy enough to understand. Macpherson gave him what he wanted and what he felt ought to be right. *Ossian* fits Arnold's formula for Celticity far better than any authentic Celtic poetry would—

as in turn Arnold's formula fitted the needs of the Celtic Revivalists better than did the history of any Irish period since the coming of Christianity. And once more we are indebted to Nutt for
reminding us that *Ossian* reflects, through Macpherson's mind,
the atmosphere of melancholy and defeat that pervaded the
Scotch Highlands after 1745.[11] We have then a reasonably clear
recurrence of a similar emotional tone, first in Scotland in the
mid-eighteenth century, thereafter in Macpherson, then in that
part of Arnold's temperament which sensed the world as

> a darkling plain
> Swept with confused alarms of struggle and flight
> Where ignorant armies clash by night,

and at last in the general feeling of disheartenment in Ireland
after Parnell. And at no point in the series is real Celtic literature
brought in for the primary effect. The concern is always with the
present emotion and the conception it leads to. The emotions are
similar and decisive.

IV

Before we come to Arnold's formula, it is but fair that we
consider his motives in writing the *Study of Celtic Literature*. In
his recent *Matthew Arnold: A Study in Conflict*, E. K. Brown
has shown very clearly that the motives were generous and sin-
cere: his strictures on Celtic weaknesses, part of the "strategy of
disinterestedness."

There is no doubt that he does dispel distrust, that he does pre-
serve the appearance of disinterestedness; but, on the other hand, he
does clutch at every shred of evidence he can find to sustain his argument—his dependence on current theories of race must now appear
astonishingly uncritical—he is in his heart an advocate for the Celt
and not a dispassionate judge. The disinterestedness is one of
strategy rather than of essential disposition. He wishes to know the
Celt; he wishes no less to exalt him.[12]

To all of which we can agree, except for his clutching at "every
shred of evidence." If one means only such evidence as would
bolster the Celtic claim to greatness, it is true. If one means evi-

dence concerning Celtic literature, it is not true. Arnold took astonishingly little pains about that, and by no means for lack of evidence. For Irish literature alone the amount of recent, scholarly translation available in the 1860's was very considerable. Yet all his Irish references can be traced to four sources, two of which are more grammatical than literary. I refer to O'Curry's *Manuscript Materials*, mentioned before as the chief Irish source; to Whitley Stokes's *Three Irish Glossaries* (1862), from which he took the etymology of *triath*, "the sea," which he misspells as *traith;*[13] and to Johann Kaspar Zeuss's *Grammatica Celtica* (1853), from which he quoted two prefatory footnotes and Zeuss's discussion of the *destitutio tenuium* as a measure for the age of linguistic forms. The fourth is probably Stokes's early edition of the "Félire of Angus the Culdee," published in India in 1863, which is likely the source of the two stanzas from the "Leabhar Breac" poem on Angus quoted in the fifth lecture.[14] It must readily be admitted that, as an argument for recognition of Celtic worth, the *Study of Celtic Literature* is a fine, large-hearted plea. More the pity that the title is so irrelevant.

The formula, when we get to it, is not so distinctively Arnold's own as one might expect from the very Arnoldesque approach to it. As most of the illustrations of Celtic poetry in the *Study* are from Nash's *Taliesin*, so many of the touchstones are from Renan's "La Poésie des races celtiques" (1859). The mixture is Arnold's, mixed at his common-sensical British best. Renan had observed the Celts in Brittany and on a flying trip to Wales, and Arnold, plainly without an eye to the Irish vote, reminded his audience that Renan had not seen the Celt at his least tamed.

M. Renan, with his eyes fixed on the Bretons and the Welsh is struck with the timidity, the shyness, the delicacy of the Celtic nature . . . He talks of the *douce petite race naturellement chrétienne*, his *race fière et timide, à la extérieur gauche et embarrassée*. But it is evident that this description, however well it may do for the Cymri, will never do for the typical Irishman of Donnybrook fair. Again, M. Renan's *infinie délicatesse de sentiment qui caractérise la race Celtique*, how little that accords with the popular conception of an Irishman who wants to borrow money![15]

But at once he adds that "sentiment" is the key word for the Celtic nature, the word "which marks where the Celtic races really touch and are one." And with that, he is off—without, however, quite warning his audience that he uses "sentimentality" in a double sense, both as the French *sentimentalité* and in a special meaning of his own: "Sentimental,—*always ready to react against the despotism of fact*," a phrase taken from Henri Martin's chapter on the Celts in his *Histoire de France* (1855–1860).[16] Its effect, too, was as double as its meaning. It gave the Celt an "organisation quick to feel impressions, and feeling them very strongly; a lively personality . . . keenly sensitive to joy and sorrow," but at the same time it deprived him of "balance, measure, and patience . . . the eternal conditions . . . of high success." [17]

"The Celtic genius," Arnold thought, had "sentiment as its main basis, with love of beauty, charm, and spirituality for its excellence, ineffectualness and self-will for its defect." [18] It contrasted sharply and, one must admit, not altogether favorably against German "steadiness with honesty" and English "energy with honesty." Much as Arnold appreciated Celtic passion, he did not think the Celts could do much with it, for in business and politics it became evident that "the skillful and resolute appliance of means to end which is needed both to make progress in material civilisation, and also to form powerful states, is just what the Celt has least turn for." [19] "Sensuousness" betrayed them: the sensuousness of the Celt proper that had made Ireland. Even in the realm of art failure dogged them for the same reasons.

In . . . poetry which the Celt has so passionately, so nobly loved; poetry where emotion counts for so much, but where reason, too, reason, measure, sanity, also count for so much,—the Celt has shown genius, indeed, splendid genius; but even here his faults have clung to him, and hindered him from producing great works . . . he has only produced poetry with an air of greatness investing it all, and sometimes giving . . . to short pieces, or to passages . . . singular beauty and power.

The Celt had not patience for the "steady, deep-searching survey," the "firm conception of the facts of human life," on which true art was based.

So he runs off into technic, where he employs the utmost elaboration, and attains astonishing skill; but in the contents of his poetry you have only so much interpretation of the world as the first dash of a quick, strong perception, and then sentiment, infinite sentiment, can bring you.[20]

So much then for the deficiencies of Celtic poetry. They were hardly what must have attracted Arnold's interest. He had as much again to say of its excellencies; and though he may have annoyed patriotic Celts by appropriating all these virtues for English verse, he was charmingly particular about acknowledging where they had come from.

"Celtic poetry," he said, "seems to make up to itself for being unable to master the world and give an adequate interpretation of it, by throwing all its force into style, by bending language at any rate to its will, and expressing the ideas it has with unsurpassable intensity, elevation and effect." [21] And this style was itself induced by what it had to control: the penetrating passion and melancholy bred into the Celts by their "sensuous nature, their manifold striving, their adverse destiny, their immense calamities," and issuing in what Arnold could only call *Titanism*.[22] There was still more, for this Titanism might have created a deep and deeper gloom ending in a depression too compacted for poetical release; and this, Arnold pointed out, had not happened. Celtic literature had a "lightness and brightness" as native as its gloom: a radiance magical in its effect. "Magic is the word to insist upon,—a vivid and near interpretation of nature," [23] an observation that went beyond faithful description of observed fact, beyond even the Greek interpretation where clarity of vision is implemented by an additional human radiance, to a perception of an interior and wayward life in the object itself, so that Celtic interpretation became as much a venture into magical revelation as into description.

v

Here, then, was a thoughtful analysis of Celtic literature, made with sympathy and good will—though with notably insufficient evidence—and published twenty-five years before the appearance of the Celtic school in English. It provided even the dullest critic with a set of tools guaranteed to give the measure-

ments of any work called "Celtic"; and the critics used it grate-
fully when the need and opportunity came. So did the young
Irish and Scottish authors whose work, the critics noticed, could
thus be measured. The writers did not use it, however, precisely
in its original form: they had to reinterpret and get rid of Arnold's
strategical qualifications. The virtues he praised could be accepted at face value; the faults and weaknesses he deplored had
to be explained, and, in the explanation, be shown as hidden but
distinctive merits. After all, it was hardly fair that the English
should wreck Celtic life and then complain of its lack of wholeness. More than a thousand years of steady, energetic Teutonic
mayhem stood between the unbroken Celtic world and modern-
ity. It would be enough, therefore, for Arnold to note the grace
and indestructible vitality of the Celtic spirit—Celtic competence
was not his proper concern.

It might be, as he said, that the steady Teuton or energetic
Anglo-Saxon, blessed with balance, measure, and patience, was
responsible for "doors that open, windows that shut, razors that
shave, coats that wear, and a thousand more such good things." [24]
What had the Celt to do with these or these to do with the Celt
while Ireland remained unfree? The intense spirituality of the
Celt could not be shackled to such material concerns: magic and
mechanics do not go together. (Besides, as Sinn Fein began
presently to argue, Ireland had only to be free, and then the
world would see such watches, razors, coats, and household ap-
pliances as were never seen before.)

As for Arnold's queer suggestion (it was really a remarkable
insight, considering how little he knew of it) that Celtic poetry
was wanting *architectonicé*, what did he expect? Was there—as
any indignant patriot could ask—but one structure for great
poetry, one manner of indicating that the poet's survey and conception of the facts of human life were steady, deep searching,
and firm? It was quite true that the Celtic poet did not imitate
the heavy didacticism of the English. He didn't need to. His
audience preferred the thing "half-said," their quick response
completing his subtly sketched allusion. Or so the neo-Celt of
1890 might argue, forgetting, if he had ever known, the tedious
acres of bardic verse stretching out to a gray garrulous infinity.

At the same time, it is significant that those who essayed the "Celtic mode" did not often attempt any of the larger forms. Irish poetry has till now remained pretty much content with the lyric, the shorter poem of any type, satisfied apparently to depend for its effects, as Arnold said it did, on "quick, strong perception," style, and intensity.

Besides these, there was his charge of "ineffectualness and self-will." The latter seemed to require little apology. If the Celt was self-willed, he had a right to be; it was not for the humdrum Saxon to pass on that. Ineffectualness was a more pointed indictment, for it could not, on the face of it, be easily denied—particularly by a people who had just wrecked the most powerful political movement they had ever had. It was, as a matter of fact, never really disposed of by the Celtic Revivalists. About as close as they got to a satisfactory answer was the romanticized paradoxical statement of Celtic wisdom and spirit, a way of hinting that the Celt was defeated by his own superiority. That device was, as we shall see, a favorite with the lesser poets and poetesses.

Of course, in speaking of formulas and conventions, we must understand that the convention of the Celtic school was not an elaborate, well-defined set of rules for the sure and easy production of "Celtic" literature. Rather, such a convention is a sort of lowest common denominator, made up of those elements most frequently to be found in the work of a group of writers who are related in a general way by elements of style and choice of subject. And since those authors who begin such a convention and contribute most to it are usually those most independent of it, it is not among the works of the best Irish writers that we must look for the most complete and indicative examples. It is the minor bards, the imitators, who may write little individually, but whose numbers are as the sands of the sea or the stars on a winter's night, who can give us the convention entire in a sigh. Yeats, for instance, though he created most of the elements of the convention, never wrote a perfect Celtic Revival poem or play—though some of his early things come pretty close to it. AE's opalescent language of vision and his hazy pantheon of Celtic divinities were widely borrowed: his concern with spiritual discipline and human liberty and decency did not fit into any nationalistic school. Lady Gregory had too much common sense and humor. Synge had too much reserve. They could not, in any case, be bothered with exploiting a particular literary mode beyond the point of diminishing returns, and what was good in the Revival was very soon worked out. In 1904 Yeats discovered Padraic Colum, and the new generation began to speak, to the surprise of all, in terms of "peasant realism." After that the Celtic mode was the property of the third-string writers.

There are many reasons why we do not find the pure convention in Yeats's work at any period of his life. The most obvious, of course, is that he was too big to be contained by it. As important is that he disagreed with Arnold on perhaps the most important detail of Arnold's description of Celtic literature. He held that the "mystery and magic charm" Arnold had so praised was not simply the product of the Celtic imagination, with its "passionate, turbulent, indomitable reaction against the despotism of fact"—it was not even specifically Celtic.

> When Matthew Arnold wrote it was not easy to know as much as we know now of folk song and folk belief, and I do not think he understood that our "natural magic" is but the ancient religion of the world, the ancient worship of nature and the troubled ecstacy before her, that certainty of all beautiful places being haunted, which it brought into men's minds.[25]

That being so, the magic and mystery could not be evoked, the obscurely preserved fragments of the ancient belief recovered, by any vague Celticism. They could be interpreted and understood only by analogy with European and Oriental occult lore, derived presumably from the same antiquity. And only when they had thus been given meaning could they be used again for sure poetical effect. That belief and the laborious practice it called for gave Yeats's poetry the discipline and intensity of symbolistic suggestion that increasingly distinguished it, a richness that could not be imitated without equal skill and labor.

It was not successfully imitated, but it could be counterfeited —and the counterfeiting resulted in the fanciest hogwash ever manufactured in Ireland. In scores of slim green volumes the discovery of popular Celtic mysticism was celebrated. It was a great time for the feeble-minded: never before had it been so easy and practicable to be wise without wisdom, visionary without visions, acutely sensitive without feeling. As mentioned before, the romanticized paradox was the secret means. Equipped with it, the common or garden Irish poet began to hear the inaudible, see the invisible, comprehend the unintelligible, apparently with no more elaborate qualification for all this than his presumably Celtic paternity. (Scotsmen could do all this, too, as "Fiona Macleod" demonstrated.) And presently it began to be done on a grand scale, for about this time the last of Arnold's Celtic touchstones was brought up and set in place. That was *Titanism*, which Arnold had defined as that "vein of piercing regret and passion . . . [which] Macpherson's *Ossian* carried in the last century . . . like a flood of lava through Europe." [26] Most of the lesser poets seem to have mistaken it, however, as an appellation for sheer size. The nine-foot Gaelic hero came into vogue:

> A fighting man he was,
> Guts and soul;
> His blood as hot and red
> As that on Cain's hand-towel.
>
> .   .   .   .   .   .
>
> I've seen him swing an anvil
> Fifty feet,
> Break a bough in two,
> And tear a twisted sheet.
>
> And the music of his roar—
> Like oaks in thunder cleaving;
> Lips foaming red froth,
> And flanks heaving.
>
> God! a goodly man,
> A Gael, the last
> Of those that stood with Dan
> On Mullach-Maist! [27]

That, incidentally, is by a poet who wrote some of the loveliest and most tender lyrics in the literature, when he eschewed the convention and worked his own vein.

By this time, the convention had become so elaborate and so

embarrassingly empty that it was beyond even the salutary aid of parody. One cannot parody the funny; and despite the fierce patriotism that undoubtedly justified this poetry in the minds of its creators, it could no longer be taken seriously by those not drunk on the same brew.

Or could it? There is one really skillful poem of this mode which still survives as an established anthology piece—used to illustrate the Celtic Revival, though it was written, not by one of the Dublin group, but by a young New Yorker. I refer to Shaemas O'Sheel's "They Went Forth to Battle But They Always Fell," a poem published in 1911 and written in a style and with a smooth facility Yeats might have envied twenty years before. In three stanzas it reproduces practically the entire formula. All of Arnold's Celtic touchstones are there: Titanism and magic and piercing melancholy and doomed bravery and ineffectualness and verbal sensuality and splendid dream-haunted failure and the exquisite spiritual sensitivity of the Celt. And there is sentiment, "infinite sentiment," too, though perhaps not of the sort Arnold meant. The title is that quotation from *Ossian* with which Arnold had headed his lectures. For the meaning it will probably be enough to quote the second stanza:

> It was a secret music that they heard,
> A sad sweet plea for pity and for peace;
> And that which pierced the heart was but a word,
> Though the white breast was red-lipped where the sword
> Pressed a fierce cruel kiss, to put surcease
> On its hot thirst, but drank a hot increase.
> Ah, they by some strange troubling doubt were stirred,
> And died for hearing what no foeman heard.[28]

Here then is the new view of Irish history which explains defeat and removes its sting. It suggests that Irish were beaten not because they were divided, or badly led, or armed with obsolete weapons, or even seriously outnumbered, but because they were distracted by more important, if less pressing, matters: matters indeed so profound that only a Celt could understand them or even be aware of them, and then only when he was not attending to business. They were beaten because, in other words, they were *fey*, doomed by their own spiritual sensitivity. One notes that the music or the word that did the dirty work was inaudible to the crass but competent enemy. Yet there was nothing weak or cowardly about the fallen. The poem goes on to imply that once they got over being doomed, by, for instance, being dead, they could conquer even the powers of darkness:

> Yet they will scatter the red hordes of Hell,
> Who went to battle forth and always fell.

A heartening statement for those who were now preparing themselves for the last revolt. And considering the odds these rebels faced, and the bravery with which they faced them, it would be a poor thing for outraged sense to begrudge them what comfort such poetry may have given. We need note it here only as the ultimate expression of the train of ideas Arnold had so carefully, so moderately, set going, in a different age, on a different theme. Except of course as a theological problem, moral responsibility in the chain of cause and effect, it has almost nothing whatever to do with what Arnold had said or thought—as Arnold certainly would have had nothing to do with it.

VI

One can only repeat that he had not predicted or desired a Celtic literary revival. He had wanted the Celts fully to enter the Anglo-Saxon cultural and political system, bringing with them their great spiritual and artistic gifts. His lectures were in large part a plea that they be welcomed as coequal citizens, valued for the qualities they alone possessed and without which, he felt, English literature and English life would lack savor. It was a noble intent. It did not, however, have much to do with the literature which was his ostensible subject, or induce him to go beyond a cursory inspection of that literature. What he saw of it, he probably saw steadily and saw whole; but he saw only fragments, and the picture he drew, while distantly recognizable, lacks depth and outline. He seems, for instance, totally unaware of that quality of reserved emotion that gives the best Gaelic poetry a whiplash sting, particularly when, as in so many of the poems translated by Frank O'Connor, it is set down in language so severely objective as to seem at first impassive. On the other hand, one would never gather from what he says of it that much Celtic poetry is very dull stuff indeed. He saw the technical intricacy of standard Celtic verse, without, however, seeing that inspiration could be killed by the tradition that required this mathematical intricacy, or rather, be smothered by it before birth. But then Celtic dullness was not part of his argument. Since the argument came first, one may question whether he would have cared for, or used, fuller information. He did not, at any rate, seek it out.

And yet, in the *Study of Celtic Literature* we are dealing with the observations of a great critic. The book can never be unconsidered by anyone dealing with the subject, or be taken lightly, or—in the end—be read with anything but recurrent admiration. Whether or not one agrees with his estimate of Celtic literature, one's own estimate is bound to be affected by his, as it is affected also by Yeats's. When the great critic or the great writer speaks on literature, we must listen with avid attention. It does not matter how much or how little he knows. We do not listen to him, hoping for information. We listen for insight. If he knew more, he would probably see into more, and that would be better; but we are grateful for what we can get. It is thus with Joyce in the *Portrait of the Artist* when he explains why he, as a young man, rejected what the Celtic Revival admired: "the broken lights of Irish myth . . . the myth upon which no individual mind had ever drawn out a line of beauty . . . its unwieldy tales that divided against themselves as they moved down the cycles." [29] It is thus with Arnold. Does it matter, in the end, how much they knew? Certainly, all the scholarly interpretation in the world, so long as it is uncombined with the genuine critical faculty, can never by itself give us the insights we need for an artistic valuation. The field of Celtic studies has not been particularly blessed with the critical gift. Arnold's book is still unique—a fact which he would undoubtedly have deplored.

As for the Celtic Revival, the period it spans brought about an enormous improvement in the quality of Irish writing. It saw, too, the secure establishment of an Irish literature in English. This, however, was not an effect of the Celtic convention: it was the result of Yeats's insistence on that care and finish and economy which had been conspicuously missing from Irish writing up until that time. By precept and example he forced the Irish writers to learn the tools of their trade, to respect their words and emotions, to say what they had to say and no more. For the first time in English, Irish poetry could lay a general claim to "intensity, elevation, and effect."

There were two great writers, Yeats and Synge, and a dozen fine ones associated with the Revival in the years when it won international respect. When its convention withered and grew stale, the withering did not affect the tradition of excellent workmanship that they had created. At its peak—and the peak came early—the Celtic convention was embodied in a great deal of fine writing. The inanity we have examined was the later phase, when nearly every writer worth his salt had outgrown it or deserted it. One thing was sure. No longer would there be one or two good Irish writers in each generation, working alone, without sympathy or a sound native canon of style, doomed to idiosyncracy, wasting their sweetness in a howling desert of rhetoric and easy tears. If the Celtic convention played any part in ending that over-prolonged condition, it justified itself a thousand times.

Notes

References to *On the Study of Celtic Literature* are to the first edition (London: Smith, Elder and Co., 1867), referred to below as *Celtic Literature*.

1. *Celtic Literature*, pp. 105–06.

2. The first quoted lines by Yeats are from "September 1913," *Responsibilities* (New York: The Macmillan Company, 1916, 1944); the second quoted lines are from "Man and the Echo," *Last Poems and Plays* (copyright 1940, by Georgie Yeats). Both quotations are used by permission of The Macmillan Company. The prose is from W. B. Yeats, *Letters to the New Island*, ed. Horace Reynolds (Cambridge, Mass.: Harvard University Press, 1934), pp. 156–57.

3. Quoted in W. P. Ryan, *The Irish Literary Revival* (London, 1894), pp. 127–28.

4. W. B. Yeats, *Ideas of Good and Evil* (London, 1907), p. 272.

5. *Celtic Literature*, p. 161.

6. Lady Charlotte Guest, *The Mabinogion* (London, 1838–1849). The first passage is from II, 112–13; the second, from I, 344.

7. *Celtic Literature*, p. 37. In *Britannia After the Romans* (London, 1836), II, 6, Herbert gives the translation as follows: "Without the ape,

heb eppa, says Taliesin, without the milch-cow's stall, without the world's incomplete rampart (go-vur), the world would be desolate." He gives it again with slightly different wording in *An Essay on the Neodruidic Heresy in Britannia,* part I (London, 1838), p. 113. The translation Arnold cites is actually from Edward Davies, *The Mythology and Rites of the British Druids* (London, 1809), appendix xii, p. 568. It concludes with the line, "not requiring the cuckoos to convene the appointed dance over the green," which does not appear in either of Herbert's versions.

8. See *Celtic Literature,* pp. 39–40, where Arnold credits the following passage to Turner:

"The strange poem of Taliesin, called the *Spoils of Annwn,* implies the existence (in the sixth century, he means) of mythological tales about Arthur; and the frequent allusion of the old Welsh bards to the persons and incidents which we find in the *Mabinogion,* are further proofs that there have been such stories in circulation amongst the Welsh."

I have not, after a careful search, been able to find this passage in Turner's book. Arnold was trying to prove that Turner was tainted with the "Celt-lover's" gullibility. Where Turner does discuss the "Spoils of Annwn" his tone is quite different from that of the above passage. Cf. his *Vindication,* p. 238:

"If its allusions are at all historical, they are too much involved in mythology to be comprehended. In [Taliesin's] mead/song, there is a connected train of thought. In the following poem ["The Spoils of Annwn"], all connection of thought, seems to have been studiously avoided."

And Turner adds in a footnote:

"It is, however, fair to remark, that if the Mabinogion and all the Welsh remains were to be accurately studied; it is probable, that enough might be gathered from them to elucidate some of the allusions of Taliesin to the opinions, tales, and traditions of his date. This would make intelligible many passages now obscure."

9. *Celtic Literature,* pp. 152–53.

10. *Ibid.,* p. 96. The quotation is from *English Writers,* vol. I, part i, p. 80.

11. *The Study of Celtic Literature,* by Matthew Arnold, with Introduction, Notes, and Appendix by Alfred Nutt (London, 1910), p. 90n. Nutt credits the idea to Smart in his *Macpherson.*

12. E. K. Brown, *Matthew Arnold: A Study in Conflict* (Chicago: University of Chicago Press, 1948), pp. 110–11.

13. *Celtic Literature,* p. 83, cited from *Three Irish Glossaries,* p. xix n. The misspelling occurs in all editions of *Celtic Literature,* including Nutt's.

14. I have not seen this edition. Stokes mentions it in *Revue Celtique,* VI, 364n. The translation cited by Arnold, *Celtic Literature,* p. 146, seems pretty obviously to be by Stokes; cf. his "On the Calendar of Oengus," Transactions of the Royal Irish Academy, Irish MSS Series, vol. I, part i, p. 4n., where the wording is nearly identical with that of the stanzas quoted by Arnold.

15. *Celtic Literature,* p. 100.

16. *Ibid.,* p. 102. The phrase occurs in *Histoire de France,* I, 36.

17. *Ibid.,* p. 102.

18. *Ibid.,* p. 115.

19. *Ibid.,* p. 106.

20. *Ibid.*, p. 104.
21. *Ibid.*, p. 144.
22. *Ibid.*, p. 152.
23. *Ibid.*, pp. 161–62.
24. *Ibid.*, p. 111.
25. Yeats, *Ideas of Good and Evil*, p. 275.
26. *Celtic Literature*, p. 152.
27. Seosamh MacCathmhaoil (Joseph Campbell), "The Fighting Man," *The Mountainy Singer* (Boston: The Four Seas Company, 1919). Used by permission of Bruce Humphries, Inc.
28. From *Jealous of Dead Leaves* by Shaemas O'Sheel (New York: Boni and Liveright, Inc., 1928). Used by permission of Liveright Publishing Corporation.
29. James Joyce, *A Portrait of the Artist as a Young Man* (New York: Modern Library edition, 1928), p. 210.

A CORRESPONDENCE
FROM OPPOSITE CORNERS

Renato Poggioli

I

Between 1919 and 1921, during the years of the civil war, the Soviet government was afraid of the effects of foreign intervention and rather sensitive to the shifts of public opinion abroad. The new regime was also painfully aware of the obvious fact that the leaders of the old-fashioned intelligentsia, after having flirted for years with a vague and dreamy revolutionary ideal, after having created their own brand of the radical-populist myth, were now disappointed and dissatisfied. They were reacting with outspoken indignation against the hard facts of revolutionary reality, or were remaining disdainfully aloof in the fight which the party was waging with the claim of establishing the dictatorship of the proletariat. The first steps undertaken by the Soviet government toward what was later to be called the cultural or literary policy of the regime (now, at least in that respect, *quantum mutatus ab illo!*) were dictated by a spirit of prudence and compromise, by tactics of expedience and opportunism, by the methods of nonintervention and appeasement. This policy at first even took the form of granting generous help and special privileges to the members of that class, dubbed with the rather amusing name of workers in letters, sciences, and the arts.

Such a policy was strongly supported by Gorky, who used for such a purpose the prestige of his name, and even subordinated, to the fulfillment of such a program, his ideological acceptance of the regime, toward which he had felt so doubtful and dubious at first. It was through Gorky and his project of publishing a collection of classical masterpieces, entitled "Universal Literature," that many of the older and younger writers got paid for their work as editors and translators and were more or less able to

weather the storm. The living conditions of the Russian intel-
lectuals remained, however, still difficult, even tragic; and the
Soviet government decided to open for their benefit a few comfortable dwellings of dispossessed aristocrats, industrialists, and
merchants. These buildings were transformed into sanitariums
where artists, writers, scholars, and scientists—old, weak, or sick—
could be given an opportunity either to improve their physical
conditions and to recover their health, or merely to work or rest
in peace. In the summer of 1920, in one of these sanitariums recently opened in Moscow, two extraordinary patients, already
acquainted with each other, the poet, scholar, and thinker
Vyacheslav Ivanov, and the historian, philosopher, and critic
Mikhail Herschensohn, spent together the period of their treatment, living in the same room. From their meeting and sojourn
together, the work originated which is the object of this study,
and for the understanding of which the reader must first be supplied with some information about the personality, background,
and career of each of its authors.

At the time of that meeting, Vyacheslav Ivanov was fifty-four
years old, having been born in Moscow in the year 1866. As a
young student at the University of Moscow, he had shown so
much promise in the field of classical scholarship that he had
been sent to study under Mommsen at the University of Berlin.
A thesis in Latin, about some of the most practical aspects of
civic and communal life in ancient Rome, had shown so much
learning and such thorough archaeological training that it seemed
to open for him a brilliant academic career in the west. But the
reading of *The Birth of Tragedy* and the later works of another
deserter from the field of classical philology, Friedrich Nietzsche,
led him to the literary and philosophical study of Hellenism, especially of the meaning and origin of the Dionysiac cult. This interest in religious history brought him back to modern Russian
culture, which, at the end of the past century and at the beginning of ours, was absorbed in questions of faith and mysticism, in
strange and eclectic creeds, in the attempt to build a kind of
syncretic religion, and was then indulging in mythical and allegorical, in heterodoxical and heretical beliefs. In brief, Ivanov

turned to the problematic metaphysics of Dostoevsky, to the liberal Christianity of Solovyov, to the erotic mysticism of Rozanov, to the "religion of the Holy Ghost" which was to be developed later by Bulgakov and Berdyaev, and, last but not least, to the pedantic and vulgar, literary and naïve Manicheanism of Merezhkovsky. Less inclined than his contemporaries to believe that Orthodox Christendom was the highest achievement of Christianity, Ivanov was on the other hand ready to accept literally and determined to prove, with more learning and imagination than they, their belief in the dogmatic statement of Tertullian, that Christianity is not only above history, but also that it has always existed, even within history itself. Even the Dionysiac cult was for him an announcement of the coming of the Redeeming Son.

All these thinkers were also literary men, and Solovyov was, like Ivanov, a poet. As a matter of fact, the mystical allegories of Solovyov's verse were to be more influential than the systematic doctrines he had expounded in his philosophical works. His poetic adoration of Sophia, a pale and vague incarnation of the *Ewig-Weibliches*, of the feminine component of the Divine Substance, was going to be the dominant inspiration of the school, or rather sect, of poets, who affirmed themselves after 1905. These poets were recognized as the second generation of Russian Symbolism, and later were to be called the Russian Symbolists *tout court*, while the poets of the first generation (Balmont, Bryusov, and *tutti quanti*) were instead to be considered the Russian counterpart of the European *Décadence*. The Symbolists merited their name because they were a more exact historical equivalent of the Symbolist movement as it had developed in France and in the west, and also because they were "symbolists" in the permanent and traditional meaning of that word.

Vyacheslav Ivanov became not only a disciple of the philosophy of Solovyov (who before his death in 1900 had seen the early verse of his young admirer and had recommended its publication), but also a poet and a Symbolist. After his return to Russia in 1905, Ivanov settled in St. Petersburg, opening his famous "tower," a house in Tavricheskaya Street, making of it both a literary *salon* and the *cénacle* of the school. The differences between his poetry and the poetry of the two younger masters of Russian Symbolism, Andrey Bely and Alexander Blok, could be briefly summed up as follows: Ivanov was a more cultivated artist and a less genuine poet than Blok, a more classical and less experimental writer than Bely, a less literal and less naïve writer than either of them. For a while he shared some of their vaguest and wildest dreams, passing, at the epoch of the "little revolution" of 1905, through a period of mystical anarchism, longing for a social crisis which could be at the same time a moral palingenesis and a spiritual apocalypse. It was to literature, however, that he devoted his best efforts. Between 1903 and 1912, in addition to his "classical" tragedies, his excellent translations, his suggestive critical, philological, philosophical, and religious essays, he published five important collections of poems. The mystical and metaphorical inspiration of his poetry, his predilection for classical themes, his sibylline and oracular style, his learned and archaic diction, often filled with ancient Slavonic words, the liturgical solemnity and ornamental richness of his verse, all those qualities for which Leo Shestov gave him, not without irony, the epithet of "Vyacheslav the Magnificent," are revealed even by the titles of his books of poems: *Pilot-Stars, Translucidity, Eros, Cor Ardens, The Tender Secret,* and so forth.[1]

Such had been the career of Vyacheslav Ivanov up to the moment of his meeting with Mikhail Herschensohn, and of his sojourn with him, under the same circumstances, in the same room. But since the knowledge of the turning points of his future development may have some bearing on the study of the work which is the object of this essay, it is perhaps worth while to acquaint the reader with the later phases of Ivanov's *curriculum vitae.* In the fall of 1920 he went to Baku, where he remained for four years as professor of classical philology at the local university. There he published his *magnum opus* on the Dionysiac cult and wrote perhaps his most human and poignant lyrical masterpiece, the *Winter Sonnets.* This work is a sequence of twelve pieces for which he chose the form, rare in Russian verse, of the Italian sonnet, and where, under the symbol of winter, with eloquent simplicity, in direct images and in intimate, almost private

terms, the poet expressed the feeling of a cosmic and human
tragedy, with which he was already viewing the historical tragedy
of the Russian revolution. In 1924 he emigrated to Italy where
he has been living ever since, crossing recently the advanced
landmark of eighty years of age, surviving the crisis of the war
and its aftermath, perhaps smiling at the false news that reached
the Russian circles in New York of his own death. During the last
twenty years, he has been living by teaching the classics in private
schools, and writing and publishing essays in Italian, German, and
French. But he has not abandoned his poetry: one of his most
important lyrical works, the philosophical cycle *Man*, appeared in
the complete and original text, after having been reworked for
almost a quarter of a century, only a few years ago. The most
significant event of the later phase of his life has been his conversion to the faith of Catholic Rome, which took place in 1926,
and which had been preceded shortly by the literary anticipation
of his *Roman Sonnets*.[2]

Mikhail Herschensohn (or Gershenson, in a more exact trans-
literation of the spelling in Russian script of his surname) was
three years younger than Ivanov, having been born in 1869, to a
Jewish family, in the capital city of the province of Bessarabia,
Kishinyov. Like Ivanov, he had studied classical and Greek philosophy at the University of Moscow, but he had been unable to
follow an academic career because of his race and creed. Like
Ivanov, his interests turned from classical antiquity to modern
Russian culture, where he showed a marked preference for its
few representatives of the tradition of romantic and idealistic
liberal thought. From 1900 to 1914 he wrote a series of outstand-
ing historical works and biographical essays, devoted to such figures as Pushkin and Griboedov, Chaadaev and Ogaryov. In 1909
he was one of those writers who contributed articles to *Landmarks*, a collection of critical and polemical studies on the role
played by the radical intelligentsia in Russian history and culture.[3] During the First World War and the early period of the
revolution, Herschensohn wrote a few more formal and ambitious
philosophical works, in the vein of what now could be called religious and optimistic existentialism.[4] When he died in Moscow

in 1926, he left an immense number of letters, printed only in part (merely a few to his brother), which promise to be—when it is possible to publish them in their entirety—his literary master-piece, and perhaps one of the most important historical docu-ments left to posterity by his generation and epoch.

This uncommon gift for letter writing, for a more intimate and private kind of communication, and this predilection for the psychological and biographical essay, give us a clear indication of what kind of writer and man Herschensohn was, and empha-size the contrast between his nature and Ivanov's. In spite of the fact that Herschensohn considered Carlyle as his master, and that he was called the "Russian Macaulay," as a biographer he resembles rather Lytton Strachey, not because of any anecdotal predilection, since he is essentially interested in the intellectual and sentimental portrait of his model, but because of his earnest concern for personal traits, his curiosity in seeking for individual peculiarities, his deep and yet discreet insight into the secrets of private life, his keen intuition of what might be called the origi-nality of the soul. That is, of course, an essentially Russian trait, and it shows how this historian and biographer was a worthy compatriot of the great masters of Russian psychological fiction.

Summing up the characters of these two men, we see on one side a poet and scholar; on the other, a biographer and letter writer; in Ivanov, a lofty passion for the metaphysics of history and culture; in Herschensohn, a love of intimate detail, a great interest in the daily chronicle of life. The former hides in the liturgical aloofness of the priest of poetry, the hierophant of cul-ture; the latter shows the lively enthusiasms of a man interested in political ideas, in social ideologies, in radical thought. The poet reveals the impassioned and archaic solemnity of a mind equally versed in the philosophical and religious lore of the ancient East and the eternal West; the biographer betrays the in-quietude of a modern man, troubled by the question of the day. The Jew, with his Talmudic strain, with his zest for life, and with his human warmth, is psychologically more Russian than the Slav, who, having spent so many years of his life in distant lands and in remote ages, confesses here to his friend that he is only "half-Russian." [5] Ivanov, so much more deeply and widely cultivated, is on the other hand too much a learned Slavophile to be the more cosmopolite of the two; furthermore, he belongs, rather than to the Republic of Letters, to the Brahmin caste of the chosen ones, the happy few. It is still very easy to find individualities to whom Herschensohn, whom we have already compared to Lytton Strachey (a far lesser figure than he), may be compared within the tradition of Russian culture: he resembles Herzen very much; he is a Herzen and a westerner of his time. As for Ivanov, in spite of his deep understanding of spirits like Pushkin and Tyutchev, Dostoevsky and Solovyov, we cannot find any adequate spiritual peer of his in Russian culture: if we discard the national and political implications of our parallel, if we remember that Ivanov is not a lesser poet than he, we may say that the German Stefan George is, among his literary brethren, the figure he resembles most.

The stay together of two men like Ivanov and Herschensohn, the meeting of two minds like theirs under the impact of such a historical emergency as the Russian revolution, could not but be an excellent opportunity for exchanging ideas, for an intellectual discussion of the validity of culture and its chances of transcending through its epiphanies the tragedy of history itself. The conversation of the two men could not dwell on any other object, and this prevented them from devoting the greater part of their time to their private meditation and intellectual research. Both immediately realized that their views were diametrically opposed, and this made their dialogue more difficult, but even more necessary. They were still trying to find a common ground for their fears and hopes, doubts and beliefs, when one day one of them proposed to the other that they exchange their ideas through the medium of the written, rather than the spoken, word. The other accepted this proposal, adding that from their written dialogue there would perhaps come out a "correspondence between the opposite corners" of the same room.[6]

Ivanov wrote the first of his six letters on June 17, 1920, during an absence of his friend, who found it, at his return, on his desk; Herschensohn penned the last one on July 19. These letters, covering a period of a little over one month, take no more printed

space than a fifty-page pamphlet. They were published under the
title of *Perepiska iz dvukh uglov*, or *Correspondence between* [7]
Two Corners, at Petrograd, in 1921; a reprint of the original edition appeared in Berlin the following year. In Russia, for obvious
reasons, the book did not receive the attention it deserved; as
for the circles of the Russian emigration, they were too busy, like
all exiles at the beginning of their exile, with the pettiness of the
everyday chronicle of political events for them to take seriously
such lofty and impassioned meditations over history itself.

Abroad, even the first translation (into German) of the *Correspondence*, which appeared in 1926, passed unnoticed, and
western consciousness awakened to it only when Ernst Robert
Curtius commented upon it from the rather biased perspective,
and in the rather dubious light, of the German problem. The
French translation appeared in a Catholic literary review, and one
year later was reprinted in book form, with a preface by the
philosopher Gabriel Marcel, now an existentialist of the moderate,
religious wing, and with an important exchange of letters between
Vyacheslav Ivanov and Charles Du Bos. The Italian translation,
particularly important because made under the supervision of
Vyacheslav Ivanov, who made also a few changes in his own text,
followed soon.[8] The letters of only one of these two correspondents
(Ivanov) have recently been brought to the attention of the English reading public: [9] and I hope that, together with them, the
present essay will contribute to the acquaintanceship, on the part
of the American public, with a work which is one of the most
important cultural documents of our epoch.

II

This investigation will begin by a detailed reading of the
Correspondence, by means of a logical rather than critical *résumé*,
and by making use, in the words of their authors, of the passages
which seem the highlights of this lofty dialogue. The very first
sentence of Ivanov's opening letter must have made a strong impression on his friend. "I know," says Ivanov to Herschensohn,
"that you are overtaken by doubts about man's immortality and
the person of God," and he proceeds by affirming the presence

within man's soul of a "luminous guest" who is like the promise
of our future rebirth, a guarantee given by God the Father to all
his sons.[10] In his reply Herschensohn, after accepting the principle of personality as the supreme value, as the only reality,
confesses candidly his temperamental dislike of metaphysics; and
he adds that, in the present human and historical condition, his
instinctive and fundamental distrust involves something more
solid and substantial than metaphysics alone, that is, culture itself.
Under the impact of present experience, culture seems to him
not merely useless, but harmful:

> For some time I have been finding oppressive, like an excessive
> load, or too heavy clothes, all the intellectual conquests of mankind,
> the entire treasure of notions and knowledge, of values collected and
> crystallized by the centuries . . . Such a feeling began to trouble my
> soul a long time ago, but it has now become customary with me. It
> must be a great happiness, I think, to dive into the river Lethe, clean-
> ing one's soul within its waters, clearing away the remembrances of
> all religious and philosophical systems, of all wisdom and doctrine, of
> poetry and the arts, and land again naked on the shore, naked as the
> first man, light and merry, freely stretching and raising one's naked
> arms, remembering of the past but one thing, how one felt burdened
> by those clothes, and how one now feels easy and free without them
> . . . Our elegant clothing did not weigh upon us as long as it remained
> unsoiled and unspoiled, but since during these years it has been torn
> and now hangs in rags from our shoulders, we would like to take it
> off our body and throw it away.[11]

In his answer, Ivanov does not defend reason, the usual object
of hatred on the part of instinct, which seems to him deserving
of being hated, although for different causes; he rather defends
the spirit, not culture alone, but that ultimate and primordial
kind of culture which cannot be conceived outside religion, because it rests on religion and is nourished by it. Herschensohn is
reproached by his friend for thinking of culture in the usual,
modern terms; it is for this reason that culture is to him the
slavery of the letter instead of being the freedom of the spirit:

> That state of mind now dominating, and greatly torturing you,
> that excruciating feeling of the intolerable load of the cultural inheri-
> tance weighing on your soul, is essentially due to the fact that culture
> is being experienced by you not as a living treasure of gifts, but as a

system of the subtlest restrictions. No wonder, since culture has aimed at being no more than that. But for me it is the stairs of Eros and a hierarchy of venerations.[12]

Herschensohn replies by referring to Ivanov's "work in progress" (a translation of Dante's *Purgatorio*), and by expressing a feeling of nostalgia for the "harmonic" civilization of the Middle Ages, but turns immediately back to the present, asking a rhetorical question:

How in such circumstances can we trust our reason when we realize that reason itself has derived from culture and, naturally enough, bows before it, as a slave to the master who has raised him? . . . I am not judging culture, I merely witness that I suffocate within it. Like to Rousseau, there appears in my dreams a condition of bliss, of perfect freedom, where the unburdened soul lives in an Edenic thoughtlessness. I know too many things, and this load tortures me.

Herschensohn's criticism of culture seems here dictated by the desire of escaping from history, by the wish to live in the individual passions of the moment: "As for that knowledge, I have no use for it when I am in love or in sorrow." An attack follows against philosophical idealism, which Herschensohn accuses of having destroyed the immediate sense of reality and of having reduced the experience of life to a ghost: "That century-long illusion has passed away, but how many awful traces it has left behind!" After the attack against modern culture, there follows the attack against modern civilization and its technology, against the *embarras de richesses* of modern industry, which in itself is merely a consequence of that "cultural inheritance weighing on our personality with the pressure of sixty atmospheres." [13]

Ivanov's reply is still inspired by his belief in the syncretism of religion and culture, by his definition of religion as a kind of transcendental culture:

It seems to me that you are unable to conceive of the permanence of culture without one's substantial fusion with it, without one's merging within it. As for myself, I believe that our consciousness must at least partly transcend culture itself . . . The man believing in God would not consent at any price to consider his faith as a part of culture: this is what I believe, although I am convinced that every great historical culture springs forth from a primordial religious fact. A man enslaved by culture (such is the conception of modern thought) will instead consider his faith as a manifestation of culture, whatever his definition of faith might be . . . Only through faith is man able to transcend the "temptation" of culture . . . The dream of Rousseau sprang forth from his disbelief.[14]

The dream of the *tabula rasa*, says Ivanov, is not the dream of a new culture, or of a life liberated from it: it is the dream of a new morality, or of the destruction of traditional morality, even of morality itself—in other words, an attempt to erase from the soul of man the traces of original sin. Herschensohn replies by denying the possibility of a coexistence of culture and faith: "But it is not of this that I wish to speak . . . I do not know or wish to know what man will find beyond the wall of the jail he is going to leave, and openly acknowledge my indifference toward 'the work of preparing freedom's roads'. . . I merely *feel* . . . an urgent need of liberty for my spirit and conscience."[15] Herschensohn ends by comparing himself to a Greek of the sixth century, oppressed by the complexity of his pantheon of gods; and to an Australian aborigine, tired under the weight of his totems and taboos.

In the following letter we find the first discreet hint, on the part of Ivanov, that his friend's viewpoint is due to Herschensohn's desire to share in the cave of his soul the collective and historical experience now taking place outside its walls: "Perhaps the last of Faust's temptations ought to become for you the first: the enchanted dream of the canals and the new world, the illusion of a free land for a free people." It is the revolutionary illusion that leads Herschensohn, in Ivanov's judgment, to think that culture is an abandoned temple, a ruined city, or simply an empty shell. Ivanov sees that Herschensohn's denial of culture had been dictated by his wish to merge morbidly, unconsciously, and passively, into the stream of historical contingency. It is the convulsive force of contemporary events, Ivanov tells his friend, that makes him feel that culture is a static weight, though it really is a dynamic power: "not only a monument, but also an instrument of spiritual initiation."[16]

But Herschensohn has no use for that monument or instru-

ment: "The revelations of truth which descended on our fore-
fathers have changed into mummies"; modern man is tyrannized
by objectivized and abstract values, which may be classified into
"fetish-values," that is, the traditional taboos of morality and religion; and into "vampire-values," that is, the bloodless totems
of metaphysical and philosophical abstractions. "It may be that
the last war has been but a hecatomb never witnessed before,
forced upon Europe by a few intelligible values allied to each
other through their priests." It is to real, personal, immediate,
everlasting, and metacultural values that man must return. "When
around a simple prayer one has built an immense structure of
theology, religion, and church," Herschensohn says, we need a
religious revolution, as it happened with the Reformation; and
when similar structures have been built also in the field of social
life, we need a political revolution, as it happened in France in
1789. A similar house cleaning or clearing of the air is taking
place at the present time: "Now a new storm is shaking the world:
the individual right to work and property forces us to go out,
into the open, into the free air, from century-long complications,
from the monstrous complexities of abstract social ideas." [17]

Ivanov's answer is an argument *ad hominem:* "Yesterday's
values are now shaken from their roots, and you are one of those
who feel joy in this earthquake"; but it is also a keen criticism
of his friend's presuppositions about the acultural or anticultural
essence of the Russian revolution. Ivanov sees in it not merely a
mystical, popular outburst, but the plan of a new civilization, of
a new culture to be built: "The anarchistic current does not seem
to predominate within it." [18] Herschensohn feels he has been
touched on a sore spot and reacts by accusing Ivanov of treating
him as a physician treats a sick man, unaware that his diagnosis
is wrong. He too finds a weak spot in the armor of his friend,
whose great learning, in spite of his transcendental religious beliefs, leads him to historicism, that is, to an attitude which implies a justification rather than a judgment of culture. And he
takes upon himself again the task of the judge: culture was created by man as an instrument to make it possible for him to live
better in his environment, but now the instrument is so com-

plicated and heavy that it has become harmful. "The deer developed horns as a means to frighten his enemies and to defend himself, but in some species they have reached such dimensions as to prevent him from running through the woods, and the species is dying. Is it not the same thing with your culture? Are not your values those horns?"[19] Perhaps the proletariat will destroy those horns; perhaps it will adapt them to changed conditions; perhaps it will create better organs for the new men.

In his answer, Ivanov recognizes that the controversy has reached a dead end, that from now on it will be only a repetition of opposite statements. He sees that there is no meeting ground for his "humanism and mysticism," and for the "anarchic utopianism and cultural nihilism" of his friend.[20] Herschensohn, discovering signs of bad humor, and even of bad temper, in their dialogue, concludes it with an apparent compromise, postulating a new culture, different from the old one, which is only "a daily habit . . . not a cultural food." [21] The correspondence can go no further; and Herschensohn, defining himself as a stranger and a pilgrim searching for the promised land, while Ivanov feels at home on the native soil of history and culture, ends by saying that their brotherly souls will find, in the house of the Father, a common abode.

III

It is indeed difficult to conceive of a loftier discussion, of an exchange of ideas on a higher plane, of a polemic about history more detached from the superficial passions aroused by current events, and at the same time more concerned with the absolute and essential reality underlying the facts that take place before one's eyes, within the relativity of time and of human things. The war and the revolution, Russia and Bolshevism, are hardly mentioned, or referred to only a few times; still, their presence is deeply and constantly felt, and the sense of this presence has a direct bearing on what each of these two speakers says, thinks, or feels. But the *Correspondence* does not need our praise; our task is rather to appraise it, to attempt a critical interpretation of this text, even more to extract from this discussion useful lessons for ourselves, valid conclusions for the present manifestations of the same crisis, still torturing the West and the world.

The position of Herschensohn is easier to deal with, and even to find fault with: and this task of faultfinding is expertly performed by the other writer, Ivanov himself. Ivanov is right when he maintains that Herschensohn's viewpoint is not new: that a similar palingenesis, beyond culture or without it, with identical intellectual and ethical implications (the longing for a simplification of life, for the regained paradise of primitivism, for an escape from any tie and any bond) had already fascinated Leo Tolstoy, who, as Ivanov tells his friend, "must naturally attract you." [22] Even before, the same dream had possessed the soul and mind of Rousseau, in whom Ivanov recognizes a decadent *avant la lettre*.[23] In this, too, it is easy to agree with him, since Rousseau's ethical, political, and social ideal is nothing but the projection into the future of a retrospective utopia, of an Eldorado dimly seen in a distant time, discovered by looking backwards into the darkness of the past. Ivanov is equally right when implying that a "transvaluation of all values" succeeds only in achieving the destruction, or at least the dethronement, of the values of the past, but it always fails to transform them into new values, or to create values of its own. Any transvaluation of this kind is another symptom of decadence of the nihilistic or cynical type; and Ivanov is again in the right when, after the names of Tolstoy and Rousseau, he brings in, to explain or rather to judge the viewpoint of his friend, a far more dangerous and suggestive name—the name of Friedrich Nietzsche: "At bottom, the problem of Nietzsche is your own: culture, personality, values, decadence, and health— above everything, health." [24] We could add that while Nietzsche aims at being the "physician of culture," at becoming its regenerator and healer, Herschensohn would rather be the priest performing the burial rites of culture, singing over its body a requiem for the peace of its soul. For, in spite of the fact that he says, "Let the dead bury their dead," we know that he, too, is one of the living dead.

Herschensohn is rather perplexed at this kind of criticism. His reactions are varied: now he denies, now he accepts, now he modifies or qualifies Ivanov's critiques. For instance, he answers

the reference to Rousseau in a rather conciliatory way: "It seems
to me that even Rousseau, who shook Europe with his dream, did
not contemplate a *tabula rasa*." [25] We may accuse Herschensohn
of many such inconsistencies and perplexities; we may admit
that his dreamed-of palingenesis may be conceived as pointing
at a cultural renaissance of its own; we may give him credit for
candidly recognizing, more than once, the absurdity of a denial
of culture based on culture itself; [26] and yet, in spite of all this,
we must say that there is no doubt that the idea of the *tabula rasa*
coincides with his utopia or promised land, with his ideal aim,
with the object of his dreams.

To agree with Ivanov's criticism of Herschensohn's position,
to accept the *pars destruens* of his argument, does not mean an
approval of his positive viewpoint, an acceptance of the *pars
construens* of his system. After all, the dream of the *tabula rasa*
is dialectically [27] the cultural equivalent of the socialist ideal, as
Dostoevsky was able to demonstrate and anticipate in his *Possessed*. On the other hand, provided that ideal be realized without becoming totalitarian, we must admit that it springs forth
(and it is only on that soil that it may flourish and live) from
the human need for a terrestrial and historical justice: a need, to
be sure, not easily satisfied with theological and metaphysical
justice, the only kinds offered to us by religion and by historicism.
It is only in this sense that, against the cultural and religious
consciousness of Ivanov, against what he calls the "vertical line,"
in a given epoch of crisis, in a given historical experience, man's
conscience may have its good reasons for preferring the solutions
of intuition and sentiment, Herschensohn's "horizontal line." This
means that the controversy is not merely a philosophical one, as
Ivanov seems to think, and as he felt it necessary to restate, many
years later, by defining the *Correspondence* as "a peculiar re-
evocation of the everlasting and protean dispute between *realism*
and *nominalism*." [28]

That medieval dispute was a scholastic replica of the Platonic-
Aristotelian alternative: were ideas, that is, the names of things,
the only real essences, the only authentic values contained in
those appearances, in those non-values that are the concrete objects? Or were those ideas only names, *flatus vocis*, mere conven-

tional or practical labels, deprived of any existence of their own, while reality belongs to solid objects and to concrete things? The realist considered as true the first hypothesis; the nominalist, the second one. In such a sense, there is no doubt that Ivanov is the realist, and Herschensohn the nominalist, for the former considers culture, which is a collection of ideas, of name-things, as the human equivalent of the Logos, which, in culture as in religion, is made flesh; while, for the latter, culture is the dead letter, and life the living spirit. Ivanov is of course nearer than his friend to Goethe, whom he often quotes or refers to, but here Herschensohn restates as his own the poetic truth of Goethe that "the tree of knowledge is gray, and the tree of life is green." And, like Goethe, Herschensohn does not care too much, either for the eternal archetypes or for the *Ding an Sich*.

If Herschensohn were merely a nominalist, he would not take issue with culture, exactly because he would consider it only as a collection of labels, a dictionary of names and nouns, a heap of dead or at least lifeless words. In such a case, he would not feel it necessary or worth while to make such a sweep of all the cultural traditions of the past, since human reality would remain outside them: one does not fight phantoms or kill ghosts. But Herschensohn is a modern man, and he knows, or thinks, that names, labels, ideas may not only be different from human realities, but possess a validity, solidity, and vitality of their own, and be filled with such an explosive energy as to act and react upon life, converting or perverting it. Herschensohn would agree with such different thinkers as Burckhardt, Benda, and Ortega y Gasset, for whom modern history and modern politics have been and still are a politics and a history of ideas: and, at least for one of them, of bad and harmful ideas at that. Herschensohn states as much when he says that the First World War had perhaps been a hecatomb forced upon mankind by ideas, that is, by the intellectual dogmas and the ethical creeds of the past.

In spite of the fact that Herschensohn's moral position and sentimental attitude differ very much from Sorel's and Marx's, to those ideas which he calls "fetish-values" one could easily give the Sorelian name of myths; and to those ideas which he calls "vampire-values" one could with equal justice give the Marxist name of ideologies. Sorel approves of social myths because of his Machiavellian sympathy for political activism; Marx, who naïvely expected that his so-called scientific socialism would not have any use or need for them, condemns ideologies as the intellectual weapons of the classes or of the social system he attacks. Unlike Sorel, we fear myths and hate ideologies, either of the Right or of the Left—for very different reasons from Marx's, and also because in this case we know better than he. We agree therefore with Herschensohn's condemnation of myths and ideologies; but we differ from him through our awareness that the revolution in which he saw the dawn of a reborn human innocence is as guilty as any established society, and even more so, of creating or perpetuating "fetish-values" or "vampire-values," enslaving the soul and destroying the dignity of man.

Ivanov stands on solid ground when he tells Herschensohn that Bolshevism is also culture, even if this is a culture of its own, and that those anarchistic tendencies of which Herschensohn is so fond are absent from the revolution and seem alien to it. We could add that technology,[29] that the very technology that he condemns at least with harshness equal to his condemnation of culture itself, will be the most important economic and political business of the society of iron and blood that the revolution, in which he sees only "sweetness and light," will finally build. At any rate, as Ivanov rightly maintains, iconoclasm does not lead anywhere, not even to the city of Utopia, to that Erewhon which is a Nowhere. On the other hand, we may think that Ivanov commits the opposite sin, the sin of spiritual and cultural idolatry, and we are ready to recognize that his idolatry of religion and historicism is essentially indifferent to the tragedy of history, to the social condition of man. But we repeat that we must accept the principle inherent in his position, that it is not through the iconoclasm of culture and history that man will be able to build a better house or a better life for himself. On the stage where the tragedy of history is performed, we reject the intervention of a *deus ex machina,* which is Ivanov's theatrical trick; but we refuse also that too easy catharsis, which Herschensohn offers naïvely to us, in his belief that it will compensate for the catastrophe, for that unhappy ending which always involves grief, death, and bloodshed. We feel rather skeptical and doubtful of those who wish, like Herschensohn, mystically and morbidly to merge one's self into an elementary and telluric force, merely because it may clear the air in the old, dusty, and unhealthy dwellings of man. We dislike equally the purely symbolical interpretation of Ivanov, and the too literal acceptance by Herschensohn, of the truth contained in Goethe's *Stirb und werde,* which after all is a command for man to act and to live.[30]

On one side, Ivanov's defense of culture and religion, within and without history, *pro et contra,* for or above man, and, on the other side, Herschensohn's desire to throw away culture in order to be better able to embrace the womb of mankind (suffering— who knows?—either the pangs of childbirth or the agony of death), prove to us that the real issue at stake in this text is a question of vital importance not so much for the intelligentsia as for the intelligence of the West. The real theme of the *Correspondence* is not the antinomy of realism and nominalism, but the antithesis of two ideals: the humanistic and the humanitarian. It matters very little that Ivanov is a religious humanist, perhaps far more religious and far more of a humanist than Irving Babbitt himself—two good reasons why his position would certainly please the keen, earnest, and educated mind of T. S. Eliot. Despite his affirmation of the supremacy of religion, Ivanov has certainly yielded to the temptation of culture, which he condemns, and the judgment pronounced by him against the humanist, which we must quote again, applies to the judge himself: "A man enslaved by culture . . . will consider . . . his faith as a manifestation of culture, whatever his definition of faith might be."[31]

As for Ivanov's attempt at a conciliation of the humanistic and religious traditions, it is nothing new. Heine, Nietzsche, and Renan had already praised the Catholic Church for having achieved that conciliation during the Renaissance, and condemned the Reformation for having broken that ideal relationship. From Marsilio Ficino and Pico della Mirandola up to Cardinal Bessarion, the European mind had often tried, as Ivanov does, to create a synthesis of the two antiquities, the classical and the biblical, to harmonize Paganism and Christianity, Plato and Jesus, Hebraism and Hellenism, the civilization of Rome and the

West and the culture of Byzantium and the East. Such a synthesis is still essentially humanistic in character, and therefore unable to change the essence of humanism, the ideal of which had been already perfectly stated by a pagan writer of the third century, Aulus Gellius, in a famous passage of his *Attic Nights* still worth quoting: "Those who created the Latin tongue and spoke it well never gave *humanitas* the notion inherent in the Greek word *philanthropia*. They gave that word the meaning of what the Greeks call *paideia*, i.e., knowledge of the fine arts."

But the humanitarian, Christian or not, radical or mystic, follower of Tolstoy or of Gandhi, is interested in philanthropy, both the word and the thing. Sometimes he is interested also in the humanities, but only when he thinks that there is no conflict between them and humanity. In a few short periods of western history, in the eighteenth and in part of the nineteenth centuries, the two ideals coincided, the former being considered as the cultural instrument and the intellectual counterpart of the latter. But this coincidence between the humanistic and the humanitarian ideal broke down during the second half of the nineteenth century, when a few spirits, in their reaction against rationalism, historicism, scienticism, and positivism, forced the humanitarian ideal to cope with the problem of personality and to find other foundations for its faith.

The mission of modern culture has been to react against four historical kinds of reason: *Verstand* or the *raison raisonnante*, that is, "mathematical" reason; *Vernunft*, or "critical" or "idealistic" reason; and, derived respectively from the former and the latter, "scientific" and "historic" reason. In other words, modern culture has reacted against Descartes, Comte, and Taine, and against Kant, Schelling, and Hegel. Such a reaction had already been anticipated by Rousseau, and was going to culminate in the work of Dostoevsky: two men who were dear to the heart of Herschensohn, a humanitarian basing his faith upon sentiment, intuition, and instinct. Such is the meaning of his attack against philosophical idealism, against historic and ideal reason: after all, Dostoevsky had already aimed his telling blows at mathematical and scientific reason, in the first part of the *Notes from Underground*. If it is superfluous to note that Ivanov had no use for mathematical and scientific reason, it is perhaps worth while to remark that many words and ideas have, in Herschensohn's attack against philosophical idealism, a Bergsonian ring.

The humanitarian of the rationalistic, practical, utilitarian kind (as Dostoevsky had already noted, in the book mentioned above) is active and positive, at least in thought; while the humanitarian of the sentimental, intuitive, and instinctive type, à la Herschensohn, is negative and passive in character: feminine and pacifistic, so to say. As a natural consequence, he is destined to be disappointed by that revolution he falls in love with, and which he greets, as Herschensohn does, in the name of personal freedom and the dignity of man—or, as he says, in the name of "the individual right to work and property," [32] as a liberation of all human faculties, as an opportunity for the self-development and self-expression of Everyman. He was dreaming of a Crystal Palace where there could be room also for the dissident and the heretic, for private life and individual idiosyncrasies, not only for the will, but even for the whims of man. If he had understood the dialectic of Dostoevsky, the ironical inventor of that myth, he would have seen that in the Crystal Palace there is no room for this. The humanitarian must find out this truth by himself. The mystical humanitarian awakens only when he survives his dream, and then he is not only disappointed, but crushed, because unlike his more logical rivals or mathematical colleagues, he is unable to rationalize the cruel reality now oppressing him and his fellow men. Herschensohn was perhaps fortunate in being spared by death from witnessing the awful metamorphosis of the figure of his dream into a new Leviathan.

Exactly because of the blindness of his irrational hopes about the kind of future which the present will bring forth, Herschensohn's iconoclasm becomes a new idolatry, and Ivanov is right in condemning it. On the other hand, as we have already hinted, there is an idolatry in Ivanov too, the idolatry of the eternal, which is very often only the apotheosis of what is merely old. The iconoclast, Ivanov implies, is a decadent, and we agree, provided we are granted the right to affirm that the idolater is a decadent, too. The cultural idolatry of Ivanov and the cultural iconoclasm of Herschensohn have the same origin: both come from Nietzsche, who is the common spiritual master of their generation and of both men, even if both disciples later discarded him. Nietzsche condemned decadence, although he was a decadent himself, and this is what both Ivanov and Herschensohn do. This point is proved merely by quoting and using the beautiful definition of decadence given in this text by Ivanov himself: "What is decadence? The awareness of one's subtlest organic bonds with the lofty cultural tradition of the past, but an awareness tied up with the feeling, both *oppressive* and *exalting*, of being the last of the series." [33] It is that oppressive feeling which leads the decadent Herschensohn to the blind and mystical acceptance of a new series, the series of a resurgent barbarousness, replacing the traditions and beliefs of a tired and dying civilization; it is that exalting feeling which impels the proud Ivanov to keep faith with the cultural values and the spiritual creeds of the old series, and later to accept as his own the creed of the most dogmatic and canonic, ancient and permanent Church of the West, Roman Catholicism, the most compact system of revelations ever devised by man.

Thus, in spite of the fact that both Ivanov and Herschensohn are, as the former accuses the latter of being, two "monologists"; [34] in spite of the fact that they stand, as Herschensohn says, "at the opposite ends of a diagonal not only in our room, but also in the spiritual world," [35] a dialogue between them is, up to a certain point, still natural and possible, owing to their common decadent background. It is decadent to believe that the only alternative left to man is between cultural traditionalism and religious conservatism on one side, and revolutionary messianism on the other. It is a symptom of decadent psychology to feel that man's fate, at this historical stage, does not offer any other choice but being, as Herschensohn and Ivanov equally are, prisoners in a kind of Platonic cave, which resembles more than they think the corners of those squalid St. Petersburg flats where Dostoevsky's heroes— or better, victims—live, suffer, and die. Both in their room and in their minds, like Dostoevsky's "underground man," Ivanov and Herschensohn are cornered: as were their younger brothers of the lost generation after the First World War; as we are, too, members of another lost generation, unstable and unsafe sur-

vivors of so many social and political floods. Their discarded
master, Nietzsche, was more right than they when he prophesied
the advent, in a not too distant future, of what he cynically calls
"war's classical age." We are even more oppressed and cornered
than they are, because we feel more remorse for the past and
more fears for the future of man.

We have therefore no right to dismiss either one of them with
a curt *medice, cura te ipse.* And yet we cannot afford to share
the traditional faith, the metaphysical beliefs, the preëstablished
harmony of Ivanov; nor are we able to indulge Herschensohn's
desire to merge with the present, with those physical bodies
which are called parties or masses, or even less, with that mystical
body which is called revolution, or what you wish. For me it is
easy to confess that I feel more at home (for professional reasons,
if for no other, and perhaps also because of my desire to avoid
the "treason of the clerks") with Ivanov's position. I am, moreover, aware that Ivanov is the more consistent thinker and the
more powerful intellect of the two: and also the more virile and
logical mind, able to avoid the contradictions, paradoxes, and anti-
climaxes of the position of Herschensohn—which is that of a
man of culture who, by denying it, hopes to save his soul. And if
I think that Herschensohn's testimonial is the more important
and poignant of the two, it is merely because his illusion is candid
and fresh; and also because we were lucky or unlucky enough to
see it shattered before our own eyes. Only because we were young
enough to become such eyewitnesses are we also able to recognize that the obscure dialectics of Herschensohn's ideal involves
not merely the "great betrayal" of culture, or even a betrayal of
the revolution in Trotsky's sense, but man's treason to man.

On the other hand, we are equally dissatisfied with any brand
of ecclesiastical culture or of cultural religion, with intellectual
mysticism, which is always fated to become an intellectual super-
stition, and like all superstitions, to end unconsciously in a kind
of worldly and universal skepticism. The utopian and anarchistic
messianism of Herschensohn is, of course, a religion, too, but not
in the literal and positive sense of a sect or a church; and at bottom we sympathize with his unconcern, or even disdain, not for
the religious or the divine, but for theological and metaphysical

problems, for the golden chains of revelations and dogmas, canons and myths. For this we are ready to forgive his confession of a medievalistic nostalgia, and even the final, eucharistic appeal to his friend. The important fact is that we agree with him that Jacob's ladder, the vertical line of transcendence, even if it may become the stairway of individual ascensions, is, like contemplation and prayer, unable to save us. We think that the only way to save our souls is to save our world. This is exactly what Herschensohn is asking for, but his horizontal line is different from ours.

We want a horizontal line able to take into account the irregularities of history, the accidents of geography, the idiosyncrasies of psychology, the peculiarities of life, and the absurdities of man; we reject his *tabula rasa*, that *tabula rasa* which, through that very culture, those very values he wanted to destroy, may be created only by the steam roller of revolution, by the juggernaut of the totalitarian state, or by the most radical and nihilistic leveler ever invented by man, the atomic bomb. Even in this case, we owe our attitude not to insight, but to hindsight, and therefore we feel as if we have no right to reproach Herschensohn for having failed to foresee what we have seen. But the vertical line of Ivanov may also be the one along which both the Ivory Tower and the Tower of Babel are built; in a certain sense, it is also the line along which the atomic bomb may fall. Idolatry of culture implies also the idolatry of science and, in the long run, of technology; and transcendental, not less than immanent, historicism is only a metaphysical justification of all of history's acts and deeds, and therefore also of the atomic bomb. At all events, not everyone is able, like Ivanov, to find a shelter in the Vatican, which was at least spared by aerial bombs.

What we are looking for is a conciliation, a synthesis, of the vertical and horizontal lines, between the respect for what is transcendental in man and the respect for what is immanent in society, in history, in the world. It is our duty to remember that the vertical line of humanism is a good corrective for the horizontal line of humanitarianism. Even if he cares only for the happy few, the humanist is often able to respect the value of the person in its concrete forms, in its separate beings, while the humanitarian very often loves mankind only in the general and in the abstract; sometimes, by looking at the masses, at the forest of men, he loses sight of the tree, of that suffering and thinking reed which is man. Only too often, as Dostoevsky says in *A Raw Youth,* " 'love for humanity' is to be understood as love for that humanity which you have yourself created in your soul." In other words, almost as easily as the humanist, the humanitarian may become the Narcissus of his own idea. If humanism is too easily satisfied with being merely humane, humanitarianism may frequently become inhuman, antihuman, too. Even more than the modern humanist, the modern humanitarian is too easily inclined to be a mere anthropologist.

Man's life must be built in extension and depth, on the cornerstones of the Others and of the Self: only in such a shelter, temporary or not, will man no longer feel that his back is against the wall. We want a house where we shall never feel cornered, either by the waves of the future or the waves of the past. This means that we are not ready to discard, as Herschensohn advises us to do, the theoretical, practical, and ethical wisdom of our western and Christian past; and on the other hand, we are not resigned, as Ivanov is, merely to conserve that tradition. We want to respect both values and life, or, in political terms, to enjoy the fruits of those ideals of spiritual freedom which are the legacy left to us by Ivanov and his peers; but we also feel a longing for that ideal of justice which, in spite of so many deviations and errors, still is the truthful message carried by Herschensohn to us. Liberty and justice are but different names for the vertical and the horizontal lines, which we want to see united again into a symbol of redemption, into the sign with which we shall conquer. In this year of our Lord, the Son of Man, either *homo sapiens* or *homo faber,* does not want to be crucified on any other cross.

Notes

1. *Pilot-Stars* (*Kormchie Zvezdy*) was published in St. Petersburg, 1903; *Translucidity* (*Prozrachnost*), in Moscow, 1904; *Eros,* in St. Petersburg, 1907; the two series of *Cor Ardens* (both consecrated to the poet's grief at his wife's death), in Moscow, 1911 and 1912; *The Tender Secret* (*Nezhnaya Tayna*), in St. Petersburg, 1912.

2. The dates of publication or composition for the most important poetic works of Vyacheslav Ivanov's later period are the following: *Winter Sonnets* (*Zimnie Sonety*), published in Ilya Ehrenburg's anthology, *Poeziya Revolyutsionnoy Moskvy* (*The Poetry of Revolutionary Moscow*), Berlin, 1921; *Man* (*Chelovek*), published in Paris, 1939; *Roman Sonnets* (*Rimskie Sonety*), written in Rome, 1925. Vyacheslav Ivanov died in Rome on July 16, 1949, after this essay was written.

3. *Landmarks* (*Vekhi*) was published in Moscow, 1909. In this book, the former Marxist, later a western liberal, Peter Struve, the religious thinkers Bulgakov and Berdyaev, on the left wing of orthodox theology, and, finally, Herschensohn himself, attacked the shallow and superficial thinking of contemporary Russian revolutionary ideology, its cultural and spiritual nihilism.

4. One of these books, *The Source of Faith*, published in 1922, appeared later in an English translation and in an American edition (New York, 1926).

5. Letter XI.

6. This testimonial is given (without revealing the author of the statement) by a friend of Vyacheslav Ivanov, O. Deschartes, in her introduction to the Italian translation of the *Correspondence* (see note 8).

7. Literally: *from*.

8. The German translation, *Briefwechsel aus zwei Ecken*, appeared in the little-known organ of a mystical group, the review *Die Kreatur*, I (1926), 2. The observations of Ernst Robert Curtius on the *Correspondence* are contained in an essay entitled "Humanismus als Initiative," which was included in his book *Der deutsche Geist in Gefahr* (Berlin, 1932). After having appeared in *Vigile*, I (1930), 4, the French translation was published in book form under this title: *Correspondance d'un coin à l'autre, précédée d'une introduction de Gabriel Marcel et suivie d'une lettre de Viacheslav Ivanov à Charles Du Bos* (Paris, 1931). The Italian translation has the following title: *Corrispondenza da un angolo all'altro. Traduzione . . . riveduta da Venceslao Ivanov*. Introduzione di O. Deschartes (Lanciano, 1932).

9. While this essay was being prepared for publication, the letters of Ivanov alone had appeared in English, under the title *Correspondence between Two Corners of a Room*, in the third issue (Winter 1947, pp. 4–22) of the international review, *Mesa*, edited and published in this country, at Pennsylvania State College, by Herbert Steiner. Unhappily, the issue was printed in a very limited number of copies, and a new edition of the *Correspondence* was required also for this reason, without speaking of the need to put before American readers the letters of Herschensohn. After this article was finished, a complete edition, under the title *Correspondence between Two Corners*, was brought out by the *Partisan Review*, IX (1948), 951–965; 1028–1048. The *Mesa* translation of the Ivanov half of the *Correspondence*, made by Miss Eleanor Wolff, is very good: if I preferred to keep my own renderings for quotations from that writer, it was owing to a desire for terminological consistency and stylistic coherence between the passages and statements quoted from each of the two authors of this text. As for the *Partisan Review* translation, made by Mr. Norbert Guterman, it appeared too late to be of any use to me; at all events, it would have been of little help, because the translator failed to take into account the changes that

Ivanov had introduced into the text of his own letters through his revision
of the Italian translation of the *Correspondence*.

10. Letter I.   18. Letter IX.
11. Letter II.   19. Letter X.
12. Letter III.   20. Letter XI.
13. Letter IV.   21. Letter XII.
14. Letter V.   22. Letter XI.
15. Letter VI.   23. Letter V.
16. Letter VII.   24. Letter IX.
17. Letter VIII.   25. Letter VIII.

26. As for instance in Letter VIII, where, confessing that he is listening
with enchantment to the siren voice of culture speaking to him through the
words of his friend, Herschensohn asks himself the rhetorical question:
"Am I not myself one of her sons?"

27. In a dialectic which is neither Hegelian nor Marxist, neither idealistic
nor materialistic, but historical and empirical.

28. In his letter to Charles Du Bos, published together with the French
translation of the *Correspondence* (see note 8).

29. Technology and science are what Spengler would call a "civilization." Herschensohn, however (and I agree with him), would refuse to
consider the technological concept of "civilization" as an antithetic value in
regard to that spiritual "culture" from which technology is derived.

30. Letters III and IV.   33. Letter VII.
31. Letter V.   34. Letter IX.
32. Letter VIII.   35. Letter II.